LOOK BEFORE YOU LEAD

How *to* Discern and Shape Your Church Culture

AUBREY MALPHURS

BakerBooks

a division of Baker Publishing Group
Grand Rapids, Michigan

Published by Baker Books
a division of Baker Publishing Group
P.O. Box 6287, Grand Rapids, MI 49516-6287
www.bakerbooks.com

Printed in the United States of America

Library of Congress Cataloging-in-Publication Data
Malphurs, Aubrey.
    Look before you lead : how to discern and shape your church culture / Aubrey Malphurs.
        p.   cm.
    Includes bibliographical references and index.
    ISBN 978-0-8010-1507-6
    1. Pastoral theology. 2. Church. 3. Christian leadership. 4. Corporate culture. I. Title.
BV4011.3.M35 2013
253—dc23   2012031876

13 14 15 16 17 18 19   7 6 5 4 3 2 1

"Aubrey Malphurs was one of the seminary professors who shaped my thinking in ministry twenty-five years ago. I have read everything he has written. Why? You would have to read two dozen books to get what you get in just one of Aubrey's. He is a master of boiling a big idea down to the essential action steps. He has done it again with *Look Before You Lead*."

Randy Frazee, author of *The Heart of the Story*; senior minister of Oak Hills Church

"There's no one better to bring a step-by-step leadership guide to pastors than Aubrey Malphurs. *Look Before You Lead* sheds practical and biblical light on the subject of church culture, a concept that many writers leave in the dark."

Will Mancini, founder of Auxano; author of *Church Unique*

"A half century ago, no one in the US was talking about church culture. Today church culture is a popular, but often misunderstood, concept. In *Look Before You Lead*, Aubrey Malphurs assists church leaders to define, discover, and design a church culture that wins people to faith in Jesus Christ. Whether you are a church planter, pastor, or consultant, this book will help you develop a spiritually healthy organizational church culture."

Gary L. McIntosh, professor of Christian ministry and leadership, Talbot School of Theology, Biola University; author of *There's Hope for Your Church*

Contents

Introduction   7

Part 1 The Basics of Congregational Culture

1 Why Leaders Should Read This Book: The Importance of
Culture   13

2 What Are We Talking About? The Definition of Culture   19

3 What We Do: The Church's Expression of Culture   25

4 Why We Do What We Do: The Church's Cultural Values   34

5 What We Believe: The Church's Beliefs   56

6 How We Respond: The Church's Relationship to Culture   68

Part 2 Reading Congregational Culture

7 Reading the Church: Understanding Its Culture Apple   83

8 Reading the Pastor: Discovering the Pastor's Culture   97

Part 3 Shaping Congregational Culture

9 The Church Planter as Culture Architect: Creating a New Church
Culture   111

10 The Church Pastor as Culture Sculptor: Part 1 Preparation   129

11 The Church Pastor as Culture Sculptor: Part 2 Personnel   154

12 The Church Pastor as Culture Sculptor: Part 3 The Process   175

13   The Church Pastor as Culture Blender: Adopting Established
Church Cultures   199

Appendixes

A   Behaviors Audit   209

B   Core Values Audit   220

C   Core Values Statements   222

D   Beliefs Audit   224

E   Faith Statement   231

F   The Culture Matrix: Beliefs, Values, Behavior   233

G   Spiritual Maturity Audit   234

H   Character Assessment for Leadership   239

I   Spiritual Gifts Inventory for Leaders   243

J   Temperament Indicator 1   248

K   The Personal Profile: The Persuader Pattern   249

L   Temperament Indicator 2   251

M   Temperament Indicator 2: Further Explanation   254

N   Implementation Team Worksheet   256

Notes   267

Index   269

Introduction

A primary responsibility of today's strategic church leaders is to create, implement, and re-implement an organizational culture that rewards and encourages movement toward the church's mission and vision. The church's culture falls under the category of organizational culture. But what is organizational culture? How does it affect a congregation? How might a leader discover his culture? And how might leaders shape or change a culture for the better? These are all questions that church leaders must be on top of if they are to have a chance of intentionally impacting their ministry communities for Christ. A leader's success will depend to a great extent on his or her understanding and shaping of the church's culture.

Have you noticed that everybody is talking about culture? I have tuned my ear to listen for the term, and almost everywhere I go, I hear it being used daily. In the ministry world hardly a conference goes by or a leadership book is published without someone making reference to or using the term *culture*. I suspect that it exceeds *vision, kingdom, disciple*, and *missional* in occurrence. But what is culture? When we make mention of culture, what are we talking about? It's a most elusive term, and I believe that anyone who uses the term is obligated to define it. Should we do so, we would find that we're all using *culture* differently, which means we aren't communicating with clarity. In fact, we're probably not even talking about the same thing.

If someone takes my advice and attempts to define *culture*, he or she will discover that it's not an easy concept to grasp. When people do try to define *culture*, it is often difficult to understand their definition. And I must admit that the most difficult task in writing this book has been defining what I mean by *culture*.

At the same time, I find it a critical concept that must be mentally digested and then applied if we're really to understand and lead our churches well. I argue that it's most important that every leader in general and pastors in particular be able to define *culture* and understand the culture in which they lead and minister. The way to understand culture is to read or exegete it. Just as we exegete the Scriptures to better understand the Bible, so we exegete a culture to better understand it, shape it, and move it toward accomplishing God's mission and vision for his church.

The primary purpose of this book is to help current and emerging leaders explore how to form spiritually healthy organizational cultures in the context of church planting, church revitalization, and church adoptions. We will focus specifically on how a church culture's shared beliefs and values interact to explain its behavior in general and display its uniqueness in particular.

My Unique Perspective

If you are under the age of forty, I want to warn you that this book takes a unique perspective. I've noticed that a number of younger pastors—church planters in particular—listen to and read only what's been written or taught by other, mostly younger, popular pastors. I suspect that they—like so many young people in America—are somewhat suspicious of those who are older and in or once were in authority. They assume that older leaders are out of touch with what it takes to reach today's unchurched generations.

While there may be some truth to this assumption, my perspective is to look to old and young alike. For example, we hear very little anymore from the proponents of the church growth movement. Whether you agree with them or not, we can learn much from these ministry pioneers who introduced the church to ministry research and shaped much of our early thinking on leadership. So you won't hear me putting down these people, as some authors do. If we listen only to what's new or consider only the latest ministry model or attend only the conferences put on by these people, then we severely limit our exposure to what God is doing in numerous different contexts in America and around the world.

What I Bring to This Table

While still in my twenties, I was involved in planting a church in Miami, Florida. Since then I've pastored two established churches, and over the last thirty years, I've had the wonderful privilege of training future pastors and leaders at Dallas Theological Seminary in Dallas, Texas. Finally, I lead a consulting ministry called TMG or The Malphurs Group. Why do I mention this? Now that I look back on God's pathway for me, I see where he has prepared me to lead and minister in a unique way. I have one foot in academia (the seminary) and the other in practicality (the church). That's another way of saying that I live in and benefit from both worlds. On the one hand, I work regularly with pastors and their churches in seeking biblical and practical solutions to the issues they face daily. On the other, I work regularly with students and faculty who wrestle with theoretical issues. We seek to understand questions like: What is a leader? Can leadership be learned? What's the future for Christ's church? What does Scripture teach about Christ's church? Consequently, when I write or speak, my goal is to bring together the best of both worlds to glorify the Savior and provide you with practical tools that will make a difference.

This Book Is for You!

I wrote this book for any church leader whose heartbeat is for Christ's church. God has chosen to present his saving message of Christ through the church. Thus the church as a vehicle for the gospel is the hope of the world. However, leadership is the hope of Christ's church. This leadership includes senior pastors of large churches, pastors of small churches, other church staff, governing boards, congregants, consultants, professors, seminarians, and denominational executives and staff. I believe they all need to have a clear definition of congregational culture and know how to discover and shape that culture if they wish to understand and lead today's churches well. This is the essence and ultimate challenge of leadership. If leaders are to meet this challenge and lead, they must understand the dynamics of organizational or congregational culture.

Three Parts

I have divided this book into three parts. Part 1 prepares you for wrestling with your or another's congregational culture and prepares you for parts 2 and 3. Part 1 addresses the basics of congregational culture. Chapter 1 stresses the importance of this culture, and chapters 2 through 6 define it, using the Culture Apple.

Part 2 guides church leaders in reading or discovering congregational culture. Chapter 7 addresses how to discover a church's culture, and chapter 8 addresses how a church leader, such as a pastor, can discover the culture that he brings with him to the church he seeks to lead.

Part 3 moves the leader from reading to shaping culture. It isn't enough just to understand a congregation's culture; the leader needs to help a church change and shape or form a more robust, vibrant Christ-honoring culture. Chapter 9 addresses how to shape a new church's culture in the context of church planting. Chapters 10–12 speak to how to shape an established church's culture in the context of revitalization. I suspect that the majority of readers will work through the book quickly to get to these three chapters that will become three dog-eared chapters, because they speak to the situation of so many leaders. Finally, chapter 13 speaks to the issue of forming a new church culture through merging or adopting several church cultures.

How to Get the Most Out of This Book

I have included discussion questions at the end of the chapters to help you as leaders grasp and apply the concepts in each chapter. I recommend that pastors and board members as well as church ministry staff read this book together and discuss the ideas as a group. Getting these issues out in the open and discussing them together could lead to a more open attitude toward change on the part of some change-resistant people. The same goes for seminarians, who may find themselves resistant to change. The questions will also help you wrestle with the tough issues that might otherwise be missed or even avoided. Finally, it is my desire that women in ministry read this book as well. I have used the masculine pronoun throughout this book not to exclude women but to avoid using "his or her" and variations, which can prove cumbersome.

THE BASICS OF CONGREGATIONAL CULTURE

1

Why Leaders Should Read This Book

The Importance of Culture

Everyone lives in and thus has a culture, and none of us can separate ourselves from that culture. We are part of it, and it is part of us. So how does it affect us and we it? Most people aren't aware of the profound influence that culture has on us. We use culture to order our lives, interpret our experiences, validate our beliefs, and evaluate behavior—ours and that of those who share the culture. It's our resource for understanding our experiences and making sense of our lives as well as this world. Since this is largely a mental reflex—an unconscious process—we're hardly aware it's taking place. It simply happens.

Vital to Effective Ministry

To effectively minister to people in a culture, whether it's a church or parachurch organization, we must understand culture in general and organizational culture in particular. We will better reach people when we understand their culture and are aware of how it is similar to or vastly different from our own. One simple example is language. If we speak English and people we're attempting to reach only speak Spanish, we need not only to be aware of this but to make adjustments to our culture and learn Spanish. At issue here is how much we're willing to change our culture to reach others with a different culture. In 1 Corinthians 9:19–23 Paul challenges us to consider this important principle, which I'll address in chapter 6.

Affecting Our Conduct of Ministry

Our own cultural context—both past and present—has shaped much of our practice of the faith as well as our understanding of the faith. From a cultural perspective, many of our older, traditional churches across North America were "made in Europe," whereas the new, emerging churches were "made in America." For example, many of our European-influenced churches view the church as a building that "looks like a church." This means that it has arches, possibly columns, and a steeple with a cross on top. Their organization is hierarchical, they emphasize the role and training of the clergy, they're more formal in dress and traditional in worship, they focus more on the past, and their music was written before the 1960s. None of this is wrong—just cultural. What is frightening is that some believe that Jesus and Paul worshiped in churches like this. And if it was good enough for them, it should be good enough for us.

Some churches that have been influenced primarily by American culture view the church more as people. Their organization is more horizontal, they emphasize the role and training of the laity, they are more casual in dress and contemporary in worship, their focus is on the future, and their music was written after 1960.

At the end of the twentieth century, many of the European-influenced churches were in decline, while some American-influenced churches were growing. In addition, a number of European-influenced churches have experienced a push by their younger people to transition to a more culturally current American-influenced format. This has been met with strong resistance, and in some instances, churches have split over it. The problem is that some of these people in the European-influenced churches believe they're defending the faith when in reality they're defending their cultural heritage. So they fight as if the entire future of orthodox Christianity depends on them. This is most unfortunate and very damaging to the cause of Christ.

A Multicultural America

We live at a time of growing cultural diversity. Consequently, we're reaching out and ministering the gospel to an increasingly multicultural America. This diversity is seen both within and outside ethnic boundaries. For example, within ethnic boundaries, white younger generations live in and experience a different culture than do white Baby Boomers. And both embrace a culture that is totally different from that of their parents and grandparents. So we shouldn't be too surprised when the younger generation fails to embrace the cultural aspects of their parents' and grandparents' Christianity. The same holds true for African Americans, Hispanics, Asians, and others.

America has become a global, multicultural nation. North America isn't a melting pot any longer; it's a salad bowl. Today we commonly speak of Mexican Americans, African Americans, and Asian Americans. And in some cities, one of these groups is the dominant racial group, not whites.

Whereas once many North American companies conducted their business only in America, now many have business interests in other countries. Along with improved communication technology, this has brought us into contact with people from all over the world. All this should press the church to ask, How can we best reach these people for Christ?

The Importance of Cultural Understanding

Established Churches

When pastors are hired to lead existing churches, they go into and have to adjust to an already established church culture. The better they read and understand that culture, as well as their own, the better their potential to shape or lead and minister well in that culture. If they fail to read the culture well, it will mean that the culture of the church will lead and manage them.

In my work with churches in general and pastors in particular, I have found that most don't realize this. One major purpose of this book is to help pastors understand their own culture preferences and an established church's culture before they accept a position to lead it. Thus early in the pastoral candidating phase, the pastor should read or exegete the church's culture. If he decides to accept a call to pastor the church, he will go in with his eyes wide open—he knows what he's getting into. He has the cultural navigational tools in place to ply the congregational waters that lie before him. He sees many of the cultural sandbars before he encounters them along the ministry journey. Every pastor must understand that to a great degree his job is to lead and manage the congregational culture, but if he doesn't understand that culture as well as his own, he won't be able to do the job.

Because of this dynamic, many leaders who have already taken and are pastoring established churches find themselves struggling. They don't realize they are butting heads with the culture. Again, the answer is found in understanding their own preferences and their church's culture. The better a pastor knows his church's culture, the better he'll be able to lead his church. To a great degree, leadership decisions are based on the knowledge of one's culture as well as one's gifts and abilities as a leader. This knowledge will provide the leader with the information necessary to make the very best decisions regarding the ministry and outreach of the church.

Planted Churches

Church planters are involved in what I refer to as either a "cold start" or "hot start." A cold start involves gathering a core group to help plant a church. A hot start involves gathering and working with a group of people who have already begun to meet before the church planter arrives on the scene. In a cold start, church planters create their own congregational culture; thus the culture they bring with them affects and shapes the new congregation's culture. They should consider what culture they bring to their new church, because it will consciously or unconsciously dictate the culture of the newly planted church. Often this will be the culture of a church that has strongly influenced them in the past—the culture of the church where they came to faith or where they were powerfully challenged to serve Christ. I'll say more about this in chapter 7.

In a hot start the church planter will discover that a culture has already started to form around those who have begun to meet prior to his arrival. The longer they've been meeting, the more the culture will have formed. This is a lot like pouring concrete. When you first start pouring concrete, it's soft and very manageable. However, the longer it has had time to set up, the more difficult it is to change. And so it is with culture. Eventually over time the culture of the church plant will become set and, rightly or wrongly, define acceptable leadership.

Church planters should be aware of the development of culture when going into either situation. They may want to opt for a cold start over a hot start if they would rather not contend with a culture that has already formed significantly without their influence. In addition, they must realize that maintaining a certain degree of cultural adaptivity is the goal and challenge of their leadership. Can they accomplish this in a context where the concrete has already begun to harden significantly?

Culture and Strategic Planning

It's critical that church leaders do strategic envisioning (planning) if their churches are to meet all the challenges that are washing up on the ministry beach. I lead a church-consulting organization called The Malphurs Group (TMG). Most of what we do is help churches with strategic envisioning and leader development. However, we've discovered that it's a waste of time and money to attempt to lead a culturally toxic church that clings to the traditions of men rather than the clear teaching of Scripture through the strategic-envisioning process. In the magazine *Executive Leadership*, Dick Clark explains, "The fact is, culture eats strategy for lunch. You can have a good strategy in place, but if you don't have the culture and the enabling systems, the culture of the organization will defeat the strategy."[1] And the church is no exception to the rule. Many leaders who attempt to implement strategic envisioning in a church discover that a toxic culture cannibalizes the strategic envisioning meat off its organizational bones.

Coping with Change

Churches are faced with problems from their external environment that affect their very survival as a culture. It's critical to the life and thus the future of a culture that it learn how to cope with a constantly changing external environment. The culture that is aware of and adapts well to these changes and challenges is more likely to survive. If it cannot adapt to change, it will die. Coping with the changes involves detecting the problems from without that affect a cultural shift, and then adapting or changing the church's culture accordingly. I will address this in chapter 12.

The Importance of Culture

- Culture shapes our lives and all our beliefs.
- Culture is vital to effective ministry.
- Our culture affects the way we conduct our ministries in the church.
- Culture helps us understand better the different people we seek to reach for Christ.
- Cultural understanding is essential to leaders if they are to lead their established churches well.
- Cultural understanding is essential to leaders if they are to lead their planted churches well.
- Culture may cannibalize strategic planning.
- Understanding culture helps the church cope with changes in its external environment.

Questions for Reflection and Discussion

1. In this chapter the author's purpose is to convince you that culture plays an important role in our lives and ministries. Did he convince you? Why or why not?

2. Of the eight reasons for the importance of culture in this chapter, which do you believe are the most important? Why? Which specifically address your church situation? Do any seem not so important? Why?
3. Do you want to know more about how culture affects the church? Why or why not?

2

What Are We Talking About?

The Definition of Culture

Now that we know how important congregational culture is and that it plays a critical role in leadership and the very survival of our churches, it's time to define what we're talking about. I refer to this as a "clarity moment." It's a time when we pause and make sure that we are all talking about the same thing. So we must define *culture*. What is our working definition? When defining a concept, I find that for maximum clarity it's often helpful to talk about what it isn't as well as what it is. We'll begin by focusing on what culture is and then move to what it isn't.

What Culture Is

What picture forms in your mind when you hear the term *culture*? Most likely, the answer is nothing. Because it's an abstract concept, you may struggle to come up with any picture at all. And that does not help us understand the concept. In fact, as I've researched the concept, I've found that people who write on organizational or church culture also struggle in their attempts simply to define the term. It has proved to be a difficult concept to wrap our minds around, and I suspect this is the reason there are so many different definitions. Indeed, a colleague argues there are more than two hundred definitions of

culture. However, for the sake of clarity, it's imperative that I provide a definition of *culture* as I use it in this book.

I define the church's *congregational culture* as the *unique expression of
the interaction of the church's shared beliefs and its values, which explain its
behavior in general and display its unique identity in particular*. This is what
I refer to as my long definition. However, I have condensed it into a short definition. In short, a church's *congregational culture* is *its unique expression of
its shared values and beliefs*.

I realize that initially you may not know what I mean by some of the terms.
And this may cause you some concern. Thus I will explain them briefly in this
chapter and more in depth in chapters 3–5. So stick with me. At this point, I
want to acknowledge the influence of Edgar Schein (the Sloan Fellows Professor of Management Emeritus and senior lecturer at the MIT Sloan School of
Management) on my thinking.[1]

Congregational Culture

In this book my concern is with *congregational culture*, which is a type of
organizational culture. I'm not writing about culture in general, but organizational culture in particular, and about a specific organization—the church.
Thus I will refer to this culture throughout this work as both organizational
and congregational culture.

The Culture Apple: Three Layers of Congregational Culture

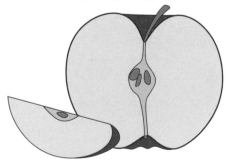

My definition of congregational culture includes beliefs, values, and their
expression (some form of outward behavior), which we can think of as three
levels or layers. To truly analyze and understand a congregation's culture, we
must differentiate between these three critical layers, while discerning how they
relate and contribute to one another. In short, what does each contribute or
bring to the culture as a whole that makes that culture unique?

I like to think of culture as an apple—the Culture Apple. When you hear the term *culture*, rather than go blank, picture an apple. The Culture Apple will help us picture and understand what a leader does as he seeks to discover a congregation's culture. Reading a congregation's culture is similar to peeling back and examining the layers of an apple. The Culture Apple consists of three layers or levels.

THE APPLE'S SKIN: THE CHURCH'S OUTWARD BEHAVIOR

The organization's beliefs and values intermingle and are seen in the church's behavior or outward expression of itself. This is the first layer that is represented by the apple's skin. Churches express themselves through their behaviors and outward appearance. We can say that they are behavior-expressed. The behaviors and outward expressions are what an observer, such as a visitor, would see, sense, and hear as he or she encounters a church's culture. Some examples are the church's physical presence (facilities), language (multi- or monolingual), clothing, symbols, rituals, ceremonies, ordinances, technology, and so forth. What is important here is that it's easy to observe the expression or behavior but more difficult to understand it. The pastor or leader who wishes to discover the church's culture must not only observe its expression but uncover its beliefs and values, which explain the behavior. I will say more about this aspect of culture in chapter 3.

THE APPLE'S FLESH: THE CHURCH'S VALUES

Congregational culture includes at the second level the church's shared values, which are represented by the apple's flesh. Churches are behavior-expressed but values-driven. The inward values drive and explain the church's outward behavior. These values explain why the church does what it does at the first behavioral level and why it doesn't do what it should do. When a church culture acts on its beliefs, they become its actual values. Until then they are aspirational in nature and inconsistent with the church's actual observed presence and expressed behavior. I'll say more about congregational values in chapter 4.

THE APPLE'S CORE: THE CHURCH'S BELIEFS

As you work your way into the apple's core, the third and most fundamental level, you find the shared beliefs on which the church's culture is based. Churches are behavior-expressed, values-driven, and beliefs-based. When Christians hear the term *beliefs*, they often think of the doctrines of the Christian faith that might be found in the church's doctrinal statement, creed, bylaws, and constitution. Certainly these beliefs or convictions are an important part of the church's culture. However, the church's beliefs also include other fundamental aspects of the church's life, such as how it views time (is the church living in the past or the present?), how it views human nature (is man good or bad?), how it communicates internally and externally (the bulletin, announcements), how it handles power (who has the power and who doesn't?), what the role of tradition is, what the church believes is the proper role of women, what it believes about the use of technology (is it high-tech or low-tech?), what it believes about the use of musical instruments in worship, and other similar views.

I will also refer to these beliefs or convictions as *assumptions*, because they are taken for granted as well as shared by the majority of the congregation. If those who seek to understand or read a church's culture don't properly identify its basic beliefs, they will not know how to read its actual values nor interpret the congregation's outward expression of itself. They will have missed the true nature—the very essence—of that culture and what makes it unique. I'll say more about the church's beliefs in chapter 5.

The Church's Uniqueness

These three elements of organizational culture—beliefs, values, and their expression—work together to display the church's unique identity. Thus they answer these questions: How is our church unique? What makes us different? Because no church has the exact same beliefs, values, and behavior, each church will have its own individual, unique nature or identity. (It's interesting that the same is true of apples—each type has its unique attributes.) And as we probe the culture, we will discover what that unique nature is.

What Culture Isn't

Now that we have a working definition of *culture* and an image (the apple) that will help us remember it, let's explore what culture isn't. The purpose is to further clarify the definition.

I'm aware of some misconceptions that Christians and churched people hold about culture, which I believe have led to some unfair criticism of church models. Let's examine some.

Culture Isn't Evil

The most common misconception is that culture is inherently evil. I've noted that whenever Christian people—especially teachers and ministry leaders who are well-known on television and radio—mention culture, it's often in a negative context. Far too many equate it with Satan's world system. When many critics hear someone say that the church needs to be culturally relevant, they interpret that to mean that the church is supposed to be like the world—to buy into and embrace Satan's world system. This represents a total misunderstanding of what the Scriptures teach about culture. Rather than jump to conclusions, it's imperative that we study carefully what God's Word says about these matters. (It's also important that we define our terms for better understanding. In this arena, teachers and leaders must define *culture* if we're to have an intelligent discussion. However, few do.)

Culture Isn't a Product of the Fall

We must realize that culture was not the result of the fall but an intrinsic part of the lives of Adam and Eve before the fall. You can find the Culture Apple in the Garden (and it's not the forbidden fruit). This was because God embedded in Adam a number of beliefs and values, as we see in Genesis 2. For example, God established the belief that a man shouldn't be alone but needs a helper (wife) to complete him and with whom to face life (v. 18). And as men act on this belief and seek that helper, they demonstrate that this is a value to them and an expression of that belief and value. Another embedded belief is God's creation of Eve (wife) and her role as man's helper (vv. 20–22). And as Adam and men who follow him seek such a helper (wife), they demonstrate that this is a value and an expression of that value. Since God accomplished all this and more, in effect, he created culture. In addition, Genesis 1:31 says that "God saw all that he had made, and it was very good." Thus God created culture, and it was very good.

Culture Isn't Independent of the Godhead

Not only did Adam and Eve operate in a cultural context, it's obvious that the Godhead does the same. In Genesis 1–2 it was the Godhead's creative acts that established the various beliefs and values that were the result of their creative thought and planning (Acts 4:24). If this is the case, and I think that it's obvious, then the Godhead relates and operates in a cultural context.

Culture Isn't Temporal

Furthermore, the evidence seems to indicate that culture will be an intrinsic part of our future state in heaven. It isn't limited to this world. For instance, Revelation 7:9–10 reveals that people's cultural distinctives or unique expression of their beliefs and values, such as their ethnicity and language, will be preserved in heaven. We see much the same later in Revelation 20–22, specifically Revelation 21:26.

Culture Isn't Always Good

The points I have made about culture do not mean, however, that culture is always good. Culture can be good or bad. We see a very different culture after the fall. In essence, the culture was devastated by the fall. Sin pervaded everything, including culture (Gen. 3:14–19; 6:5). It wreaked havoc on people's beliefs and values.

Culture Isn't an End in Itself

It is a problem if we view culture as an end in itself. It's not an end but a means or vehicle to an end. Paul indicates this in Romans 14:14 when he refers to food, a vital aspect of culture, as not unclean in itself. However, if someone believes that a particular food is unclean, then for him or her it's unclean. Therefore, as a means to an end, it can be used for good or bad. Another example is language. In James 3:9–12 James distinguishes two usages of the tongue, which is a figure of speech for language (v. 10). On the one hand, people use it for good, such as praising God; on the other hand, people may use it to curse others who've been created in God's image (v. 9). A hunter can use a gun to provide food for his family, while a criminal may use it to rob a store. The same scalpel can correct a baby's malfunctioning heart valve or take the baby's life through an abortion.

Questions for Reflection and Discussion

1. What is the author's definition of culture? How well do you understand this definition? Does the apple metaphor help?
2. Does this definition make sense? Do you agree with it? If not, why not? How would you change the definition? How might the author's definition help you understand culture better?
3. Why is it helpful to know what culture isn't? Are you aware of certain misunderstandings of culture? Have you heard of any that the author addresses? Are you aware of any he didn't include? What are they?

3

What We Do

The Church's Expression of Culture

In the last chapter, I defined congregational culture as a church's unique expression of its shared beliefs and values. This unique expression is the church's behavior that a visitor might observe on a typical Sunday. The church's culture is behavior-expressed. Next I suggested that when you hear the term *culture*, you picture an apple in your mind, and I briefly addressed the three vital concepts that make up the Culture Apple: expression (behavior), values, and beliefs. I hope you now have a much better idea of how I define *culture* and how I'm using this concept in this book. I doubt that the concept is now crystal clear, because it's such an abstract concept. So I want to extend and expand my "clarity moment" into this chapter and the next two.

I've set aside these three chapters to explain further and to expand my definition. The plan is to peel the Culture Apple, sample its flesh, and observe its core. I would compare the process to adjusting the lens on a microscope. Somewhere in your early education it's likely you took a biology class where you learned how to operate a microscope. When you first placed a bug or a piece of leaf on a slide under a microscope, you may have been able to see the object, but it was out of focus. You corrected this by adjusting the focus until it was clear. And that's the major purpose of these three chapters—to adjust the focus on culture until the definition is clear and workable.

Through these chapters, I'll begin to erect what I refer to as the *Culture Matrix*. It will appear at the end of chapters 3 and 4 and will make up appendix F. Don't let the term *matrix* concern you, because you will see an example of a matrix later in this chapter. It provides a way to capture and summarize the contents of the chapters as a visual comparison of what behavior, values, and beliefs contribute to the culture.

Culture Apple

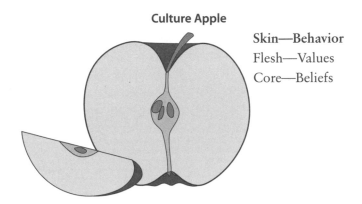

Skin—Behavior
Flesh—Values
Core—Beliefs

To better understand my definition of *culture* in chapter 2 and the impact of congregational culture, imagine that you're a candidating pastor or an unchurched lost person visiting a church for the first time. What would you experience? What are the cultural layers that lie before you? And what might you learn by peeling back the layers, much as a chef might peel an apple for one's favorite pie or strudel?

In this chapter our goal is to peel back the first layer and examine it. This first layer will help you think through your congregational first impression—how your congregational culture impacts "outsiders" as well as "insiders" as they attempt to understand what's taking place. We will peel the Culture Apple by identifying the skin or first layer, by providing a number of examples of what you might see at this layer, by addressing how people respond, by observing and understanding the layer (cultural exegesis), and by using the Culture Matrix to summarize the layer.

The Identity of the First Layer

The first layer of the church's culture is its expression or presentation of itself in terms of what it does. It consists of its overt behavior or actions and artifacts (the results of behavior). It's that aspect of the culture that is perceived by one's senses, including all that you would see, hear, and feel as you first encounter the congregation. In defining culture, some have used the illustration of the old-timer who when asked for a definition of culture responded, "It's the way we do things around here!" This is true, but true only of the first layer or the skin of the apple. It doesn't reveal enough. For example, it doesn't address why they do things the way they do—their values—or the beliefs or assumptions on which they're based. Both are vital to discovering culture.

How might a culture sculptor identify the first layer? The answer is twofold. First, I have found the following format to be helpful in discovering and identifying the apple's skin. If it will fit in the sentence below, it's most likely a first-layer feature of the culture:

> *Expressions Format*: "We see, hear, feel, sense _____."

Second, I have provided some general cultural practices or expressions early in chapter 7 where I address how to exegete a culture. They will help you identify your culture when you begin to study it. Should you desire a more exhaustive list, see the Behaviors Audit in appendix A.

It's important to note that it is easy to observe expressions of a church's culture but more difficult to understand them. You can't tell much about an apple simply by observing its outer layer or skin. It's like the tip of an iceberg. Anyone who knows anything about icebergs knows that the part you see above the water—only 10 percent of the iceberg—isn't representative of the entire iceberg. Most of it (90 percent) lies below the surface. The church's behavior or expression of itself is what you can observe. It's the tip of the cultural iceberg. Remember that while the culture is behavior-expressed, it is values-driven and beliefs-based. For you to really understand the congregational culture, you must explore below the waterline at the values and beliefs levels. They will tell you much about the culture.

Some Examples of the First Layer

To better understand the first layer of a church's culture, let's visit a fictional church and see what we observe, hear, feel, and sense out in the parking lot, during the worship service, in a Bible study, and so forth. Following is a list of the more common cultural expressions or behavior that a visitor would experience at the first layer of a church's Culture Apple. Should you peel off and examine the skin, here is what you might see (see appendix A for more examples).

Neighborhood or community. Is the neighborhood new, old, or in between? Does it consist of apartments, houses, businesses, or a combination? Are the people who live in the community Anglo, Hispanic, Black, Asian, other, or a combination? Are the people in the community of the same ethnicity as those who attend the church or are they different? Does the neighborhood seem to be declining or growing?

Demographics. Is the congregation made up of Anglos, Blacks, Hispanics, Asians, other, or a combination (multiethnic)? Are the people poor, affluent, or somewhere between? Are people mostly young, middle-aged, or elderly? Are there young families with kids? How does the congregation's demographics align or not align with those you've observed in the neighborhood?

Language. What do you hear? What languages do people speak? Is the church mono- or multilingual? What languages are spoken in the service? Do you understand what's being said?

Facilities. Usually the facilities include educational space, the worship center/sanctuary, and offices. Do the buildings have drive-by appeal? Are the facilities clean and well maintained, especially the nursery, the bathrooms, and the kitchen? Are the facilities safe? During worship, do people sit in pews, chairs, or both?

Parking. Is adequate parking available? Does the church provide visitor and handicapped parking? Is there special parking for the elderly and for expectant moms? Are parking places reserved for the pastor, other staff, and their spouses? Are security or police vehicles present?

Grounds. Are the grounds clean and well kept? Is the grass mowed? Are the leaves raked? Are there adequate flowers and foliage?

Signage. Is there signage showing where to turn in to the church? Is there adequate signage so that visitors know where to park? Are there signs inside the building for the bathrooms and classrooms?

Attendants. Are there friendly, helpful attendants located in the parking lots to direct people where to park their cars? Are there people available to direct visitors to the nursery or Sunday school classes?

Vehicles. What types of vehicles are in the parking lots? Are they new, expensive cars or are they older and possibly not well kept? Are there trucks (in Texas they call pickup trucks Texas Cadillacs)? Are there church vehicles, such as a church van or bus?

Clothing. Is the dress casual, dressy, or business formal? Do the men wear suits? Are the people stylish—do they seem to care about or wear the latest styles? Is there a particular style of clothing, such as Western wear, that many wear?

Friendliness. Are people friendly? For example, do they greet you, say hello, smile, answer questions, and offer to help visitors find their way around the church?

Emotions. Do people show their emotions? For example, are they emotionally expressive during worship time (do they wave their hands and/or shout amen)? Or are they unemotional (they keep their hands in their pockets)? Do they ever shout, speak out, fall over, stand, weep, dance, and so forth?

Security. Are there police or security people wandering the facilities? Are there security cameras? Are the facilities and grounds well lighted? Do people appear to feel safe when at this church?

Manner of address. Do people call one another by their first names? How do people address the senior pastor or other pastors and staff members?

Technology. Is the church technologically astute? Does it have front or rear screen projection? Is there a soundboard? Do you see people using computers or other electronic devices?

Communication. How does the church communicate with people? Does it use bulletins, make announcements, use U.S. Postal Service, or use email? Does it have a website?

Ordinances. Does the church practice the ordinances (baptism and the Lord's Supper)? How often? Does it baptize by immersion or sprinkling? Does it use wine or grape juice, cracker or matzo in communion?

Symbols. Does the worship area or sanctuary contain symbols, such as a cross, a religious tapestry, stained-glass windows?

Worship. Is the church's worship style traditional or contemporary? Does it use a liturgy? What musical instruments, if any, are used in worship? Is there a choir? Are people free to express their emotions during worship? Does the church sing using hymnals, words on a screen, or both?

Disciple-making ministries. Does the church evidence a clear, simple pathway for making disciples? Does it offer Sunday school, small groups, men's and women's Bible studies, and other learning opportunities? Does the church appear to have the same or similar ministries for children and young people?

Outreach ministries. Does the church have and make known its community outreach ministries? Do they advertise them well? Does the church reach out to poor and oppressed people in or outside its community?

Missions. Does the church support in some way international missions? Does it support local missions? Does the church ever do a fund-raiser or capital campaign to raise funds for missions?

The Scriptures. Does the church teach and preach from the Bible? Do people carry their Bibles to church, classes, and small group meetings?

Discipline. Does the church practice church discipline? Have you ever observed someone being disciplined?

Visible behavior. Do people in general manifest the fruit of the Spirit as found in Galatians 5:22–23 (love, joy, peace, patience, kindness, goodness, faithfulness, gentleness, and self-control)? Do the majority of the people appear on the surface to be spiritually mature people?

Vision. Does the church appear to have and communicate a vision? Is it written down anywhere? Do you hear it regularly from the pastor or clergyperson when preaching?

Values. Has the church identified and does it communicate well its values? Has it done the same with its core values? Are they written down somewhere?

Atmosphere. Do you sense that the church is warm and welcoming or cold and aloof? Do you feel tension in the air?

Ceremonies. What does the church celebrate? Does it have baby dedications, infant baptisms, and ordination services?

Women. Does the church appear to have more women than men in the congregation? How do women express themselves in the church?

Myths and stories. Is there any particular person or persons that the church tells stories about—who are its heroes? Is this person the pastor or a past pastor, such as the founding pastor? Does the church make heroes of some of its missionaries or longtime members?

Visitors. Does the church seem prepared for visitors? Do they have parking reserved for visitors? Do they have greeters who look for visitors and direct them to where they want or need to go? Does the church follow up visitors with a phone call and/or letter?

Pastor. Is the senior pastor friendly? Is he a good preacher? Is he a good leader? What does he appear to value most? Do you like him?

Staff. Does the church have any staff people (paid ministry people other than the senior pastor) who lead ministries? What ministries do they lead?

Doctrinal beliefs. Does the church have and communicate its doctrinal beliefs as based on the Scriptures? Do the pastor and other teachers regularly teach and preach the church's doctrinal beliefs from the Bible?

Leadership development. Does the church have a process for developing leaders churchwide? Does the church have a process for developing its small group leaders? Does the church have a governing board and provide leadership training for it?

Finances. Do the pastor and others preach and teach on stewardship at least annually? Is the church struggling financially? Is the church doing well financially? Do leaders say little about the church's finances?

How People Respond to the First Layer

Those who are visiting the church for the first time (believers who are looking for a good church, unbelievers who have been invited to attend the church, or potential pastors or staff) experience the first layer as expressed above. Practically everything they see, hear, or feel is somewhat unique to the church and new to them. They will likely be comfortable with some of it and uncomfortable with other aspects of the first layer. They are there to check out the church to see if it's the kind of culture they want to be a part of. Often they're looking for a culture similar to one that has had a powerful impact on their lives in the past.

Those, however, who have been at the church for a while tend, with some exceptions, to have accepted the culture the way it is and hardly notice it until someone calls it into question or attempts to change it. They go through the motions that are part of the culture without thinking much about what they're doing or experiencing. For example, there was a time in my ministry when I did a lot of interim pastoring. I found that when I questioned the church about some aspect of their culture, such as the upkeep of their facilities or the lack thereof, people would be surprised by my observation. They were operating on automatic pilot and basically were unaware of what they were or were not doing.

Observing the First Layer

Wise leaders don't operate on automatic pilot or the status quo. We'll learn that regularly they observe the congregational culture of other churches as well as their own. The goal is for this observation to become second nature. I'll fully address this topic in chapters 7 and 8. As a culture detective, your job at this point is simply to observe and experience what a church does or what you see when you visit the church. Be a visitor. Make a list. Take copious notes of the congregation's behavior. Resist the urge to ask why they do what they do, trying to interpret their behavior. This is the values question that we'll ask at the next level. Simply observe as much as possible. Early in chapter 7 there is a brief exercise to help you in your observation of your culture.

Summarizing the First Layer: The Culture Matrix

At the beginning of this chapter, I briefed you on the Culture Matrix. I want to make it clear what I mean by the term *matrix*. The matrix I have designed is a summary of what chapters 3, 4, and 5 contribute to our understanding of a church's culture. As we go through the chapters, the summaries will appear side by side for easy comparison. The first part of the matrix focuses on the expressions or actions of the culture.

Behaviors or Expressions

Definition	The results of acting on a value.
Action	The resulting behavior—what we do.
Number	Organizations have numerous actions, behaviors, or expressions.
Purpose	How a value affects life.
Change	Subject to change.
Synonyms	*Actions, presentation; what we do*

Expressions Format: "We see, hear, feel, sense _____."

Questions for Reflection and Discussion

1. Do you find that using a figure, such as an apple, helps you better grasp the definition of congregational culture? Why or why not? Is there another figure that would be more helpful? If so, what is it and how does it help?
2. The first layer of a congregation's culture—the apple peel—is its expression or presentation of itself. Would you agree that, much like the tip of an iceberg, it doesn't tell you enough about a particular congregation's culture? Why or why not?
3. In this chapter, the author supplies you with a number of examples of the first layer of a culture. Do you find these helpful? Why or why not? Are there any examples you feel the author might have missed or left out? If so, what are they?
4. If a guest were to visit your church, what do you believe he or she would observe, hear, feel, and sense? Use the Behaviors Audit in appendix A to help you answer this question.

5. Conduct your own tour of your church. Take several leaders in your church on a tour of what takes place on a typical Sunday or at other times when people meet. Ask what they see, hear, and feel.

6. Ask outsiders to visit and point out what they see, hear, and feel. Ask them for the unvarnished truth.

7. Do you believe that this chapter can help a pastor, a visitor, or some other person to begin exegeting or reading a congregation's culture? Why or why not?

8. Would you agree that many of the people who attend a particular church regularly over a period of time don't think much about what they are doing and why? Why is this the case? Could this be true of a church that you are a part of?

$$4$$

Why We Do What We Do

The Church's Cultural Values

A s you peel off and observe the first layer or skin of the Culture Apple, you have a sense that something is happening at the next layer, which is directing the church's behavior or expression of itself. This second layer—the apple's flesh—is the church's organizational values in general and its core values in particular that are most critical to its culture. In this chapter I will address the reason values are so important to the culture, the definition of a value, kinds of values, how to discover your culture's values, the development of a values statement for your ministry, and how to communicate your values. At the end of the chapter, I have added values to the Culture Matrix.

Culture Apple

Skin—Behavior

Flesh—Values

Core—Beliefs

The Importance of Values

Values are a vital part of any ministry's culture, the very threads that make up its organizational fabric. Lyle Schaller writes: "The most important single element of any corporate, congregational, or denominational culture . . . is the value system."[1] If pastors fully grasped this, they would know that they should not become the pastors of some churches. While churches and pastors differ in many areas, most significantly, their views of ministry may rest on different foundational values. If this is true, it's only a matter of time before the winds of turbulence test and eventually collapse the church's organizational structure. Any pastor or church that overlooks the importance of core values to the culture does so to its detriment. Following are nine essential reasons that core values are so important to a church's culture.

1. Values Determine Ministry Distinctives

God has not cut all churches from the same bolt of cloth. Your church or ministry culture is unique—like no other. This is good because it takes all kinds of churches to reach all kinds of people. What makes each ministry different is its organizational culture. And as Schaller notes above, the most important ingredients in any cultural recipe is the values system. A ministry based on clearly articulated core values drives a fixed stake in the ground that says to all, "This is what we stand for; this is what we are all about; this is who we are; this is what we can do for you." Thus values define each church's unique identity in the ministry world.

2. Values Dictate Personal Involvement

Values help people such as a pastor, a pastor candidate, or a potential member determine his or her personal involvement in a particular ministry culture. A potential member, pastor, or ministry staff person should discover if his or her core ministry values align closely with the organization's values. I call this ministry values alignment based on shared ministry values. The key questions are: Do we have the same values? How close are we in what we value? Can we passionately commit to the same precepts? These questions help people find common cause that leads to ministry community. People involve themselves more and last longer in a ministry culture if they know from the beginning that they share the same or similar core values. When people walk through the church's front door, understanding clearly both their own and the church's values, it promotes their assimilation, closing the church's back door.

3. Values Communicate What Is Important

An organization's core values signal its bottom line. They dictate what it stands for, what truly matters, what is worthwhile and desirous. They determine what is inviolate for it; they define what it believes is God's heart for its ministry. While every ministry culture has a set of values, not all of the values are of equal importance. Some take priority over others. These high-priority values represent a watershed, or point of no return, for the culture.

4. Values Guide Change

More than at any other time in its history, North America is exploding with accelerating change. America and all of Western society have climbed on board the roller coaster of change only to find that they cannot climb off. And no end to the convoluted, chaotic ride is in sight.

The important questions for Christian churches are: How can we know what to change in our culture and what not to change? How can we know what is good or bad change for the organization? With the increasing speed of change, a wrong move would not only prove costly, it could prove deadly to the ministry. The only sacred cows in the ministry are those based on Scripture: its mission, its core values, and its doctrinal beliefs.

The church's primary values provide a useful anchor in a wider culture that is constantly in a state of accelerating flux. The church organization must have a set of values that provides it with a common and consistent sense of direction. These core values serve as glue and a guiding force that hold a visionary ministry culture together in the midst of transition. As the culture changes rapidly around it, the organization must learn to adapt to change, but only within the context of its unchanging beliefs. How does it accomplish this? How does it choose what change to embrace and what to reject? The answer lies in the question, Does this change agree with or contradict the core values and mission of this culture? The answer will guide the church to positive change.

5. Values Influence Overall Behavior

A ministry's key values are the shaping force of the entire institutional culture. They beget attitudes that determine behavior. They affect everything about the organization: the decisions made, the goals set, the priorities established, the problems solved, the conflicts resolved, and more. Someone has compared key values to an aroma that permeates every aspect of the institution. Schaller writes: "The values of any organization control priorities, provide the foundation for formulating goals, and set the tone and direction of the organization."[2] Values are the basis for all your behavior, the bottom line for what you will or will not do in your unique culture.

6. *Values Inspire People to Action*

You can tell Christians to share their faith with the lost. You can insist that they volunteer for ministry in their churches. You can offer them stipends and tease them with perks in an attempt to increase their effectiveness in what they are already doing. Yet until they make a personal commitment to do evangelism on the local college campus or volunteer to serve in an inner-city soup kitchen, nothing much will happen. What is the missing ingredient to the recipe that stimulates and sustains this kind of cultural transformation within a person? What moves a church member from a passive pew position to persistent participation? People need and want something they can commit to, something they feel is worthy of their best efforts. They are willing, even eager, to commit voluntarily and work for that which is truly worthwhile, that which is larger than themselves, that which creates meaning in their lives. Churches can play an enormous role in infusing their people's lives with such meaning.

How does a ministry culture accomplish this? How can it play a role in infusing people's lives with meaning that, in turn, inspires them to action? The answer, as expected, has everything to do with its core values as well as its mission and vision. Values give servants a greater sense of meaning in their service, but not just any values and not just biblical values. The values must be shared, biblical core values. The shared beliefs of both the leaders and their followers catalyze—energize—people. They are the invisible motivators that move people's hearts toward meaningful ministry. If any church culture desires to capture the great energies and gifts of its people, it must share to some degree their common core values, so that its people, in turn, find common cause with the organization, which leads to authentic biblical community.

7. *Values Enhance Credible Leadership*

As the leadership goes, so goes the organizational culture. Good leadership is essential to any successful Christian ministry. A core element in any definition of leadership is influence; good leaders influence people. The ability to influence followers has characterized the excellent leadership of people like Abraham, Moses, Joshua, Deborah, Nehemiah, Esther, Peter, Paul, Martin Luther, John Calvin, Abraham Lincoln, Martin Luther King Jr., Elisabeth Elliot, Billy Graham, Joni Eareckson Tada, and Charles Swindoll.

VALUES-DRIVEN LEADERS

All leaders are values-driven, and the ministry cultures they build are expressions of their values. Because they identify closely with their organizations and because they have committed so much of themselves to them, their ministries reflect their key, vital values. Therefore, leaders must decide what they stand for. They must determine their bottom line. Not just any bottom line will do. It is imperative that Christian leaders opt for a strong Bible-based values system. This is because strong values make for strong leaders, and strong leaders make for strong ministry cultures.

VALUES-CONSISTENT LIFESTYLE

When leaders have a set of core values for their churches as well as for themselves, it is equally important that they model a lifestyle consistent with these values. This is key to leadership credibility. Leaders shape people's values, and they instill these values more through what they do than through what they say. If their behavior is consistent with their values, they infuse their leadership with large doses of credibility. If, however, their walk does not match their talk, if they articulate one set of values for the organization's culture but live with a different set, followers will view them as hypocrites, and they will lose all credibility. In 1 Timothy 4:12 this is made very clear to Timothy, a young leader and mentor of leaders, when Paul writes to him: "Don't let anyone look down on you because you are young, but set an example for the believers in speech, in conduct, in love, in faith and in purity." In 1 Corinthians 11:1 he writes to the Corinthian church: "Follow my example, as I follow the example of Christ."

8. Values Shape Ministry Character

People's character, whether good or bad, directly affects how they conduct their life. People of poor character tend to live life poorly in that they may fudge on the truth or cut corners to accomplish their goals. People of good character live life well in that they are honest, moral, and upright. In either case it is their values that directly affect their character. A person's character is the direct descendant of his or her values; personal character rests on the foundation of personal values.

The same is true for any church culture. Its values are character defining. Core values are the qualities that make up and establish an organization's character, and that character determines how the organization conducts its ministry. It is essential that the pastor of a church have a vision of where the organization is going and a strategy for how it will get there. However, he must understand that the members and the attendees will use certain standards to judge his performance and that of the staff as they pursue and lead others in the pursuit of the church's vision. It is actually the character of both the pastor and the ministry team that is being judged, and key to their character are their core precepts.

9. Values Contribute to Ministry Success

Any organization, Christian or non-Christian, must have and adhere to a sound set of fundamental beliefs if it is to achieve success. It is the culture's ingrained understanding of its core values more than its technical skills that makes it possible for its people to have a successful ministry culture.

But what is success? What makes a ministry culture such as a church successful? Success is the accomplishment of the ministry's mission and vision (Matt. 28:19–20) without compromising its vital, bottom-line values. A church that is winning lost people in its ministry community and is moving its new converts and older converts toward maturity—Christlikeness—while maintaining its distinctive, primary biblical values is successful because it is accomplishing its biblical mission and vision without sacrificing its core values.

Nine Reasons Values Are Important

1. They determine ministry distinctives.
2. They dictate personal involvement.
3. They communicate what is important.
4. They guide change.
5. They influence overall behavior.
6. They inspire people to action.
7. They enhance credible leadership.
8. They shape ministry character.
9. They contribute to ministry success.

Defining Values

One of my personal core values is clarity. I find that some ministry leaders use terms without defining them and thus don't communicate as well as they could. I referred to this problem in the introduction and again in chapter 2. Sometimes I want to lead a clarity parade where we all stop marching long enough to define our terms so that people know what we're talking about. Otherwise we may discover that we're not even talking about the same thing, even though we are using the same or similar terms.

This is certainly true of *values*. What does the term mean as I'm using it in this book in general and culture in particular? This calls for a "clarity moment." I've made the point that values are important; now I must pause to define what I mean by *values*. It's imperative that I practice what I preach, so here is my definition: *Core values are the constant, passionate shared core beliefs that drive and guide the culture.* The following will further explain or illuminate my definition by addressing key ingredients that make up the values pie.

Constant

First, a culture's values are constant. That is, they don't change easily or quickly. They hang on tenaciously to life. This could be bad or good. It can be bad when cultures need to change but resist changing and often fail to do so. I'm convinced this is one of the reasons so many churches are plateaued or in decline. They either don't change or don't change fast enough to keep up with the church's surrounding environment.

On the other hand, resisting change is good when a church has embraced good, biblical core values, such as those in Acts 2:42–47.

Passionate

Core values are passionate. *Passion* is a feeling word. It's what you feel strongly and care deeply about. Discover a person's passion and you unearth his or her cause. And cause is critical to one's life and ministry. Take away a person's cause, and you strip him or her of the drive to do what the person wants to do in life. Good core values get at an organization's cause—they touch the heart as well as the head and elicit strong emotions from a congregational culture. If your soul isn't stirred by your stated core values, they aren't at the culture's core.

Shared

The core values of a culture must be shared. If people don't share them, they're not core. Another term for this is *common cause*. Shared values become the common cause that is so vital to realizing a ministry culture's vision. However, if congregants don't share these values, the mission and vision will not happen.

Core Beliefs

Core values are beliefs, but not just any beliefs. Values are rooted in your core beliefs. But what is a belief? Again, clarity is needed here. *A belief is*

WHY WE DO WHAT WE DO

a conviction or opinion that you hold to be true, though based on limited proof. There may not be a lot of evidence to support it. It is a view that you take by faith. Most congregational cultures have numerous beliefs that make up their core or third layer. The beliefs that the culture acts on become actual values as well as beliefs. Those the culture doesn't act on remain beliefs and aspirational values at best. A classic example is evangelism. Theologically conservative churches believe in evangelism. It's a core belief. However, it's not a core value until many in the culture begin to share their faith. I'll say more about this in the next chapter on beliefs and assumptions.

Whereas the church's behavior (the first or outer layer) communicates what it does, the congregation's values (second layer) are its beliefs that it actually acts on; they explain why the organization does what it does or behaves the way it behaves at the first layer. As you recall, the first layer asks and answers the question, What are you doing? It's behavior-expressed. The second layer addresses what you value or *why* you do what you do. It's values-driven. The third asks what you believe or assume. It's beliefs-based.

Driving and Guiding the Church

Finally, the church is values-driven and values-guided. Core values are to the church what an engine is to a ship. Just as the engine drives the ship toward its destination, so a church's core values drive the ministry toward its mission and ultimately its vision. Not only do values drive the church, they guide or give direction to the congregation, much as a ship's rudder guides a ship. They make sure the culture ship is moving in the right direction, and they are the red flag that waves when it isn't.

The Definition of a Value

A value is constant.
A value is passionate.
A value is shared.
A value is a core belief.
A value drives and guides the church.

Kinds of Values

In defining core values, it has been helpful to consider what they are. We can further hone and refine the definition by examining different types of values. We will discuss four kinds of values that exist in tension.

Conscious versus Unconscious Values

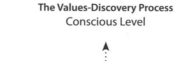

The Values-Discovery Process
Conscious Level

Values
Unconscious Level

The core organizational values of all Christian ministry cultures exist at both a conscious and an unconscious level. To some degree those involved in the culture are aware of the values that are most important and of high priority. An evangelistic organization is well aware that it values evangelism; a school or seminary knows that it values teaching. Most ministries, however, hold the majority of their values at a subconscious level. This is because they have numerous values, and even though these values influence decisions made every day, the ministry participants have not actually stopped to think about or discuss most of them.

Leaders are responsible for discovering and articulating the institution's primary cultural values. When values are articulated—conscious—leaders know why they are doing what they are doing. If they hold some bad values or some that their ministry's constituency does not share, they will be aware of them and over time can make changes accordingly. If people in the ministry have sharp disagreements with one another, they may find solutions once they have identified their key values. Often they'll discover that their differences are due to the fact that their values do not align.

Personal versus Ministry Values

A person's organizational values resemble a ministry's organizational values. Both concern the ministry organization. One difference between them, however, is that the latter values affect all who make up the organizational culture, whereas personal values affect primarily the individual but have the potential to affect the entire organization.

MINISTRY VALUES

Every institution has a core set of organizational values. We have seen the importance of these key values in driving the organization. (I refer to these as *organizational, institutional,* or *corporate values.* These are valid terms to use in describing the values of a sacred or a secular institution. When referring specifically to a Christian organization, I may use the term *ministry,* and if it is a church, I may use the adjective *congregational.*) Individuals who make up the institution also have a set of core values. (I call them *personal, individual,* or *private organizational values.*) These are values that concern the organization as a whole. Every person brings to a ministry his or her own private set of core beliefs concerning what should drive and guide that culture.

PERSONAL VALUES

Like the organizational values, personal or individual values can be helpful or harmful. They should ask such questions as: Are my values for this ministry going to help or harm it? Are they reasonable or unreasonable? Do most of my core values align with those of the ministry culture of which I am a part? Do few of my values align, or do some align and some not?

Actual versus Aspirational Values

Leaders and organizations have both actual and aspirational core values.

ACTUAL VALUES

Actual values stem from the beliefs at the third level or core of the culture that they own and act on daily. These values come from inside the person. They exist in the present and have to do with what is true about the ministry right now. Luke provides us with the Jerusalem Church's actual core values in Acts 2:42–47. They are worship, fellowship, biblical instruction, evangelism, and ministry. We know they are actual values, because in verse 42, he writes, "They *devoted themselves to* the apostles' teaching . . ." (italics mine).

ASPIRATIONAL VALUES

Aspirational values are beliefs that the individual or organization does not currently act on. These values identify what should or ought to be, not what is; they may be values that the leadership or culture would like to adopt in the future. Until they are adopted, however, they remain aspirational values. Today there are a number of churches who have few people involved in ministries in their church. Consequently, for them to list lay ministry as an actual value is a mistake. They should view lay ministry as a belief or an aspirational value.

Most of this book focuses on actual not aspirational values. The key to understanding what drives you or your ministry culture is not what you would like to value as much as what you do value. You cannot fake your values or your vision. Nor can you intellectualize or rationalize them. You must passionately hold your core values, as well as your vision, at a gut level right now, today.

Single versus Multiple Values

All organizations have multiple values. In larger corporations with numerous people, there can be hundreds of values. A culture's core values, however, are those that are the highest in priority, and in some institutions, a single, overriding core value exists. If you listed their values in order of priority, you would find it at the top of the list, often with some distance between it and the others. It's like an umbrella with the other values appropriately arranged under it.

In a congregational culture, a single robust value may serve to unify the church and communicate the church's central thrust. It announces what the church is all about, what it stands for. The chart in the next section presents several North American church paradigms and the unifying, dominating core value of each. We will look at the first paradigm, the classroom church, to get an idea of what the chart is communicating about each value.

Kinds of Values

Conscious versus Unconscious
Personal versus Ministry
Actual versus Aspirational
Single versus Multiple

The Power of a Value

American Evangelical Churches

Type of Church	Unifying Value	Role of Pastor	Role of People	Primary Purpose	Typical Tool	Desired Result
Classroom church	Doctrine	Teacher	Students	To know	Sermon outline	Educated Christians
Soul-winning church	Evangelism	Evangelist	Bringers	To save	Altar call	Born-again persons
Experiential church	Worship	Worship leader	Worshipers	To exalt	Liturgy	Committed Christians
Family-reunion church	Fellowship	Chaplain	Siblings	To belong	Potluck	Secure Christians

At the top of the chart is the classroom church. The overriding or unifying value is information or Bible doctrine. This is what is distinctive about this ministry culture. It communicates that if you want to know the Bible, this is the church for you. You can see how this one potent value affects the entire ministry. It clearly defines the role of the pastor and the people. It sets the key emphasis (to know) in concrete. And it dictates the desired result (an educated Christian).

A Unifying Value

A culture or church ministry would be wise to examine its essential beliefs to determine if it has a unifying or overarching value. Many do. However, this unifying value may or may not be desirable, depending on the ministry's vision and purpose. When my church-planting students at Dallas Seminary examine this chart, they view it through Great Commission eyes. The result for them is that most of the churches with a single, unifying value prove inadequate because they emphasize some aspect of the Great Commission and not the commission as a whole. Thus they specialize, more like a parachurch ministry than a church ministry.

Values and Expectations

This chart demonstrates well the power of a value in the life of a culture. Values alert you to what people's expectations of you will be if you're a pastor or the candidate to be a pastor. A pastor needs to know the congregation's values that are key to their expectations. If the pastor fails to meet these expectations, he will be looking for another church.

Of course, pastors have values as well. Their values will lead them to expect a certain response from the culture. For example, a pastor's overriding value might be Scripture or biblical teaching. However, the congregation's primary value might be pastoral care, not Bible teaching. The pastor may not last very long in such a culture.

Discovering Core Values

Whether they are aware of them or not, pastors and their churches have a set of actual core values. If they have not surfaced and articulated these values, it could prove costly to both the pastor and the congregation. Many cultures other than churches have given little or no attention to the vital, shaping values that drive the institution and underlie the behavior of the leaders and members.

These values are ever present and are vital determinants of behavior; yet rarely do leaders consciously express them, and even more rarely do they discover and discuss them in an open fashion to determine whether values are helpful or harmful to the ministry.

What if a pastor as a culture detective and a church as a culture community want to surface and discover their key congregational values? How would they go about the process? What does a leader or an organization do to probe the culture and unearth values? The answer to these questions is the values-discovery process. It consists of three elements: a decision concerning who is responsible for discovering the values, a determination of the values the church will seek to discover, and the discovery of the church's actual values.

Who Discovers the Culture's Values?

A LEAD PERSON

If an established church culture desires to discover its values, the primary responsibility to see that it takes place is with the leadership, and in particular, with the point person in the organization. The point person is the primary leader of the organization—the leader of the leaders. In the church the point person is the senior pastor. He along with a ministry team will pursue the values-discovery process.

If the organization is a new church plant, the lead church planter or culture creator will need to discover the core values of the culture that he and others are creating. Most likely they will be the church planter's values—the ones he brings with him. If you are a senior pastor or ministry staff person who is being considered for a lead position in a church, you are responsible for discovering that church culture's values. Finally, when one culture is adopting another—as in the merger of two churches—the lead pastor or lay leader along with a party from the other church culture needs to take the responsibility to discover both churches' values to see if there's alignment between the two cultures.

A MINISTRY TEAM

Let's return to the established church setting. Most people in an established culture look to the top for a definition of what is really important—the ministry's bottom line. The leader may or may not be the author of the key values, but the leader is responsible for their discovery, making them clear, and ensuring that all live up to them in the decision-making process. One of the great contributions a leader can make to a ministry culture is to help unearth, clarify, and breathe life into its significant values. The leader does not accomplish this by himself but sees to it that it is accomplished.

To discover the key values, it is imperative that the leader enlist the aid of other leaders or the leadership team in the ministry for their knowledge of the ministry culture and for their objectivity. In the old leadership paradigm the pastor does all the ministry and makes all the ministry decisions. The new paradigm looks to leaders sprinkled throughout the ministry culture to be involved in the process. I refer to them as the church's E. F. Hutton people—from the old E. F. Hutton television commercial that stated, "When E. F. Hutton [an investment broker] speaks, people listen." In the church these E. F. Hutton people have influence, no matter their ministry or position or even if they have no official position. They are people on the church board, staff, pastor, and lay leaders, such as Bible study leaders, Sunday school teachers, small group leaders, as well as long-term members with influence.

Usually the size of a church ministry dictates the number of persons involved in the values-discovery process. A small church may have five or six people. In a larger ministry I've worked with as many as thirty leaders, each with their circles of influence in the culture. If this number seems too large, keep in mind that some will always be absent from teamwork meetings due to other responsibilities. I recommend that you have at least five people and no more than twenty to twenty-five on the values-discovery team.

Finally, some research tells us that, for a person to really understand the values of a culture, he or she needs to have been a part of it for one to two years. However, there's value in asking new people to the culture what values they've observed and experienced since they've been there. Sometimes established church members tend not to perceive the values that are present or absent in the culture, while new members are more apt to notice due to their newness to and early interest in the culture. They ask, "What does this church value, and do their values align with mine?"

What Values Are Discovered?

The values-discovery process examines both personal values and organizational values.

PERSONAL VALUES

Values discovery begins at the individual or personal level of each person involved. In an entrepreneurial ministry culture, such as a church plant, the point person, especially if he is a lone ranger—not working with a team—will

usually identify and cast his personal values for the culture. Then, when others
consider joining the culture, they can look for common cause to determine
if there is a ministry fit. It is most important that the primary leader and the
key decision makers in an established ministry culture be clear about their
own individual, personal values and recognize any differences between them.

ORGANIZATIONAL VALUES

Next, values discovery moves to the ministry organization itself. This includes two levels. The first is the values set that drives the entire ministry culture
as a whole. These values make up the ministry's credo or values statement.
They communicate the uniqueness of this culture as well as what the entire
organization is all about.

The second level is the values of the organizations or ministries that make
up the broader organization—the under-the-umbrella ministry cultures or the
cultures within the culture. In the church they may include biblical instruction,
worship, outreach, evangelism, service, and so on. In the best of all worlds,
all the under-the-umbrella ministries hold to the same values as the entire
organizational culture, but they apply them to their particular ministry focus
groups. Let's use evangelism as an example (see the chart below). Assume that
the church as a whole values evangelism. The ideal and what it should strive
for is that the various age-specific ministries, such as adults, youth, and so
forth, also value evangelism but as it relates to their age group.

Ministry	Ministry Value
Church ministry	Lost people matter to God
Adult ministry	Lost adults matter to God
Youth ministry	Lost youth matter to God
Children's ministry	Lost children matter to God

How Are Values Discovered?

Values discovery attempts to determine the reasons an individual or organization does what it does. At this point in the process, it is important to
remember that people are not creating or shaping their primary values; they
are discovering them. They are attempting to bring to the surface actual,
not aspirational, values of an adopted, established, or planted church. The
process has to be authentic; they cannot fake core values nor can they intellectualize them. By looking inside, people discover the values they hold
passionately at a gut level. If they are not passionate about them, they are
not core values. In effect, discovering values is a process of dusting off their

values and taking a hard look at what they already own, not at what they plan to adopt in the future.

THE VALUES FORMAT

One way to discover values is by using the second layer Values Format. In the last chapter we discovered the culture's first layer—the culture's behavior or expression—by using the Expressions Format.

Values Format: "We value_____."

What you write in the blank will most likely be your values.

THE CORE VALUES AUDIT

Another way to discover values is through the Core Values Audit, which you will find in appendix B. A leader may use this audit to discover his personal core values or with a congregation to discover congregational values. The senior pastor and other leaders in the established church culture should use this audit to surface the church's core congregational values. Church planters should use this audit to discover their own personal core values, understanding that these will most likely become the congregational values of the future church. A senior pastor or staff person who is being considered for a lead position in a church would use it to discover the church's values. Leaders considering a merger of cultures would use it to see the compatibility of the values of the churches involved.

Since organizational values exist on both the personal and the corporate level, when I work with an established church culture, I ask the ministry leadership team to take the Core Values Audit twice. The first time, I ask them to take it from their personal perspective to discover what their personal core values are for a congregational culture. The second time, I ask them to take it from the perspective of the church culture as a whole. Most likely these leaders are the ones who will unearth the ministry's values. They may discover that their personal values for their church do not always align with the church's congregational values. Thus they need to be clear about their own personal credos and any differences they may have with other leaders and decision makers as well as with the church. When there are large differences in values, these leaders will likely move on to a culture that holds values similar to their own.

When seeking to discover personal or congregational core values, one must be careful to distinguish between a church's functions and its forms.

Functions

On the one hand, the functions are timeless, unchanging, and nonnegotiable, because they are based on Scripture. Some examples would be evangelism, worship, biblical instruction, and service. *The church's values are functions.*

Forms

On the other hand, the forms are timely, changing, and negotiable, because they are based on culture, not Scripture. *The forms are not values but expressions of values.* They are the means that accomplish the functions or values. Some examples would be contemporary or traditional worship music and friendship or confrontational evangelism. The forms are what you would detect when you first encounter a church culture. They are found at the first layer of the Culture Apple. When you peel them back, you find the values underneath.

Discovering Values

Functions/Values	Forms
Example: Evangelism	Friendship evangelism
Example: Worship	Contemporary worship

THE CHURCH BUDGET

A third way to discover a church's core values is to read a copy of its current budget. Unfortunately budgets can be difficult to read, because many are written in "accountantese." However, the fact that you know what you're looking for—core values—will help you find them.

Start by looking for the core values of the Jerusalem Church in Acts 2:41–47 (worship, fellowship, biblical instruction, evangelism, and ministry or service). Note the amount of money that has been budgeted for each of these values. How much has the church budgeted for missions? Is this under evangelism or is missions a substitute for evangelism? How well is the church paying its personnel? This will tell you if they value their ministry staff. I have ministered in at least one situation where the church gave more money to its missionaries than its staff but couldn't figure out why it had a morale problem with the staff. It's wonderful that they could give so much to missions, but it was at the expense of their staff. Finally, how much money is budgeted for its facilities? Is this a high or low value for the church? Do they value the facilities more than they should or do they need to put aside more funds for facilities upkeep?

The point is, while there will be exceptions, often you can discover the higher values by the amount of money budgeted to an area. I have included the following to help you discover good guidelines for developing budgets that reflect good values across the board.

Missions and Evangelism	10 percent
Personnel	50 percent
Ministries	20 percent
Facilities	20 percent

THE CHURCH'S VALUES STATEMENT

I advise a pastor who is considering a call to a church or is in the midst of candidating for a lead or staff position in a church to unearth its values if he really wants to know what the church believes at a values level. Request a copy of the church's core values, but don't be surprised if you are greeted with a "Huh?" Most likely the church won't know what you're talking about. If it doesn't, then send a copy of the Core Values Audit in appendix B and ask your contact at the church to complete it. If it is completed, that speaks well of the church.

The Malphurs Group has worked with a number of churches that are looking for a pastor, and one of the exercises we conduct with the church is that of discovering the church's core values. Should you candidate at one of them, the church would inquire as to what your ministry core values are. This is due diligence. They are checking for critical values alignment.

How to Develop a Core Values Statement

Since values are so important to a church's culture, it would be wise to develop a core values statement. (The same is true for a pastor who desires to plant or lead an established church.) Once the team members have discovered their ministry's core values, the next step is to articulate them for the rest of the congregation. This will take the form of a values statement or credo much like the two in appendix C.

In preparation for articulating the values, the team should determine who will develop the credo. My answer is the senior pastor. However, ministry staff people, lay leaders, and board members may be involved in the process. Their fingerprints need to be on the document. This allows them to provide valuable input and gain ownership.

Before you begin, you should think through the reasons for writing or crafting the statement. A written values statement benefits the ministry in several ways. One is that it infuses these values with leadership authority. Also, writing out the primary beliefs gives them greater clarity. And in a multisensory culture, writing remains fundamental to good communication.

The process of developing the values statement takes four steps.

Step 1. Distinguish between Values and Forms

The first step involves making sure the team is working with the value and not its form. I addressed the difference between functions and forms above. One more example should suffice. Often churches list small groups as a value. Actually a small group is a form that expresses or implements a value, but a small group itself is not a value. You may think small groups are important as a form, but that does not make them a value. Do not confuse what you think is important with the actual value. Remember, core values are constant, passionate, biblical core beliefs that drive or empower and guide the ministry. The value behind small groups could be fellowship, biblical community, evangelism, or some other function.

Another way to make the distinction is to ask if the item in question is an end or a means to an end. Small groups are not an end in themselves. They are a means to an end—biblical community or some other function. Or ask, Why are we doing what we are doing? The answer is the value.

Determining Actual Values

	Value	Form
Example:	Biblical community	Small group
Its purpose:	End	Means to an end
It answers:	Why?	What?

Step 2. Determine the Number of Values

The second step is to decide on the number of values. You will need to decide how many values will be in your statement. My research indicates that most churches have from five to ten core values. In *Built to Last*, James Collins and Jerry Porras advise that you have no more than six values and that most visionary companies have fewer.[3] Ken Blanchard and Phil Hodges write, "Research shows that people can't focus on more than three or four values if you really want to impact behavior."[4] The rule of thumb is: less is more—having fewer values is better. I too recommend six actual values and think that, for example, the statement for Northwood Community Church in appendix C contains too many values.

Step 3. Decide on a Statement Format

The third step is to determine the format. This affects how you articulate the values. Several different formats may be used for a values statement. I suggest that you peruse several statements and determine which you like best. Again look at the two examples in appendix C. The values statement for the Jerusalem Church is brief and to the point. The statement for Northwood Community Church is more articulate but has too many values and would be improved if a short one-sentence statement of application were added. See the example of Biblical Teaching below. I have added the sentence in italics, which gives the application. As you write your values statements, strive to keep them simple, clear, straightforward, and powerful.

Biblical Teaching
We strive to teach God's Word with integrity and authority so that seekers find Christ and believers mature in him (2 Tim. 3:16).

> *Therefore, we will strive for excellence in biblical instruction in our worship services and Bible studies.*

Step 4. Test the Statement

Finally, test the values statements. Ask the following: Does this statement attract interest? Is it simple, clear, straightforward, and powerful? Does it include too many values?

The Values Statement Process

1. Distinguish between values and forms.
2. Determine the number of values.
3. Decide on a statement format.
4. Test the statement.

How to Communicate Core Values

You might develop the perfect values statement for your ministry, but if your constituency never sees it, then it dies an untimely death. You should encourage everyone in the ministry to become involved in the values communication process. But it becomes the primary responsibility of the leadership team—board and staff—to see that the statement is available to all connected with the organization.

Following are some ways that churches have communicated their values:

Life and example of leadership   Slide presentation

Written statement   Audio- and videotapes

Sermons   Skits and drama

Formal and informal conversation   Newcomers' class

Stories   Newsletter

Bulletin   Performance appraisal

Framed posters   Cartoons

Church brochure   Website

Training materials

I have touched only the tip of the iceberg. The only limit to the way a church communicates its values is its creative abilities. Jerry Joplin, the pastor of Bacon Heights Baptist Church in Lubbock, Texas, built a climbing wall in the sanctuary where each foot- and handhold was labeled with a core value. What might you and your creative people come up with?

The Culture Matrix

As we work our way through chapters 3–5, we are building a Culture Matrix for the purpose of clarity. In chapter 3, the matrix summarizes and clarifies the culture's actions. Now we add the culture's values and compare them with its behavior or expression.

Values versus Behavior

	Value	Behavior
Definition	A belief that guides and drives an individual or organization to act on a belief or assumption.	The results of acting on a value.
Action	A belief that people act on. It guides/directs behavior—the reason we do what we do.	The resulting behavior—what we do.
Number	Organizations have fewer values.	Organizations have numerous actions, behaviors, or expressions.
Purpose	To guide or direct behavior that affects life.	How a value affects life.
Change	Very slow to change, but not as slow as beliefs.	Subject to change.
Synonyms	*Ideal, standard, precept; why we do what we do.*	*Action, presentation; what we do.*

Values Format: "We value _____."

Expressions Format: "We see/hear/feel _____."

Questions for Reflection and Discussion

1. The author lists nine reasons that values are important. Did he convince you of their importance? Why or why not?
2. Did any particular reason stand out from the rest? If so, which one? Can you think of any other importance of values that the author may have missed? If so, what is it?
3. Do you agree with the author's definition of a value? Why or why not? Does anything need to be added or taken out?
4. Does your church hold its values at a conscious or unconscious level? If the latter, then what is your responsibility to the church as its leader or one of its leaders?
5. How do your personal organizational values align with the church's organizational values? Are they the same, somewhat the same, or very different? If the latter, what should you do about it? What *will* you do about it?
6. Does your culture have a single controlling value that stands out from the rest? If so, what is it? How does this affect the church's ministry? If you're the pastor, how does it affect people's expectations of you? How does it affect your expectations of your people?
7. Who in your church would be the best person to lead in discovering its actual core values? Why?
8. Of the three ways to discover a church's values, which is best for you? Why? Would you prefer to use all three?
9. Would you or your church benefit by drafting a values statement? Why or why not?
10. How important is it that you communicate your values constantly? What are some ways that you might accomplish this?

5

What We Believe

The Church's Beliefs

So far, as a culture detective, you have peeled the Culture Apple's skin (outer layer or expression) and examined its flesh or meat (inner layer or values). At this point you would sense that something else is happening below the surface to influence the church's expression and values. That something else is the church's beliefs. The culture is beliefs-based. At the very core of the Culture Apple are the church's beliefs or assumptions. In this chapter I will address the reasons beliefs are so important to the culture, the definition of a belief, how to discover your culture's beliefs, and how to communicate those beliefs. I will also add beliefs as the last item in the Culture Matrix.

The Importance of Congregational Beliefs

It's imperative to identify and discover a church's core beliefs if you want to unearth its culture. There are ten reasons for this.

To Discover What a Church Truly Believes

People may be able to articulate what they believe or think they believe about their church (its doctrines, mission, practices, purpose, goals, and so on). The church may even express its views in a doctrinal statement, mission statement, covenant, or constitution and bylaws. But these may not reflect what they truly believe.

As we uncover a church's beliefs, we'll discover what they really believe, as well as what they don't believe, which can be just as important. For example, most churches would agree that the church's mission is to make disciples, according to such passages as Matthew 28:19–20. When some evangelical churches hear this, they nod their heads and say, "Yes, that's what we believe—that's our mission." However, when you probe at the belief's level, you discover that their mission is to feed the hungry, take care of the people of the church, especially the elderly, and so on. It is important for the pastor or pastoral candidate to know this.

To Discover Effective Ministry

As a rule, good beliefs such as those that align with the Bible as well as those that do not contradict the Bible lead to effective ministry. For example, we have people of all ages in the congregation but we can't please everyone's taste in worship music and instrumentation. Our older people who realize that our churches aren't keeping their young people may desire the church to pursue a more contemporary format so as to keep and minister to the young. We don't want to lose them. Here the good belief is that a contemporary as well as a traditional worship format can reflect true worship.

Poor beliefs such as those that do not align in some way with Scripture or contradict Scripture result in ineffective ministry. For example, a church has people of all ages, but most are elderly and believe that the form of worship that best honors God is traditional. Thus they'll pursue traditional worship regardless of its effectiveness or ineffectiveness. Here the poor or bad belief is that traditional worship, not contemporary, best reflects true worship.

The job of the leadership is to uncover the church's beliefs or assumptions so that it can have effective ministry for the Savior. While building on the church's good beliefs, ministry staff leaders will seek to correct mistaken beliefs that lead to less effective ministry.

To Accomplish Change

Churches cling tenaciously to their beliefs, especially their core assumptions. They are bedrock beliefs. If change is going to take place, it has to happen at the assumptions or beliefs level. To attempt change at the surface level is problematic and disruptive. People persist in their beliefs and resent the change because leaders haven't addressed it at the beliefs level. Thus the leader or change agent must discover the basic beliefs and address them as the church works through the change process. For example, some people assume that the way a traditional church conducts its worship service today is the way they did it in the first-century church, so changing how we do church would be a violation of Scripture. In this case, leaders need to teach repeatedly that we don't know how they conducted their worship services in the early church, and, if we did, there's no biblical mandate that we must do it that way.

To Explain the Presence or Absence of Core Values

Core values are built on and derived from a ministry's core beliefs. As we learned in chapter 4, a value is a belief. In strategic planning, we start with core assumptions and then go to values before moving on to other concepts, such as mission and vision. The order is important because the one leads to the others. The presence or absence of a core value can be directly traced back to the church's assumptions. If there's no belief, there will be no value.

To Discover What People Expect of the Church

People's core beliefs shape and direct their expectations of a church or a ministry or person within the church. For example, many people assume that the pastor is supposed to function as a chaplain and his primary or only role is to take care of them. Consequently, they expect the pastor to visit them at home and especially in the hospital. (Some younger pastors are not aware that this is an assumption of many church members.) If visitation doesn't happen, the pastor loses face with these people. They believe either he's not doing his job or he doesn't like them. And some would take this as a personal affront.

To Guide in Problem Solving

The assumptions people hold about a church help them understand the church and how it functions. Whenever problems surface, the church deals with them from the context of its beliefs, which often dictate the outcome. For example, a common assumption among some churches is that the deacons, elders, or trustees are to lead the church, while the pastor is to preach and take care of the people. In these churches, if the pastor desires to lead and challenges the people on this issue, he'll likely lose unless he deals with this assumption first. When people discover and believe that an assumption no longer works or simply isn't true, they're more open to change and may be willing to accept an alternative belief.

To Make Sense of the Church World

The church's beliefs provide a mental frame of reference for what its people think and ultimately act on in regard to the church. People operate within this framework whenever they think in some way about their church. Beliefs act to filter incoming information. Congregants accept thoughts and ideas that agree with their frame of reference and reject that which challenges or differs with what they view as true.

To Provide Mental and Emotional Stability

People need and seek mental and emotional stability that helps them function in the church as well as in the world. A world in general and a church that's constantly changing produce a certain amount of stress and anxiety that tend to disrupt such stability. Assumptions help explain not only the world out there but the world of the church, providing a sense of stability. This makes it most difficult to bring change to a church. Change threatens stability. It's the reason leaders may meet with strong resistance when they propose change, especially from people who have held their assumptions for a long time.

To Determine a Leader's "Fit" in a Church

Every pastor or staff person comes into an established church with a set of assumptions. The church will also have a set of assumptions that may not be consistent with those of its new pastor or staff person. Eventually the two sets will collide with one another, producing friction that will prove problematic for all involved. Usually in such instances, the pastor leaves the church and this solves nothing. The pattern will be repeated over and over until it is addressed from a beliefs perspective. Therefore leaders would be wise to know at least their core beliefs when considering a ministry change, and churches would be wise to know their shared core beliefs when seeking a new pastor or staff. There must be some beliefs alignment between them if they are to work together for future ministry success. The wise pastor and church should be aware of this and address their beliefs or assumptions in the candidating stage.

As a Product of Past Success

Churches and wise leaders take notice of what does and doesn't work. We're pragmatists at heart. What seems to work over time is taken for granted and operates as a silent filter on what a culture perceives and thinks about. The problem comes when these beliefs stop bringing success. The church's environment changes and these beliefs no longer work, but the church doesn't or won't realize this. The culture needs to regularly evaluate what it's doing, address what no longer works, and embrace what does work as long as it doesn't violate any biblical teaching.

Ten Reasons Beliefs Are Important

1. They reveal what a church does and doesn't believe.
2. They are key to effective or ineffective ministry.
3. They are vital to accomplishing change in the church.
4. They explain the presence or absence of core beliefs.
5. They are the basis for people's expectations of the church.
6. They guide the church in problem solving.
7. They help people make sense of the church world.
8. They provide people with mental and emotional stability.
9. They may determine a leader's "fit" in a church.
10. They are often a product of past success.

Defining Congregational Beliefs

As we discovered in addressing the definition of values in chapter 4, a belief is *a conviction or opinion that a person holds to be true about the church and its world as based on limited proof.* There may not be a lot of evidence to support a belief. It is a church view (which I'll explain shortly) that you take by faith.

Most congregational cultures have numerous *core beliefs* that make up their third-layer beliefs. More important, every church also has a set of *shared beliefs* that may be true, partially true, or entirely false. The church may hold them at a conscious level but holds most at an unconscious level, thus they become unquestioned assumptions. Finally, these beliefs or assumptions may or may not be consistent. So don't be surprised if some don't seem to add up. The beliefs that the culture acts on become actual values. Those the culture doesn't act on remain beliefs and aspirational values at best.

Core Beliefs

While we should be aware of most of our beliefs in general, we need to focus on core or essential beliefs in particular. Thus when we seek to discover a church's or pastor's beliefs, we will focus on the beliefs at the core. This isn't to say that other beliefs aren't important, but we need to be aware first of our essential beliefs. Then we can identify other beliefs that would score high on our list.

Shared Beliefs

People in the church may hold beliefs about the church that may or may not agree with the beliefs of others. However, the *church's beliefs*, as I'm using the term in a cultural context, are those that represent the majority of people in the church. These are their largely shared assumptions—the ones that the majority of people agree on consciously or unconsciously. These beliefs may be what attracted them to the church in the first place. Because so many agree with them, they have become mutually reinforced over the years.

Beliefs, Not Values

The church's beliefs are different from its values (see the chart on pp. 62–63). There are a number of distinctions between the two. A belief is a conviction of the existence or truth of something that's not subject to rational proof. If you applied the scientific method to a belief, it would not pass the test. Beliefs also fall under the category of assumptions. We assume them to be true. A belief becomes an actual value when it guides and drives an individual or organization to act—to do something.

ACTION

The difference in the way a belief and a value relate to action is an important distinction. Beliefs have a *predisposition* to action, whereas actual values *involve* action. We learned in chapter 4 that actual values stem from beliefs, and they drive behavior. Thus a church is beliefs-based and values-driven. In other words, when a congregation begins to act on a particular belief, it becomes an actual value that expresses itself in some behavior. If they don't act on the belief, it is an aspirational value and remains an inert belief. An example is evangelism. Most evangelical churches would argue for evangelism as a belief. However, if they don't do evangelism, it remains a belief and an aspirational value. A congregation that does evangelism holds it as an actual value as well as a belief.

MANY BELIEFS

A church or ministry culture will have many beliefs. If you were to attempt to inventory a church's beliefs, it would take all day or longer and use reams of paper. On the other hand, a church will likely have fewer actual values. In a sense, it's easier to be a belief than a value. Beliefs simply exist, whereas actual values require effort—they're beliefs that people act on.

DIFFERENT PURPOSES

Beliefs and values have different purposes. The purpose of a belief is to guide or orient people in life. They help people make sense out of life in general and their lives in particular. Values, on the other hand, are more focused. They do more than exist; they guide or direct behavior that affects or impacts a culture or a person's life.

SLOW TO CHANGE

Beliefs differ from values in terms of change. Beliefs are tenacious—they're slow to change. Once we've embraced our beliefs, it takes evidence before we move to change them. Values are also change resistant, but it takes more evidence and time to change our beliefs than our values. When a value is challenged, our first impulse is to dig in and defend it. Some people, such as Jim Collins, leadership guru and author of the bestseller *Good to Great,* would even argue that values, unlike beliefs, don't change at all. He would say that if you're part of an organization and you don't agree with its values, then you need to change organizations, because the values won't change. I suspect that he believes this because they are so slow to change in most cultures.

DIFFERENT SYNONYMS

In this work I'll use several different synonyms for beliefs, such as *convictions*, *assumptions*, and *church view*. I'll also use synonyms for values, such as *ideals*, *standards*, and *precepts*.

FORMATS

Our beliefs fit into the Beliefs Format.

"We believe/assume _____."

Our values fit into the Values Format.

"We value _____."

Beliefs versus Values

	Belief	Value
Definition	A conviction of the existence or truth of something not subject to rational proof (scientific method). It is an assumption (we assume it is true).	A belief that guides and drives an individual or organization to act on a belief or assumption.

	Belief	Value
Action	A predisposition to action (for example, people do evangelism).	A belief that people act on (people believe in evangelism and do it). It guides/directs behavior—the reason we do what we do.
Number	Organizations have many beliefs.	Organizations have fewer values.
Purpose	To guide or orient people in life—to make sense out of life.	To guide or direct behavior that affects life.
Change	Slow to change, making change in an organization difficult.	Slow to change but not as slow as beliefs.
Synonyms	*conviction, assumption, church view; what we believe or assume*	*ideal, standard, precept; why we do what we do*

Unquestioned Assumptions

A ministry's beliefs are its assumptions that largely go unquestioned by its members. Over the years the beliefs become assumptions that are so entrenched and accepted that there's little if any debate about them or challenge to them. Church people have come to believe in and share them. They're not even discussable, because people take them for granted. Actually, to question them would cause much anxiety and defensiveness. This makes them extremely difficult to change. If you want to discover how mature and patient a church is, simply challenge their assumptions.

A church's beliefs come together to form its view about the fundamental aspects of its life or existence, such as the church's nature, how it views reality, its purpose and mission, people's roles, and so on. I call this a "church view." But what does that mean? An understanding of the concept of worldview will help us understand the concept of a church view. So let's first look at worldview as the broader concept.

WORLDVIEW

A church's worldview, like its church view, has to do with its beliefs but at a much deeper, more profound level than a church view. It asks, what is real or what is reality about one's world? Thus it goes way beyond the immediate, individual congregational culture. It's interesting that many congregations, at least in the Western world, share a similar worldview. Typically North American congregations hold to theism, which is a Western worldview. The Western worldviews have been theism, deism, and currently a fading modernism (naturalism), and a rapidly encroaching postmodernism.

Our worldview provides us with the answers to the basic, fundamental questions that we ask or should ask about our world: What is real? Who are we? Where did we come from? Why are we here? What is the basis for morality and ethics? Our answers to these worldview questions inform the beliefs that influence our total belief system—what we think is true and real about our world.

James Sire's definition of a worldview is basically the same as my definition of a culture's beliefs and influenced it. A worldview is a set of assumptions (beliefs) that may be true, partially true, or entirely false, which people hold (consciously or unconsciously, consistently or inconsistently) about the basic makeup of our world.[1]

A worldview supplies answers to certain rock-bottom questions that work together to provide what seems to be a coherent frame of reference for all thought and action in regard to the world. Sire lists seven questions. Your answers to these questions make up your worldview.

1. What is really real?
2. What is the nature of the world around us?
3. What is a human being?
4. What happens to a person at death?
5. Why is it possible to know anything at all?
6. How do we know what is right or wrong?
7. What is the meaning of human history?

While some in the congregation will be conversant at the worldview level, most won't. As we go about our daily regimen, it's extremely rare that someone asks a worldview question. Exceptions would be in a college philosophy class, a seeker who is under the convicting work of the Holy Spirit (John 16:5–11), and someone who is facing a faith crisis or a life crisis, such as the death of a loved one.

CHURCH VIEW

Having examined the concept of worldview, let's focus on the concept of church view. While similar to a worldview, a church view is much narrower and focuses on the world of the church rather than the world of Western civilization.

Because a church view is another term for a church's beliefs, I would define them similarly. *A church view is a set of beliefs that may be true, partially true, or entirely false that a church holds consciously or unconsciously, consistently or inconsistently about the basic makeup of its world.* These beliefs include the doctrines of the Christian faith that you would find in a doctrinal or creedal statement, but they're much more than biblical doctrine and dogma. For example, they may address what the church believes about time, space, or language. These beliefs may or may not be based on Scripture. Often they're based on the church's traditions, what works (pragmatism), or a mixture of the two.

Whereas it's not likely that many people in the church have a consistent, coherent theology or ecclesiology, right or wrong they will have a church view. The reason is that their church beliefs supply answers to rock-bottom questions that work together to provide a seemingly coherent frame of reference for what they believe and think about the church. Together their assumptions form a paradigm—in this case a set of ecclesiastical glasses—through which people view their church and ministry world and that of others. Ultimately their beliefs help them make sense of their church world for better or worse. Not to have a church view is to be disoriented mentally and emotionally in terms of the member's church life. Consequently, to challenge or suggest altering a church view will upset people. In time, people will either adopt the church's new view, try to change the church, or leave the church.

Just as discovering one's worldview involves asking a number of basic, fundamental questions, so discovering one's church view involves asking key questions about the church. Your answers to the following questions as well as others represent a number of the beliefs or assumptions that make up your church view, which in turn provides a seemingly coherent frame of reference for all thought and action regarding the church. Note that there are more church-view than worldview questions.

- What for the church is real?
- How does the church determine truth?
- What is the nature of the church?
- What is the purpose of the church?
- What is the mission of the church?
- What are the church's theological beliefs (the church's doctrine, traditions, and so on)?
- What does the church believe about the Trinity?
- What does the church believe about Christ?
- What does the church believe about salvation?
- What is the church's polity (how does it handle authority issues)?
- What is the nature and role of the pastor?
- What is the nature and role of the congregation?

- What is the role of women?
- How does the church view time?
- How does the church view space?
- How does the church view technology?
- How does the church view change and innovation?

How to Discover Congregational Beliefs

Wise culture detectives will surface and articulate their key congregational beliefs, including both those at the core and any surrounding beliefs. Knowledge of their beliefs will be key to understanding their church culture. My experience is that rarely do congregations discover and discuss their beliefs in an open fashion to determine which are helpful or harmful to the culture. So how might a pastor as a culture detective and a church as a culture community discover their key organizational beliefs? What does a leader do to unearth ministry beliefs? He or she could do one or both of the following steps.

Step 1 The Beliefs Format

By filling in the Beliefs Format, key beliefs will be articulated.

Beliefs Format: "We believe/assume _____."

Step 2 The Beliefs Audit

Take a congregational Beliefs Audit. You will find the Beliefs Audit in appendix D most helpful. Note that each item begins with a broad, general church-view statement, followed by what the church specifically believes or assumes in regard to that statement, a place to add other views, and room to include any necessary comments.

How to Communicate Congregational Core Beliefs

You could communicate your congregational core beliefs much as you do your core values. Rather than repeat them here, I suggest you look back at the list at the end of chapter 4. One way to communicate beliefs that doesn't appear in the values list is a faith or doctrinal statement. Most such statements are limited to what the church believes the Bible teaches about angels, Christ, and other biblical teachings. An example from Northwood Community Church is in appendix E. While I've never seen a faith statement that included the church's beliefs about time, technology, space, change, and other concepts that fall under church view, there is no reason they should not be included.

The Culture Matrix

This chapter provides the last of three layers that contribute to building the Culture Matrix, which not only summarizes this chapter on beliefs but compares beliefs with behavior (chapter 3) and values (chapter 4). You can find it in appendix F.

Questions for Reflection and Discussion

1. Did the author convince you of the importance of congregational beliefs? Why or why not? If so, which were the more important reasons? Did he miss any?
2. Did you find the definition of congregational beliefs helpful? Why or why not? Anything that wasn't clear?
3. Do you struggle with the idea that a belief may not have a lot of evidence to support it? If so, why? If not, why not? Does the fact that biblical truths may be included in a church's beliefs affect your thinking in any way? Would you not agree that many biblical truths don't have a lot of evidence to support them outside of the fact that they're taught in the Scriptures?
4. Does the thought that some of your church's beliefs or assumptions may be false or only partially true alarm you? How so? What might you do about this?
5. Do you find the concept of church view in comparison to worldview helpful in understanding a culture's beliefs? How is it helpful? Do some of the church-view questions invite you to search the Scriptures for answers? Do you already know the answers to most of them?

6

How We Respond

The Church's Relationship to Culture

So far we have a definition of church culture in chapter 2 followed by an explanation of the three layers that make up that definition in chapters 3–5. These chapters present the peel, flesh, and core of the congregational Culture Apple. In part 2, we will apply this information to our reading and shaping of the church's culture (chapter 7) and to the culture architect (chapter 8). But before we do, we need to pause long enough to address the church's response to and relationship with culture in general. So we will look at how the church responds to culture, how it relates to culture and the gospel, and how culture relates to doing church. In this chapter I am switching to a discussion of culture in general.

Responding to Culture

We need to determine a Christian response to culture that will guide and direct us as we give leadership to our churches—especially new model churches— that have their own unique congregational cultures. There are three possible responses: isolation, accommodation, and contextualization.

Isolation

A view that represents one extreme is isolation. It argues that the Christian's proper response to the culture is to separate from it. Isolationists wrongly believe that the culture is always inherently evil and an enemy of the gospel. (I addressed this briefly in chapter 2.)

The Position

Many would equate *culture* with the term *world* in the Bible and believe that John is warning us to avoid culture in such passages as John 12:31; 16:11; 1 John 4:4; 5:19. Thus we should separate from culture. Supposedly Paul is doing the same thing in 2 Corinthians 4:4 and Ephesians 2:2. Separation from the world is first-degree separation. Some argue for second-degree separation as well. This view of isolation teaches that we must separate not only from the world but from anyone in Christianity we feel may have compromised the gospel and thus embraced the world. For example, some Christian pastors and other leaders would not associate with Billy Graham and his crusades because he invited some leaders they felt had questionable theology to sit on the platform with him.

A Response

I respond to isolationists in several ways. First, the New Testament does use the term *world* to refer to our culture. However, often that usage refers to lost people or humanity in general (John 3:16, 17, 19; 8:12; 9:5) as dominated by Satan and darkness (12:46). It would also include culture when under the control of Satan, his forces, or people who pursue evil, not good (Eph. 2:2). Isolationists totally miss the biblical teaching that culture can be good or bad.

Second, isolationists have difficulty explaining Christ's incarnation, when he came into this world, became a man, and embraced the good aspects of the culture. They must explain how Christ could become part of our culture if it is all bad. The truth is they cannot.

Third, they also view culture as an evil force or object "out there" that we can separate from. The truth is, while culture is "out there," it's also "within" us. Not only is culture all around us, it's part of us. The beliefs we hold and the values that direct and empower us are part of our culture. Our ethnicity, our language, even our thoughts are culturally distinctive. This presents a major dilemma for isolationists. How can you separate from that which is an intrinsic part of who you are?

Accommodation

Accommodation is the other extreme. It involves the Christian's accommodation or adoption of the culture. It has two forms.

THE FORMS

The first form is that of theological liberalism. It believes that much of the culture is a friend of the gospel and argues that we must adopt the beliefs and values of modern science, sociology, philosophy, and theology. These beliefs include the acceptance of concepts such as radical feminism, homosexuality, and abortion but would exclude biblical orthodoxy. To minister to the culture, it advocates embracing the sinful use of culture, thus conforming to culture and buying into the spirit of the age. The problem is that while leaning over to speak to the world, there's a danger we might fall in. And I believe that most liberals have.

The second form of accommodation is a conservative form. I'm surprised at the number of Christians who embrace or come very close to embracing this view. Often their arguments betray a subconscious belief that God endorses a particular culture or subculture as distinctly Christian.

For some it's the first-century culture. Those, for example, who embrace patternism—we should follow the patterns of the first-century churches or do church the way they did—tend to favor this view. These patterns or unique expressions of their beliefs and values are very much a part of the first-century culture. Some examples are the church's possible meeting on the first day of the week and the use of wine in communion.

For some, such as the Amish, it's the culture of the 1800s, when most people wore black clothing and had none of the modern conveniences we have today. Still today the Amish don't use electricity or drive cars; they use a horse and buggy.

For others the culture they consider Christian is our twentieth- or twenty-first-century European or North American church culture. They may not realize that they communicate to unbelievers and converts alike that their way of expressing themselves (through clothing, singing, "temple talk," and especially "doing church") is better than and more Christian than anyone else's. A common example is when we send the message to unchurched, lost people that they have to believe and behave like churched people to be accepted. Many of them view churched people much like Dana Carvey's character the "church lady" on *Saturday Night Live* in the 1990s. Her hair is in a bun and she wears dresses down to her ankles. She doesn't wear any makeup and is quick to tell you what she's against. And she never smiles. Lost people, and I suspect many saved people, don't want any part of that.

When lost, unchurched visitors come to church, they may not behave like those who have been in the church—they don't know all the cues, such as when to stand and sit, what to wear, how to pray, and so forth. Those who expect accommodation to twenty-first-century church culture think there's something wrong with these visitors. The message we send is that they must become like us and embrace our culture or our unique expressions of our beliefs and values to be accepted and in some cases to be saved.

A RESPONSE

The gospel, however, doesn't presuppose that any culture is superior to another. While some cultures are more advanced than others, the gospel views them not as superior or inferior but as different. We don't have to embrace some distinct Christian culture along with the gospel to be saved. The church determined this at the Jerusalem Council in Acts 15—a Gentile doesn't have to become a cultural Jew (be circumcised and so forth) to be saved! Neither was the first century nor the eighteenth century superior to the twentieth or twenty-first century. Even though much of the New Testament was written in the first century and the church grew and developed at that time, this doesn't mean that God favored or endorsed that culture any more than any other culture.

Contextualization

The third and best response to culture is contextualization, which attempts to plant or reestablish churches and communicate the gospel in language and practices that are within people's cultural context so that the biblical message is clear. Therefore it views culture as a means or vehicle that God, man, or Satan can use for his own purposes, whether good or evil. It teaches that a convert doesn't have to adopt or embrace a so-called Christian or church culture to be accepted or saved or to join a church. It uses indigenous cultural forms and practices or expressions to communicate biblical truth; otherwise the gospel isn't clear.

CULTURAL RELEVANCE

Communication and the clarity of the Christian message is what cultural relevance is all about. We must remember that culture or our unique congregational expressions of our beliefs and values communicate something. And we must ask what they communicate and how clear the message is. Cultural relevance isn't blindly succumbing to worldly practices, as some argue, but understanding a culture well enough to articulate and communicate to the people of that culture in a way that they can hear and, with the aid of the Holy Spirit, understand the gospel. To fail to be culturally relevant is to muddy the gospel with unnecessary cultural trappings or expressions that serve only to miscommunicate the Christian message. While our missionaries in foreign lands understand this (they learn a language and local customs, for example), some of our churches in North America have totally missed it. Some even argue that cultural relevance is fine for the mission field in another land but not in North America. Not only does this make absolutely no sense, but it demeans missions.

THE EXAMPLES

Though God is above and beyond human culture, he has chosen to work through man's culture and even, at times, to limit himself to that culture. For example, he chose to speak to men such as Adam, Moses, the prophets, and many others through human language. Had he used some heavenly language (1 Cor. 13:1), they wouldn't have understood him.

Jesus's incarnation is a great example of contextualization. He incarnated himself in a human body, learned a language, and lived among and learned from men (Luke 2:52). One reason he did this was to reveal himself to mankind in a way that clearly communicated to them. As he lived and spoke the message, they got the message.

Finally, Paul, rather than impose his own culture on those to whom he ministered, chose, instead, to adapt to them and the morally acceptable elements of their culture. In 1 Corinthians 9:19–22, he teaches:

> Though I am free and belong to no one, I have made myself a slave to everyone, to win as many as possible. To the Jews I became like a Jew, to win the Jews. To those under the law I became like one under the law (though I myself am not under the law), so as to win those under the law. To those not having the law I became like one not having the law (though I am not free from God's law but am under Christ's law), so as to win those not having the law. . . . I have become all things to all people so that by all possible means I might save some.

This is a profound statement! I wonder how many established churches in America and beyond would be willing to follow suit? Our approach is to form traditions around how we do church and then tenaciously cling to them, shaking our heads vigorously should someone suggest we change them. This includes both traditional and contemporary church formats, clothing, and so forth. The critical question is, How far are we willing to go in terms of changing how we do church to reach lost people in our communities? Our tendency is to bring our so-called Christian culture to them rather than embrace those aspects of their culture that are biblically and morally acceptable.

An extreme example is the missions movement in the eighteenth century when missionaries from Europe went to Africa to win tribal communities to

Christ. It is important to note that at that time, rather than embrace the African cultures, the missionaries brought their European cultures to Africa. And over time the tribes began to look strangely European—not African—in their practice of the faith. The point is that, as we reach out to our communities for Christ, we need to be students of their culture, determining what we can and cannot embrace for the gospel's sake.

Three Responses to Culture

Isolation	Contextualization	Accommodation
Attempts to withdraw from culture	Uses indigenous cultural practices to clearly communicate biblical truth and make the gospel clear	Embraces either a sinful use of culture or a particular culture as uniquely Christian

Culture and the Gospel

What is the relationship between the gospel and culture? Is the gospel above or part of the culture? How should the church relate to the gospel and to culture? The church in North America needs to answer these and other questions about the gospel and culture to accomplish Christ's mission. Following are three answers.

Both Supracultural and Cultural

First, the gospel is supracultural in its origin and essence but cultural in its interpretation and application. God, who transcends man's culture and is thus supracultural, is the source of the gospel (Gal. 1:11–12; 2 Tim. 3:16). However, Christians originally recorded and communicated the gospel in the context of the Greco-Roman culture. Today we interpret, study, and apply the gospel in the context of some culture, such as that of North America, Europe, Asia, and others. Therefore we must understand that though supracultural in function, the gospel exists in some cultural context. And the clarity of the gospel is enhanced by an understanding of that culture.

Distinguishing between Culture and the Gospel

It's imperative that Christians and churches distinguish between the gospel and their culture or unique expression of their beliefs and values. Failure to make a distinction between the gospel and culture mixes the two together in people's minds. Mixing them communicates that acceptance of the gospel also includes the acceptance of certain cultural practices or expressions, such as singing the great hymns of the faith played on a piano or organ; wearing formal clothing such as coats, ties, and long dresses; or even wearing your hair in a bun. And the same is true of a contemporary cultural mind-set as well. There were some in the early church who failed to make this distinction. They argued that a Gentile had to observe the custom of circumcision to be saved (Acts 15:1).

Use Culture to Promote the Gospel

We must discover how to use our culture and that of others to best clarify and promote the gospel. When we put the gospel into other people's cultural forms or expressions, whether North American or some other, we make it possible for them to understand it, embrace it, and communicate it to others. Consequently, we seek to express the gospel in ways and forms that our focus group—unchurched, lost North Americans, Asians, Javanese, and others— can understand. However, we must be sure that the expressions we use carry meanings themselves that convey the proper message. For example, the use of wine as a part of communion in some contexts could convey a negative message. The same could be true of the use of drums and guitars in a worship service populated mostly by the Builder generation.

Some Implications of Culture and the Gospel

- The gospel is supracultural in its origin and essence, but cultural in its interpretation and application.
- It's imperative that Christians and churches distinguish between the gospel and their culture.
- We must discover how to use our culture and that of others to best clarify and promote the gospel.

Culture and Doing Church

A proper understanding of culture, the gospel, and the Scriptures teaches us much about how we do church. What are some of these lessons? Let's look at several. Not that any of these are bad or wrong. My point is they are Western European in origin and not necessarily of biblical origins.

Culture Affects All Churches

Culture affects all churches. There are no exceptions. The question, therefore, isn't, Does culture affect what we do as a church? Rather the question is, Which culture affects what we do as a church?

Most older, established, white churches in North America still reflect a Western European culture. Their practices and customs or unique expressions of their beliefs and values were "made in Europe." Actually, Christian churches are among the few institutional vestiges of European culture that are still standing in America. Cultural expressions, such as the use of organ music, hymns, altars, pews, collection plates, kneelers, stained-glass windows, a distinct architecture, and robes are Western European, not biblical, in origin. Much the same is true of the newer emerging churches that have rejected European culture in churches. Instead, they have adopted different cultural practices or expressions that are American, not biblical, in origin. They're churches that are "made in America." Examples are the absence of the practices and customs in their services, the use of drums and guitars in worship, and the wearing of casual rather than formal clothing by clergy and congregation.

BAD OR GOOD

It isn't necessarily bad that Christian churches reflect European or American culture. Remember that culture is a means that can be used for good or bad. If the people in our churches cling to a European culture as if it were a biblical culture and refuse to adjust when the culture all around them is changing, then it's bad. When the church's culture, not the message, unnecessarily turns people off to the gospel and Christianity, then it's bad. Unfortunately, far too many of our churches did this consciously and subconsciously at the end of the twentieth century. Unchurched people visit a church only to find that it's a culturally alienating experience—they don't understand the jargon ("temple talk" or "Christianese"), can't relate to the music, and feel uncomfortable and out of place. Thus they draw the wrong conclusion that Christianity and the gospel isn't for them. They don't realize it's the culture that turns them off. Add to this the practice in some churches that requires lost people to behave like churched people before the church will accept them and in some cases even before they let them in the door, and you have a formula for spiritual disaster. That's a big part of what Acts 15 corrected in the first century but may not have corrected in the twenty-first century.

THE PURPLE-HAIRED VISITOR

When I work with a church, I like to test its response to culture. My approach is to ask the question, How would this church respond to a visitor who had purple hair and piercings? Some churches are totally unprepared and don't know how to respond. Some churches would avoid the visitor as a means of expressing their disapproval of her appearance. In some the response would be mixed—some would accept her and some would reject and avoid her. The question for your church is how your people would respond. Would they accept her for who she is and view her coming to church as a potential inroad to reach a unique culture—the culture of the purple-haired people—with the gospel?

Culture Affects Churches More than We Realize

IT'S CULTURAL

Culture affects our churches much more than we realize. I'm convinced that as much as 80 to 90 percent of what we do in our churches is culturally, not biblically, directed. An example is church music. It plays a far greater role than most realize, not only in the lives of our adults but in the lives of our young people. Musicians and their music exert a profound influence on today's youth culture. To ignore this in our churches is to risk the alienation and loss of our youth from the cause of Christ. People in our churches have got to realize that today's traditional music was yesterday's contemporary music, and today's contemporary music is tomorrow's traditional music. For an older generation to impose their tastes or unique expressions of their beliefs and values on the younger generations—no matter how innocently they do it—means that both groups suffer in the long term. Those in the church must let the newer generations develop expressions or styles and a culture that best convey Christianity to them, as long as those expressions don't clash with Scripture.

THE PROBLEM

The problem is that most pastors and congregations aren't aware that the culture of the church is turning young people off. They believe that if they change something, they are somehow violating Scripture, not changing the church's culture. As one older deacon quipped, "If the organ was good enough for Jesus and Paul, then it better be good enough for us!"

For others, unfortunately, power is the issue. They have the power in the church and want to keep things the way they are. The good news is that each church has a lot to say regarding its culture. It can choose to make changes in its culture that enhance, not hinder or compromise, the clarity of the gospel.

Here is my advice to older pastors of established churches:

1. *Be a student of the culture.* Though I'll say more about this below and in chapter 12, it means that you'll need to be a learner as well as an instructor—a listening head as well as a talking head. It's imperative that you take time out of your busy schedule to listen and observe. In

particular, learn what the younger generations are listening to, watching, and saying. You don't have to agree with it; simply be aware of it to the point that you can articulate it and discuss it with others.

2. *Be willing to lay your cultural forms or expressions on the altar.* If culture is a means or vehicle to an end, then should you not be willing to work to make changes where culture no longer communicates effectively—especially to a younger generation? I would argue that the older generations, not the younger ones, should set the example here, and without the older generation's help this isn't likely to happen.

3. *Finally, do everything within your power to work with the younger people in the church.* Let's face it, they're the future of your church. Without them your church has no future. Someone has said, "The family that prays together stays together." In the cultural context I would argue, "The church family that pulls together stays together." If we don't pull together, we'll pull apart.

Church Cultures Exclude Some People

It's inevitable that our church cultures will exclude some people. Most of us in general and younger Christians in particular desire to reach everyone, and that's good. However, I believe it was Peter Wagner who said a church that attempts to reach everyone in general will likely reach no one in particular. Face it, your church's culture or unique expression of its beliefs and values will exclude some people—it can't be helped. Keep in mind that we're talking about lost people as well as saved people. Some simply will not care for your church's style of music and so on. In effect, they're rejecting you. My point is that it's okay not to reach everybody. That's the reason so many different kinds of churches exist; it takes all kinds of churches to reach all kinds of people, and this is a powerful argument for new model or paradigm churches! The important thing is that we're *willing* to reach everyone, that we don't needlessly turn people off to the gospel, and that not only are we open to new paradigm churches but we promote starting them.

Now the question becomes, Who will we reach? Keep in mind that I'm talking specifically about unbelievers more than believers (though the same applies to believers). The answer is people who are attracted to us and our culture or expression of our values and beliefs. Those, for example, who like our style of church in general. While there will be some exceptions, this is the norm. Therefore those who are culturally attracted to us could form our initial focus. Just as Paul targeted the Gentiles and Peter targeted the Jews (Gal. 2:7), so we'll focus on certain people as well.

No Culture Is Superior

No culture is distinctively Christian and thus superior to another. While I've already commented on this earlier, it bears repeating. God hasn't endorsed any culture as uniquely Christian. He has not put his stamp of approval on any of them. The Bible in no way encourages us to strive to be like the first century or any other century.

Some people, when spreading the gospel, knowingly and unknowingly include their particular culture as part of it. Usually the culture looks strangely Western, even denominational, and often smacks of capitalistic, middle-class American values. Though some of these values are good, we must be careful to distinguish between a Christian use of culture and labeling a culture as Christian.

I do believe that some cultures are more accepting of Christianity than others. For example, the American culture has been more accepting of Christians than that of China or Russia. What I mean by this is that the American culture has reflected the teaching of the Bible and Christianity, though this is diminishing. The other cultures have never accepted the Christian teaching. Examples in America are that the Ten Commandments are posted in many public schools and manger scenes are set up at Christmas at the courthouses of many of our towns—especially in the South.

The Church Should Remain Relevant to the Culture

If a church exegetes the culture as well as the Scriptures, it should remain relevant to that culture. Like the men of Issachar, we should understand our times so that we know how to communicate well with and reach people (1 Chron. 12:32). Exegeting our culture helps us understand it, discern what is good and bad about it, and know how to minister well to those who are a part of it.

The Culture and the Church

- Culture affects all churches.
- Culture affects our churches more than we realize.
- Our church cultures will exclude some people.
- No culture is distinctly Christian and superior to all the rest.
- The church that exegetes the culture should remain relevant to that culture.

Questions for Reflection and Discussion

1. Of the three responses to culture (isolation, accommodation, and contextualization), which best describes your ministries? Why? Has this always

been your view? Why or why not? How does your current response help you do church?

2. Do you believe that culture affects all churches? If not, why? If so, how has it affected yours?

3. Have you found that your church's culture consciously or subconsciously excludes some people? If so, who and why?

4. Do you agree that no culture is necessarily Christian or superior to another? Why or why not? If not, what culture do you believe is Christian or superior?

5. Do you agree with the author's understanding of cultural relevance, or do you believe that for a church to be culturally relevant it has to embrace the world? What does "embrace the world" mean to you? Why is it so important to the author that churches be culturally relevant?

6. What are some aspects of your church's culture that might unnecessarily turn believers and unbelievers away? What will you do about this?

7. How would your church respond to a visitor with purple hair and piercings? Do you believe this response is good or bad? If bad, what would you do about it if anything?

8. How do you respond to the author's statement that your culture will exclude some people from attending your church?

READING CONGREGATIONAL CULTURE

7

Reading the Church

Understanding Its Culture Apple

Reading a church's culture involves the accurate discovery and understanding of all three layers of the Culture Apple. As we have seen, working from the outside in, the layers are the skin or the culture's outward expression of itself, the flesh or its shared values, and the core or its shared beliefs and assumptions. Together these layers form a Culture Matrix for your church that gives it its unique identity.

A knowledge of a church's culture is most important not only to the current pastor of a church but to the leader who is being considered by a church as its next pastor. (Often we refer to this as candidating.) He needs to know his culture—the culture he brings with him to the church (I'll address his culture in the next chapter)—and early on he needs to know the church's culture or what he's getting himself into. Every church has some pathology that comes with the culture, and the pastor or candidating pastor needs to know what it is. As he reads the church's culture, he should get a feel as to whether he has the skills and expertise to lead the church into the future.

A knowledge of a church's culture is also most important to the people of the church. If they truly desire to serve the Savior and his people, they need to know where as a church they are strong and weak, healthy and unhealthy, consistent and inconsistent. After the people of the church have discovered their culture, they need to work to improve and reshape that culture.

Reading a culture means exegeting it. Usually we think of exegesis when we study the Bible. First, we observe a text by asking all kinds of questions about it. We pepper it with questions. The goal is to discover what the biblical text says, not what it means. Next, we begin to interpret the text by asking what it means. And finally, we apply the text to our lives and ministries by asking what difference it makes or should make.

Exegeting the church's culture follows the same pattern. It involves observing the culture and asking questions, interpreting the culture, and then applying that knowledge to leading a church well in its culture. This chapter will walk you through the three-step cultural exegesis process. Because the term *exegesis* is a technical term and may be confusing to some, I'll mix in other synonyms along the way, such as *studying*, *deciphering*, *reading*, and *decoding*. The following chart provides you with an overview of where we're headed in this chapter.

Apple	Culture	Exegesis
Peel	Behavior	Observation
Flesh	Values	Interpretation
Core	Beliefs	Application

Step 1 Observe the Church's Culture

Apple	Culture	Exegesis
Peel	Behavior	Observation

What Do You See?

As we begin our observation, we start on the outside of the Culture Apple and work our way in. This first layer is the behavioral, observable, outward manifestation of the culture. It's what you see when you visit a church one weekend. Let's face it. Most of us aren't as observant as we think. We really don't pay much attention to what's taking place. We get in an observation rut; while seeing, we don't see. An exception is when someone is considering adopting the church as his or her church. Then he or she is "all eyes." So to read the outer layer, we must turn on our powers of observation. In essence we must become a cultural Sherlock Holmes.

THOROUGH OBSERVATION

When I was a student at Dallas Seminary, I took a course taught by Dr. Howard Hendricks in Bible study methods. He taught us the observation, interpretation, application approach to studying the Bible. When he covered the observation step, he asked us to observe Acts 1:8, come up with at least two hundred observations, write them down, and then bring them to class. (Later we referred to this exercise as "juicing" Acts 1:8.) We assumed that this was an impossible assignment. Who could come up with two hundred observations from a single verse? However, much to our surprise, we did it. At our next class, he asked us to share some of our observations with one another. Then he did an amazing thing. For our next assignment, he asked us to make an additional two hundred observations of Acts 1:8. Again, we thought this was an impossible assignment. However, we did it. And in making this assignment, Dr. Hendricks taught us the power and importance of good, thorough observation. My assignment for pastors and churches is not to make a few observations here and there but to make two hundred observations of the church culture, and once you think you can't make any more, return to the culture and make two hundred more observations.

THE OBSERVATION QUESTION

As you observe a culture, you ask the observation question: What is the church doing? (This is a question that is answered by an action or expression.) How does the church express itself? Specifically, what do you see, hear, and feel as you carefully observe the culture? The answers fit in the Expressions Format:

Expressions Format: "We see, hear, feel _____."

Take copious notes (mental, but preferably written) of what you see. A good goal would be two hundred–plus observations. Resist the urge to move too quickly to interpreting your observations or attempting to explain them. While it's human nature to do some interpretation early, the important thing is that you observe and record what's taking place. Keep in mind that at this stage, it's easy to observe and listen but difficult to decode or decipher. Remember, it's like the iceberg—what you see at the surface isn't the entire iceberg. It's only 10 percent of the whole. So focus on observation and collection, not interpretation.

An Observation Exercise

Following are some general questions that will serve as prompts and examples to help you know what to look for as you observe a culture. I introduced you to some in chapter 3. Should you want a more exhaustive list, use the Beliefs Audit in appendix D. If you've already used the Beliefs Audit, or after you've responded to the prompts below, go back and go through the audit again. Squeeze out two hundred more observations. They also serve as observational categories that make it easier to interpret and apply what you have observed. Try using them to organize your observations.

- What is the church's setting/environment (its location and facilities)? Is it rural, urban, or suburban? What is its dominant ethnicity? What do you observe about its neighborhood? What do you note about its facilities and grounds? Are the grounds attractive and well kept, or is there a lot of trash lying around? Are the facilities in good shape or in need of repair? Are there enough bathrooms? Are the bathrooms and the kitchen clean?
- Do people carry Bibles? Does the preacher preach from the Bible? Do any classes or small groups teach from the Bible?
- What ministries do they offer? Do they have a preaching/worship event, a Sunday school, small groups, men's and women's Bible studies, and other ministries? Do people seem to like and respond to the preaching and to the worship? Are there ministries for children and youth?
- How does the church do worship? Is it orderly or unplanned? Do they use musical instruments or are there no instruments? If they use instruments, what are they: piano, organ, guitars, drums, and others? Do they have an orchestra? Is there a bulletin or worship guide that helps people follow and understand the service?
- What symbols are present? Do you see any crosses, a crucifix, an ixthus (fish symbol), a tapestry, candles, a baptistery, and others?
- What kind of clothing do people wear? Are they dressed up or informal or a combination? What about the clergy? Do they wear robes or dress the same as the congregation?
- What rituals do you observe? Is there an order of worship? Do people recite a creed?
- What ceremonies do you see? Do they observe the ordinances (baptism and communion), baptize or dedicate babies, and so forth?

Step 2 Interpret the Church's Culture

Step 2 moves you from observing to interpreting what you've observed. The goal is to continue to work your way from the outside of the apple (the peel) to the inside (the flesh and then the core). Now that you've peeled or observed the apple, you move to its flesh and its core. However, you are not done with the observation phase. There will be overlap between observation and interpretation. To some degree you will continue to observe the culture during the life of the church. With each church encounter, you will observe a practice or behavior that wasn't present or obvious before. However, you reach a point where you need to move to the next step, which involves interpreting what you've observed. This point is reached when you've exhausted the questions regarding the practices above and any others that surface in the process.

The next two layers of the Culture Apple are the church's values and underlying beliefs. The second step seeks to interpret both the church's values and its beliefs or assumptions, which combine to explain its unique expression or the behaviors you observed in step 1. The values will explain the reasons the church does what it does, and the beliefs form the foundation or basis for what it does. Without the beliefs there would be no values. As we have seen, every culture is beliefs-based and values-driven. The essence of the culture lies in its fundamental values and beliefs or assumptions. Once you identify and begin to understand them, you are well on your way to understanding and explaining not only the outward practices of the church observed in step 1 but ultimately the church's culture, which is the goal of step 2.

How might you discover the church's values that affect its expression of itself? (At this point, you might want to pause, return to, and review chapter 4, which addresses cultural values.)

Apple	Culture	Exegesis
Peel	Behavior	Observation
Flesh	Values	Interpretation

Discovering the Church's Values

THE VALUES QUESTION

Interpreting the culture involves taking the first bite or asking the values question: Why does the church do what it does? The observation question asks: What does it do? The values question asks: Why does it do it? What drives and guides its behavior? The answer is the culture's values.

A VALUES INTERPRETATION EXERCISE

Examine the results of your observations and begin to ask why the church does what you've observed it doing. Ask this question of each observation. Look for the underlying or supporting values that would cause such an expression and explain why the church does what it does. For example, if you observe that a number of people carry a Bible, the pastor preaches from the

Bible, and most classes and small groups teach the Bible, then it's likely that the church values Bible teaching or biblical instruction. Your answers will fit the following Values Format:

Values Format: "We value _____."

In addition, use the Core Values Audit in appendix B. As you examine the results, do you see any alignment between the church's actions and its actual values, as discovered in the values audit? Complete the Values Format for each value, based on your interpretations and the Values Audit.

Values Format: "We value _____."

Example: "We value *evangelism*."

Note that as you unearth and interpret a church's values, you'll also discover what it doesn't value, which can be almost as important as what it values in terms of church health and any cultural pathology. For example, if the church doesn't value evangelism or lay ministry, this will inhibit its becoming a mature, spiritually healthy church. You might treat values you don't observe but deem critical to the life of the culture not as actual but aspirational values. Use a different Values Format for these and then include them along with but separate from the actual values above so as not to confuse the two.

Values Format: "We aspire to value _____."

Example: "We aspire to value *evangelism*."

A VALUES VALIDATION EXERCISE

Once you have a list of what you believe are the church's actual values, you need to validate them. There are several ways to validate your work.

1. If you're a pastoral candidate for a church, ask some of the people who have been in contact with you from the church to take the values audit, or you may want to ask them the kinds of questions that would surface values. For example, ask: On a scale of 1 to 5, where is the church in terms of doing evangelism? Or you could ask: Do you believe that the church is evangelistic? Why or why not? What's the evidence?
2. If you're the pastor of a church or a serious pastoral candidate for a church, ask some of the formal leaders in the church (board persons,

ministry staff, and others) to take the Values Audit. Note: the more people
you ask, the more likely you'll discover the ministry's actual core values.

3. Compare the results, looking for consensus.

4. With this information in hand and mind, continue to ask other people,
   such as teachers and small group leaders, about the values as you have
   opportunity. The idea here is to validate as much as possible what you
   believe to be the church's actual values.

Discovering the Church's Beliefs

THE BELIEFS QUESTION

In addition to its values, the interpretation step includes and focuses on
the church's beliefs. Now that you have observed the church's actions and
discovered the values that drive and guide those actions, it's time to examine
the apple core. You're ready to identify the beliefs or assumptions that are
foundational to the church's values and actions. Since the church is values-
driven and beliefs-based, they address the basis for or fundamental aspects of
the church's life and explain what really matters to the church culture. You'll
find them at the third layer or inner core of the Culture Apple. Interpreting
the culture involves asking not only the values question but also the beliefs
question: What does the church believe or assume is true of itself?

A BELIEFS INTERPRETATION EXERCISE

Examine the results of both the Behaviors Audit and Core Values Audit (especially those that align) and attempt to identify the basic beliefs of the church.
Do you observe any alignment between the church's behaviors and values? This
alignment points to the church's beliefs. Look for the underlying or supporting
beliefs or assumptions that would explain why the church does what it does
and values what it values. What beliefs would lead to or support these values
and the ensuing behavior? That's alignment. I pointed out above that if people
carry their Bibles to church and the preaching and teaching are done from the
Bible, then biblical instruction is likely a value of the church. And based on this
alignment between actions and values, a church's belief or assumption may be
that the Bible consists of God's revealed truth that is the basis for the church's
faith and practice. Your answers will fit the following format:

Beliefs Format: "We believe/assume _____."

You might find it helpful now to go through the Beliefs Audit in appendix D
if you haven't already. Use the information you gain here.

You may also discover the church's beliefs through its doctrinal or faith statement (see an example in appendix E) or possibly in a church creed or covenant. Another often overlooked source is the church's constitution and bylaws. As you discover beliefs, complete the following format for each one you surface.

> *Beliefs Format*: "We believe/assume _____."

> Example: "We believe the congregation should do evangelism."

As with the values-discovery process, you'll discover what the church doesn't believe, as well as what it does believe. This will be important in the third or application step.

A BELIEFS VALIDATION EXERCISE

Once you sense that you've discovered many of the culture's beliefs, seek to validate your findings.

1. If you are the pastor of the church or a pastoral candidate, either interview someone in the church and/or have them take the Beliefs Audit and see if their beliefs align with the beliefs you've surfaced. Compare the results, looking for consensus. (Note: If you're a pastoral candidate, you don't have to be at the church to accomplish this. You could interview someone by phone or send them the audit.)
2. Based on the above results, make a list of what you believe are the church's core beliefs or assumptions and any important beliefs that surround that core. Leave room to add to your list.
3. If you are the church's pastor, a pastor candidate, or a leader in the adoption of two or more congregations (where a healthy church blends with a smaller, struggling church with few if any concessions to the smaller church), continue to ask people about the culture's beliefs as you have opportunity to speak with them. Take a naive approach and ask "why" questions. For example, "Why are you doing evangelism?" The answer is, "We believe in evangelism." The goal is to validate as much as possible what you think are the church's beliefs.

Step 3 Make Application to the Church's Culture

By the time you reach the third step, you should have a fair read or understanding of the church's culture. So what do you do with this information? How can it be helpful if you're the pastor of the church, a pastoral candidate, or involved in some way in a merger of cultures? The answers are found in the following four application exercises.

Apple	Culture	Exegesis
Peel	Behavior	Observation
Flesh	Values	Interpretation
Core	Beliefs	Application

Determine the Church's Commonalities and Uniqueness

First, ask, What does the church culture have in common with other cultures? While every church is unique, all share some things in common. What do you share with other church cultures? The following questions are based on some commonalities I've observed over the years.

Is the church growing, plateaued, or declining?

Do people expect the pastor to do the work of the ministry, or are they willing to be involved?

Does the church expect the pastor to be a leader with a clear, compelling vision, or is he a chaplain who takes care of everyone?

Can the church identify its core values that empower and guide it?

Does the church have a biblical mission, or does it have little direction?

Does it have a clear simple pathway for making disciples, and do people understand and know where they are along the pathway?

The application questions for the leader are: Are you equipped to lead such a church? Can you help it develop in any of the above areas where the church might be deficient? Do you know what to do? In addition, are you open to getting outside help, such as that of a consultant or mentor?

Second, ask, In what ways is the culture unique? This is a question that needs to be asked of all churches in general and spiritually healthy, growing churches in particular. Let's use Fellowship Bible Church, located in Grapevine, Texas, as an example. This church is exploding in attendance, with between fifteen and twenty thousand attendees. So what's unique about it? The answer is their belief in creativity that's not just a value but a core value of the church. Pastor Ed Young so values creativity that he has a creativity team that works very closely with him in planning and creating his worship services and sermons.

Another example is Fellowship Bible Church in Dallas, Texas. Former pastor Bill Counts planted this church to reach upwardly mobile professional people who were struggling emotionally due to a dysfunctional childhood, divorce, and other similar heartbreaking issues. Bill's wife divorced him while he was in seminary; thus he understood the pain of divorce. But this church is so unique because Bill has an uncanny understanding of and biblical teaching on grace: God truly accepts us the way we are.

The application question for the leader is: Have you identified what is unique about the culture, and are you the best person to minister and lead in such a context? For example, chances are good you've not experienced the pain or trauma of a divorce. Will that limit your ministry to those who have? Would someone else who has ministry experience with dysfunctional people be better prepared than you? Another question to consider is, How can the church leverage its uniqueness?

Discover the Church's Strengths and Weaknesses

First, ask, What are the culture's strengths? When we at The Malphurs Group begin working with a church, we ask that its Strategic Leadership Team (SLT) take our Church Analysis. The analysis seeks to determine the culture's strengths and weaknesses. We may or may not know what they are, but they do. Some strengths that seem to repeat church after church are the following: the church's pastor and staff, the women's Bible study, the children's ministry, the ministry of the nursery, the church's worship, and world missions.

Second, ask, What are the church's weaknesses? Some weaknesses that repeat analysis after analysis are the following: communication, evangelism, leadership, leadership development, lay involvement in the ministry, organization, openness to change, follow-through, mission, vision, and strategy.

The application questions for the leader are: How well could you lead a church with these strengths and weaknesses? What are your training and experience, and how might they affect your leadership in such a culture? Do you know what to do to see the weaknesses become strengths? For example, can you help the church develop a mission and identify its core values? If your answer to these questions is no, are you willing to get outside help in addressing these issues?

Discern If the Culture Is Spiritually Mature or Immature

In a number of places, the Bible addresses maturity (for example, 1 Cor. 2–3; Gal. 6:1–2; Heb. 5:11–14; Rev. 2:6; 3:1–4). While these passages are addressing spiritual maturity, I don't think you can separate spiritual maturity from cultural maturity. A culturally mature or immature church is a spiritually mature or immature church. The two, though different, are intertwined. You won't have one without the other.

To determine the spiritual state of the church, attempt to determine whether the church is spiritually mature, immature, or somewhere in between. If you're the pastor or a leader in an established church, circle the number below that you believe best summarizes the health of the culture. Next, go through the Spiritual Maturity Audit in appendix G to determine where the church is. Then circle the number on the continuum below according to the results of the audit and any other information you might have. Are the numbers the same, close, or different?

Maturity								Immaturity	
1	2	3	4	5	6	7	8	9	10

A church can be immature for several reasons. One is that maturity takes time, and the church has not been in existence long enough. An example is the early church in Acts. It was a biblically based, spiritually strong church that simply had not been in existence long enough to become mature. This would be the case with most church plants. Another reason for immaturity is the carnal culture, a church dominated by carnal people, such as the church at Corinth and several in Revelation 2–3. A church with carnal people is toxic and does more harm than good.

If you're the pastor of a spiritually immature church, the application questions are: Should you even attempt to change this church? Is there hope for such a church? If it's a culture like the Jerusalem Church, the answer is yes! If it's carnal and toxic, the best solution may be to close its doors.

Determine Where You as a Leader Will Be Most Effective

Now that you've wrestled with the material above and have a read on the culture, discern where you fit or don't fit in leading a church culture.

1. If you are the pastor of an unhealthy, established church, do you believe you can lead the culture to health? Do you have the knowledge and experience necessary to lead in a culture turnaround? If not, are you willing to pursue the knowledge and help you will need for such a task? What is God telling you in all this? Are you listening to him? Are you the man God desires to use to point the church in a new, spiritually healthy direction? Since you are the current leader, will you do all you can to make a difference in the life of this ministry?

2. If you are a pastor candidate who is considering becoming the pastor of an established culture, determine if you have the necessary knowledge

and experience to lead this church in a turnaround to spiritual maturity.
How does the church culture align with your culture or the one you
would bring with you to the church? How do the two cultures not align?

3. If you are planting a church, you're in the early culture formation period. You need to be aware of this. What kind of culture will the church
embrace? The answer is that it will be the culture you bring to it. You
are the primary culture architect or potter. So what are your beliefs and
values? How will they express themselves when the church gathers? As
you observe the church-planting process, what do you see happening?

4. If you are part of two (or possibly more) churches that are considering
participation in an adoption—a stronger church adopting a weaker
church or churches, what does this application process tell you about the
potential success of such a venture? What are your beliefs and values?
How are they expressed in your culture and any other church's culture?
Are you very much alike or very different from the other church? If the
latter, what might God be telling you? If the former, will an adoption
be relatively easy? Is one culture spiritually healthy and the other not so
healthy? In this unique situation, would all parties be better off if you
simply let the struggling church die? Will an adoption adversely affect
the healthier church?

A Review: Reading the Church's Culture

Moving from outside to the inside of the Culture Apple.

Step 1 Observe the Church's Culture

1. Ask the observation question: What do you see?
2. Fill in the Expressions Format: "We see, hear, feel _____."

Step 2 Interpret the Church's Culture

1. Discover the church's values.
   - Ask the values question: Why do we do what we do?
   - Fill in the Values Format: "We value _____."
   - Validate the church's values.
2. Discover the church's beliefs.
   - Ask the beliefs question: What does the church believe or assume?
   - Fill in the Beliefs Format: "We believe/assume _____."
   - Validate the church's beliefs or assumptions.

Step 3 Make Application to the Church's Culture

1. Determine the church's commonalities with other churches and its uniqueness.
2. Discover the church's strengths and weaknesses.
3. Discern if the church is spiritually mature or immature.
4. Determine where you as a leader will be most effective.

Questions for Reflection and Discussion

1. What is your culture situation? Are you currently the leader of an established church, a pastoral candidate, a church planter, or a participant in an adoption?
2. As you take the first step and peel the Culture Apple, what have been some of your observations or those of others of your church? What does the Behaviors Audit tell you about the culture? What fits in the following Expressions Format:

   "We see, hear, feel _____."

3. As you take the second step and interpret the culture, what are its values? Have you taken the Values Audit? What did you learn from it? What fits in the following Values Format:

   "We value _____."

4. As you continue to interpret the culture, what are its beliefs that are foundational to its values? Have you taken the Beliefs Audit? What did you discover? What fits in the Beliefs Format:

   "We believe/assume _____."

5. As you take the third step and make application to your culture, what are some of the commonalities of your church culture with other churches? Were any similar to those the author listed? How is your situation unique? Are you finding this difficult to answer?
6. As you continue the third step, what are the culture's strengths and weaknesses? Where is it in terms of its spiritual maturity? Do you believe you have the knowledge and/or experience to lead in turning this situation around? Why or why not? If not, are you willing to work hard at acquiring this knowledge and experience? If so, how will you accomplish

this? Are you and the church willing to get some help from those who do have the knowledge and experience, such as another pastor in the area, a mentor, or a consultant?

7. Where is God in all this? Have you asked for his wisdom and help? What is he telling or trying to tell you? Are you listening? How do you know?

8

Reading the Pastor

Discovering the Pastor's Culture

A critical factor in the culture of any church is the leadership of the senior pastor and any ministry staff. The reason is that a ministry rises or falls with its leadership. As the leadership goes, so goes the church. At the same time, the role of leading a church in the early twenty-first century has become increasingly difficult. For example, people in our churches have high, often unrealistic expectations for their leaders. To compound the problem, few in the ministry world seem to be addressing the importance of leadership and how to become a better leader.

Most church leaders lack leadership training, and seminaries have become a major offender in this. The role of most schools is to prepare men and women for ministry within and outside the church. But far too many seminaries do a good job of training people in church history, theology, and the Bible and come up short in leadership training. Even though every thriving, spiritually directed church is well fed and well led, much professional ministry preparation emphasizes good preaching at the expense of good leadership. Our churches desperately need both.

Regardless of their training or lack thereof, most potential leaders and established pastors lack an understanding of congregational culture. Too many pastors aren't aware of the importance that culture plays in their lives and that of their churches. In this chapter I will focus on the primary leader's culture and what he brings with him to the culture of an established church.

What you must understand is that most if not all pastors have a cultural context that serves as the backdrop for their ministry. The problem is they don't know or tend to be unaware of it.

The solution to this problem is to help the pastor discover and then understand his personal cultural context. To some degree every pastor is a culture carrier and must exegete his culture to understand it. Sound familiar?

The last chapter took us step-by-step through the process to understand a church's culture. The emphasis was on discovering the culture of an established church on the part of its pastor or a pastor-candidate. The goal in this chapter is to unearth the culture that the pastor as a leader carries and brings with him to a church. It is written as a guide to help leaders discover their culture, but it could be adapted to be used by a church to determine a leader's culture. To discover the leader's cultural context, I use a four-step process. It's much the same process as that used to discover a church's culture but with a few differences and an additional first step.

Step 1 Discover the Source of the Leader's Culture

The first step in this process is for you as the leader to discover what has formed or shaped your culture context. Following are several potential sources of that context.

The Church Where the Leader Was Raised

The church where you grew up may be a source of your culture. If you grew up in a church, you naturally and almost unconsciously absorbed that church culture over time. This is a somewhat subtle matter of exposure. When it comes time to make a decision or act in a particular ministry context, we naturally fall back on what was modeled for us. It's our cultural default mode. We tend to think, *When this situation came up in my home church, the pastor and/or staff did this.*

Your early experiences can also have the opposite effect. You may have rejected the culture of the church in which you were raised. For example, you may be a strong, visionary-type leader who is considering the ministry. However, you have observed your pastor who has functioned largely as a chaplain and you conclude, "That's not how I believe a church should be led. I will not follow his example."

The Church Where the Leader Came to Faith

The church where you came to faith may have had a profound impact on your culture, especially if you had been unchurched and thus had little exposure to a church. Your first church as a believer would have shaped your culture. For many of us, coming to faith in Christ was a life-changing experience. This was true in my case. I was in my first year of college and trying to figure out what I was going to do with my life. I came to faith, and all that changed. I wanted to share the gospel with others just as it had been shared with me and assumed that meant going into some kind of ministry. So I began to look to the church for direction in my life. This assumes, of course, that you begin to regularly attend and become involved to some degree in the church.

A Church of Profound Impact

A church that has had a profound impact for Christ on your life and the life of its community will be instrumental in shaping your culture. A characteristic of such a church is that good things are happening—people are getting saved and the church is growing. You may or may not have come to faith in this church, but at some point (a personal crisis, a change in vocation, and so forth) you were powerfully challenged by the church to go into the ministry or to deeper involvement in ministry. Thus the church's culture largely became your culture. Often this affects in particular those who have grown up in a somewhat status quo situation. Then they discover a church that's spiritually healthy and mature that will not tolerate the status quo, and they are powerfully attracted to and embrace it.

A Combination of Sources

A combination of sources can have impact. For example, the same church where you came to faith may also have had a strong impact on your life. Thus you want to minister in a spiritually healthy church, very much like the one you've been a part of. Or you may have been strongly influenced by a church, and you like much of the church's culture but not all of it. For example, the church may be monoethnic, because those who live in the neighborhood are monoethnic. However, you desire to minister in a multiethnic context. Thus you will adopt certain aspects of the culture in the church but change other aspects of it.

Other Sources

Of course there can be other sources of one's culture. Nonetheless, your life has been changed as the result of your church's culture, and it's that culture that will strongly influence how you view the culture of another church.

Culture	Exegesis
Behavior	Observation

Step 2 Observe the Leader's Culture

Once you discover what has formed or shaped your culture, you are ready for the second step. This involves observing your culture or peeling the skin off the apple. You may have already accomplished much of step 2 in step 1. Discovering what has shaped your culture means you have had to observe your culture. However, you need to ask yourself, was it intentional observation? Do you need to revisit that church with "intentional observation eyes"? I would strongly encourage that, if possible, you go and visit the church to observe it, as directed in chapter 7. You'll likely see things you haven't seen before.

An Observation Exercise

When you visit the church, what should you look for? I would use the same observation exercise found in chapter 7, abbreviated here.

- What is the church's setting/environment (its location and facilities)?
- Do people carry Bibles?
- What ministries do they offer?
- How does the church do worship?
- What language do people speak?
- What symbols do you see (crosses, a crucifix, candles, a baptistery, and others)?
- What kind of clothing do people wear (dressed up or casual)?
- What rituals do you observe (an order of worship, reciting a creed, and so forth)?
- What ceremonies do you see (the ordinances, a baby dedication, and so forth)?

An Observation Question

What did you see, hear, feel when you experienced the church's culture as you remember it? And what do you see, hear, feel now as you observe it intentionally through a visit?

Expressions Format: "I see, hear, feel _____."

The observation exercise in chapter 7 should stimulate your memories of the culture. For additional insight, you might want to use the Behaviors Audit in appendix A.

Step 3 Interpret the Leader's Culture

You learned in chapter 7 that interpreting culture involves discovering the influencing church's values and beliefs, which make up the flesh and core of the Culture Apple. In this chapter we need to unearth the leader's values and beliefs. Most likely you will not agree with all the values and beliefs of the influencing culture, but knowing them will help you know your own.

Discover the Leader's Core Values

You have numerous values in general and should be aware of them. However, you need to focus on your four to six core values in particular and any others that might surround them but not be a part of them. Similar to discovering the culture's values, there are several steps involved in discovering your actual, not aspirational, essential values.

1. Ask the reasons why you do what you do as a leader. The answer will most likely be your core, driving values. They will fit in the following Values Format:

   Values Format: "I value _____."

2. Use the Core Values Audit in appendix B to surface your core values that make up your personal ministry values culture. Where do your values align with or not align with the church culture's core values? This tells you what is most important to you and where you place the emphasis in your ministry and leadership, whether consciously or subconsciously.
3. Evaluate the values. Are they healthy values, and are any key values missing? The answer as before is found in comparing the leader's values with those of the Jerusalem Church in Acts 2:41–47.
4. Ask how your core values align with those of the culture you're currently leading or are a candidate to lead. Where there is misalignment, there will be friction and resistance to your leadership from the culture.
5. Articulate the core values in a values statement or credo (see an example in appendix C). You could articulate these from your or another pastor's perspective. Simply replace the name of the church with your name or another's. Change the personal pronoun "we" to "I" or even "he." Place your core values in the Core Values Format. The assumption is that these are your actual values. However, if you wish to list your aspirational values as well, you could use the second format. I would suggest that if you don't already embrace any of the Jerusalem Church values,

they become your aspirational values and that you list them separately from your actual values. If you do not currently embrace the Jerusalem Church values, it's a serious matter. You will likely not do well leading any ministry connected with a church.

Values Format: "I value _____."

Values Format: "I aspire to value *evangelism*."

6. Validate your core values. Once you have discovered and articulated what you believe are your core values, you would be wise to validate those values. Sometimes we can be blinded to reality by what should be. Our aspirational values can fool us into thinking they're our actual values. There are several ways to validate one's values. One is to evaluate any past church leadership experiences. What values surfaced as core in those experiences? Second, determine if, when under pressure, you still hold to these values or if you default to other values. The latter would be your true values. Third, ask those who know you and your ministry well if the values you have identified are truly your values.

Discover the Leader's Beliefs

In addition to your ministry values, interpreting your culture involves surfacing and understanding your ministry beliefs or assumptions. Just as with the values, it's likely that you do not agree with all the beliefs of the culture that has influenced you. Thus you need to focus on your beliefs more than those of that culture.

1. To discover your beliefs, compare the observations of your influencing culture—the one you bring with you—with your personal ministry core values. It is likely that the longer you have been a Christian, the more other cultures have shaped you as well. So include them in the mix. Where is there alignment? Alignment points to ministry beliefs. For example, if your influencing culture or another culture was strong on evangelism, and evangelism is one of your core values, then evangelism is one of your bedrock beliefs. See if the beliefs fit the following Beliefs Format:

Beliefs Format: "I believe/assume _____."

2. Use the Beliefs Audit in appendix D to help you determine your beliefs. The results will go in the following Beliefs Format.

   Beliefs Format: "I believe/assume _____."

   Example: "I believe every church should be involved in evangelism."

3. Finally, you should validate your findings, simply as a double check of your beliefs discovery. Using the example of evangelism, validation questions are: Do you share your faith? What evidence is there of this? Can you point to specific, recent examples? Your answers confirm not only that evangelism is a value but that it is based on your belief in the importance of evangelism. Also ask others who know you well if evangelism is one of your bedrock beliefs as regularly displayed in your ministry. Finally, when under extreme duress, do you still share your faith?

Culture	Exegesis
Behavior	Observation
Values	Interpretation
Beliefs	Application

Step 4 Make Application to the Leader's Culture

When you reach the third step, you should have a good understanding of the church culture that you as a leader hold. How can this information be helpful if you're the pastor of the church, a pastoral candidate, or involved in some way in the merger of two churches? Four of the applications below are similar to those in the last chapter. I have added a fifth application on divine design.

Determine the Leader's Commonalities and Uniqueness

First, ask, What does my view of church culture have in common with other cultures? What problems am I likely to encounter? Do I understand the importance of mission, vision, and values to a culture? How do I know? Have I guided a church in the development of a mission and vision? In what ways is my culture unique? Do you, like Pastor Ed Young, hold to a belief in creativity that displays itself in your leadership and ministry in general and preaching in particular? Or do you, like Pastor Bill Counts, have an uncanny grasp of the biblical teaching on grace? I doubt you would have these same values. But that's not the point. What values do you hold that might be unique to you?

Discover the Leader's Strengths and Weaknesses

Ask: What are my strengths? What are my weaknesses? Am I strong or weak in any of the following: communication, evangelism, leadership, leadership development, lay involvement in the ministry, organization, openness to change, follow-through, a Great Commission mission, a compelling vision, vision casting, and strategy?

Decide If the Leader Is Spiritually Mature or Immature

Determine whether you are spiritually mature, immature, or somewhere in between. Circle the number on the maturity continuum that best represents where you are at spiritually. Using the Spiritual Maturity Audit in appendix G will help you determine your spiritual maturity. Then circle the number on the continuum that best describes or summarizes your spiritual maturity according to the audit. How do the two numbers compare? How close are they?

Maturity									Immaturity
1	2	3	4	5	6	7	8	9	10

Discern Where the Leader Will Be Most Effective

With the information that you have discovered above, discern where you fit or don't fit in leading a church. Review the questions in the last section of step 3 in chapter 7, which dealt with this question of where the leader will be most effective.

Answer the following questions: Where do I fit best in pastoral ministry? Has God wired me to plant a culture, pastor an established culture, adopt an established culture, or play some other role in church ministry, such as an assistant pastor, a youth pastor, an executive pastor, an administrative pastor, a pastor of small groups, a pastor of congregational mobilization, a pastor of evangelism, and so forth? How would you know? I've added the following application to help you understand better how God has gifted you for ministry.

Discover the Leader's Divine Design

Not only is the leader's culture important to his current or future ministry, but so is his divine design or how God has wired him for ministry. Your divine design consists of the three Ds: design, direction, and development.

DESIGN

The first D is your design. It asks: Who are you? How has God put you together? The answer is threefold. First are your natural and spiritual gifts. If you haven't identified these, then you need to do so as part of your leadership-discovery process. The Spiritual Gifts Inventory is in appendix I; it will help you with the discovery of your gifts. A critical factor is whether you're wired to be a leader. In short, do you have a gift of leadership? Also, what are your strengths? You might find Marcus Buckingham's *Now, Discover Your Strengths* (Free Press) helpful to discover strengths.

Second is your passion. Your passion is what you care deeply or feel strongly about. Often passion directs the ministry of your gifts. For example, if you have the gift of leadership, your passion may serve to identify whom you'll lead best, such as a particular age group. For a pastor it would likely be a mixed group, such as a congregation.

Third is temperament that addresses how you behave in a certain context. Studies reveal that some temperaments favor the leadership role more than others. For example, pastors who have been used of God to turn churches around or who lead growing churches are often but not always Ds and/or Is on the *Personal Profile (DiSC)*. Ds are visionary, practical, decisive, productive, and strong-willed. For more characteristics look at the items in column one in appendix J. People who are Is are warm, friendly, enthusiastic, and outgoing. For more characteristics see column two in appendix J. They tend to be ENTPs or ESTJs on the *Myers-Briggs Temperament Indicator*. For a list of these characteristics or to discover yours, turn to and read over or take appendix L (Temperament Indicator 2).

DIRECTION

The second D is direction. Once you have a good understanding of your design, you need to ask: How does God want me to use my gifts for ministry? Based on my design, what has God wired me to do? This isn't rocket science. For example, if you have a natural and/or spiritual gift of leadership, then God wants you to lead and/or train others to lead. If you have a gift of evangelism, God wants you to evangelize and/or equip others to evangelize.

DEVELOPMENT

The third D is development. Once you know your gifting and passion, how will you develop? For example, if God has designed you to be the leader of a church culture, then how will you prepare? Some attend seminary or Bible college. Others join a staff and are coached in how to grow and develop as a leader. Wise leaders do both. And most read books on various leadership topics and attend church leadership conferences.

If you would like to explore the divine design concept further, we'll revisit it in more depth in chapter 11.

A Review: Reading the Pastor's Culture

Note that in reading the pastor's culture, as with the church's culture, you are moving from outside to the inside of the Culture Apple.

Step 1 Discover the Source of the Leader's Culture

1. The church where the leader was raised
2. The church where the leader came to faith
3. A church of profound impact
4. A combination of these sources
5. Other sources

Step 2 Observe the Leader's Culture

1. Ask the observation question: What do you see?
2. Fill in the Expressions Format: "I see, hear, feel _____."

Step 3 Interpret the Leader's Culture

1. Discover the leader's core values.
   - Ask the values question: Why do you do what you do?
   - Fill in the Values Format: "I value _____."
   - Validate the leader's values.
2. Discover the leader's beliefs.
   - Ask the beliefs question: What do you believe or assume?
   - Fill in the Beliefs Format: "I believe/assume _____."
   - Validate the leader's beliefs or assumptions.

Step 4 Make Application to the Leader's Culture

1. Determine the leader's commonalities and uniqueness.
2. Discover the leader's strengths and weaknesses.
3. Decide if the leader is spiritually mature or immature.
4. Discern where the leader will be most effective.
5. Discover the leader's divine design.

Questions for Reflection and Discussion

1. Would you agree with the author that the leader-pastor brings with him his personal church culture that will shape the church where he ministers? If not, why not? If so, which of the five sources of a leader's culture would be closest to the ones that have influenced you? If none, then identify the source that has most influenced your culture.

2. Would you have an opportunity to visit the church that has most influenced your culture to observe it with "intentional observation eyes"? If possible, are you willing to learn more about the culture that has most influenced the development of your culture? Why or why not?

3. To interpret your culture, you need to know your core congregational values. If you had to limit them to five or six, what would they be? Have you validated them? According to Acts 2:41–47, is a key value missing from your core values? If so, what is it and what will you do about it?

4. To interpret your culture, you also need to know your beliefs. What are yours? Have you validated them?

5. What does your view of church culture have in common with other cultures? What is unique about your view of culture?

6. What are some of your strengths as a culture leader? What are some of your weaknesses? Where would you rank yourself in terms of your spiritual maturity on a scale of 1 to 10, 1 being mature and 10 being immature?

7. Based on what you've learned in this chapter, where do you fit or not fit in leading a church? To answer this question, review application 4: Discern Where the Leader Will Be Most Effective.

8. What is your divine design? What have you discovered to be your natural and spiritual gifts? What do you feel deeply and care strongly about? What is your temperament, and how might it affect your leadership? What do you think God wants you to do based on your design? How will you prepare for this?

SHAPING CONGREGATIONAL CULTURE

9

The Church Planter as Culture Architect

Creating a New Church Culture

The churches in America are not doing well early in the twenty-first century. As many as 80 to 85 percent of our churches are plateaued or in decline.[1] One researcher, David Olson, reports that only 17 percent of the population attend church on any given weekend.[2] In addition, we're not winning lost young people, and David Kinnaman of the Barna Group has indicated that we're not keeping those who have come to faith. And most would agree that today's young people are the future of the church. Finally, Olson concludes, "In summary, the future looks grim for the American church. The conditions that produce growth are simply not present. If present trends continue, the church will fall farther behind population growth."[3] The problem has become such that a growing number of church and other leaders refer to America now as a post-Christian nation.

This raises some questions. What can we do to reverse this trend? What can we do to make a difference? The answer is threefold. We must plant more churches, revitalize established churches, and encourage healthy churches to adopt some smaller, struggling, established churches. (Normally I include adopting churches under revitalization or turnaround ministry but want to give them special attention in this book. Thus I have devoted a chapter to adoption.) For each approach, an understanding of congregational culture is vital. This chapter focuses on the first solution—church planting that involves creating a new culture.

In essence planting a church involves shaping or creating a culture. Church planters are culture architects and builders who design and build cultures. In this chapter I will use a number of different terms for church planters for variety, such as *culture architects, culture creators, culture builders, church starters, and culture planters*. And it's these founders of the new churches that play a profound role in forming the new culture. How do they accomplish this? We learned in the last chapter that to a certain extent pastors bring a culture with them to the new church. They are not culture neutral nor do they lack culture. Instead, they are culture carriers who bring with them their own unique beliefs or assumptions and values that will become a vital part of the new organizational culture. Therefore I encourage church planters to examine and be aware of the culture they bring with them and how it will impact the new church.

Of course, the architect's culture won't be perfect. Actually, it may be fraught with problems that the architect isn't aware of. For example, it may not be a suitable fit for the particular part of the country where the new church will be located. In other words, what God is blessing in Southern California might not work elsewhere.

At the same time, culture architects also have a wonderful opportunity to move beyond what they simply bring with them to something new and vibrant. They can be culture creators. They can create culture and thus add to what they carry with them, or in some cases they can start fresh. The aim of this chapter is to explore the creation of these new cultures. As in chapters 7 and 8, this will involve working our way from outside the Culture Apple in—from the peel to the core. And again, we'll use the exegesis process, beginning with observation and working our way through interpretation and then application.

So what's new? What's different from the process we used in chapters 7 and 8? In those two chapters, we were reading an existing culture. The culture was already in place. In this chapter we're forming culture. We're involved not in discovering what's there but creating what should be there—something new. You can discern the difference between the two in noting the questions to ask when you work through the culture exegetical process in the chart below.

Reading and Shaping Congregational Culture

	Reading the Culture	Shaping the Culture
Observation	What do you see?	What should you see?
Interpretation	What does it mean?	What should it mean?
Application	What difference does it make?	What difference should it make?

So how does the culture architect shape or create the new culture? The answer involves asking and answering three questions. First: Who are culture creators? Who's good at creating culture? Can anyone plant a culture? The focus here is on the person—the culture builder. Second: What kind of culture will the culture architect create? Here the focus is on the culture product. How do you do it, and what will it look like when you're finished? We will answer this question *by observing, interpreting, and applying the new culture.* Finally we will ask: How will you implement the new culture? How will you get it done? Here the focus is on the process.

Who Creates Cultures?

Who make good culture creators? Whom has God wired to start new works? To answer these critical questions, we will work through the following four characteristics that make up the church planter's profile: strengths and weaknesses, spiritual and emotional maturity, character qualifications, and divine design.

The Planter's Strengths and Weaknesses

The church planter will need to be in touch with both his strengths and his weaknesses. A good book that helps leaders unearth their strengths is Marcus Buckingham's *Now, Discover Your Strengths* (Free Press). Not only does he include a tool that he has labeled the Strengths Finder to help you discover your strengths, but he shows you how to leverage them for results at three levels: for your own development, for your success as a manager, and for the success of your organization, such as a church. Some typical strengths that I've observed in good culture architects are the following. They are entrepreneurial, visionary, self-starters, skilled with people, flexible/adaptable, risk takers, resilient, spiritually robust, optimistic, supported by their spouse, nontraditional, emotionally healthy, have good self-esteem, like a challenge, humble, challengers of the status quo, inspirational, people magnets (attract people), servants, team players, patient, wise, adaptive, and strategic thinkers and actors. When any of these characteristics are missing from their makeup, there is weakness. No one has all these characteristics, but the more one has, the better.

The Planter's Spiritual and Emotional Maturity

The culture creator will need to discern his spiritual and emotional maturity. Is he a mature or immature Christian? Being spiritually immature would disqualify the leader. One thing to look for is the fruit of the Spirit found in

Galatians 5:22–23. In Galatians 4:19 Paul writes that he travails as in childbirth that Christ might be formed in the Galatian church. That's how important spiritual maturity is. How does it happen? The same Holy Spirit who indwelled Christ indwelled them and indwells us. It is through his work that we become more like Christ and begin to evidence the fruit of the Spirit. The more we yield ourselves to the work of the Spirit, the more mature we become. I would encourage the leader who wants to assess his spiritual maturity to use the Spiritual Maturity Audit in appendix G.

I believe that every believer walks with an emotional limp, that is, a weakness that could bring failure. However, some limp more than others. Studies of leadership failures reveal that some leaders struggle with personal insecurities, feelings of inferiority, the need for parental approval—especially the father's approval—and other dysfunctions that caused their failure. And some of the very issues that appear to bring success are the same issues that result in their failure. For example, some pastors build large churches and seem most successful. However, the primary driving motivation is to prove to their fathers that they can be successful, not to bring glory to God. If any of this describes the aspiring culture creator, he would serve best by waiting until he has grown up in Christ and is addressing well these emotional issues before becoming involved in culture creation.

The Planter's Character Qualifications

Wrapped up in the leader's maturity are his character qualities. The biblical character qualifications are no different for a culture architect than for a culture revitalizer or any other lead pastor. They are found in 1 Timothy 3:1–7 and Titus 1:5–9: above reproach, not given to drunkenness, husband of one wife, gentle, temperate, not quarrelsome, sensible, not a lover of money, respectable, manages family well, hospitable, not a recent convert, able to teach, not overbearing, not violent, not quick-tempered, a good reputation with outsiders, not pursuing dishonest gain, loves what is good, holds firmly to the faith, upright, and holy. I will return to these and address them further in chapter 10. You may want now to examine your qualifications by using the Character Assessment for Leadership in appendix H.

The Planter's Divine Design

The church planter will need to determine where he will be most effective. And the way to accomplish this is in discovering his divine design.

Who creates cultures? The answer is that God does. However, he chooses to work through people to accomplish this (1 Cor. 3:6–7). The answer to the question used to be anyone who could convince a denomination or church-planting network to sponsor him financially. Sometimes the result was a new culture, but more often it was a failed effort. Then toward the end of the twentieth century, many of us who trained church planters felt that there was a better way to select culture architects. We discovered that those whom God blessed as church planters were all "wired" or designed similarly. In particular, they had similar spiritual gifts, passions, and temperaments. Let's explore some of these.

THE PLANTER'S GIFTS

The church planter's gifts are apostleship, leadership, evangelism, preaching, and teaching. Three well-known church planters are Rick Warren, Bill Hybels, and Andy Stanley, and most of us would agree that all three have at least gifts in evangelism, preaching or biblical communication, and leadership. They are apostolic leaders (like first-century church planters) who are evangelists, preach well, and are willing to step out in faith (not risk-aversive). If you would like to pursue further your spiritual gifting, use the Spiritual Gifts Inventory in appendix I.

THE PLANTER'S PASSION

The church planter's passions tend to be for lost people, unchurched lost people, entrepreneurial ventures, and/or evangelism, among other passions. Often it's the planter's passion that provides him with a cause—to be creative in ministry or to reach dysfunctional upwardly mobile people, for example. Thus he needs to be aware of this and see what cause his passion may point him toward.

THE PLANTER'S TEMPERAMENT

On the *Personality Profile* or *DiSC*, the culture architect's temperament is usually either a D (a results-oriented, dominant, developer-type person), a D/I (an inspiring type of person who relates well to people), or an I/D (a persuader-type person). Some who plant may also have either D or I temperament in combination with some other such as C or S. The C type persons are compliant people who are sticklers for reality and like planning ahead with accuracy. The S type persons are sympathetic and cooperative. They prefer to work behind the scenes and perform in predictable ways. But they don't fare as well as the D/I combination. I will go into greater detail on temperament in chapter 11. If you wish to know more now about your temperament, use the Temperament Indicator 1 in appendix J and read through appendix K.

On the *Myers-Briggs Temperament Indicator*, the culture creator tends to be an ENTP. The E stands for extraversion, the N indicates he is a visionary, the T marks him as a thinker, and the P means he is adaptable, flexible, and spontaneous. If you wish to know more now, use Temperament Indicator 2 in appendix L and read over the information in appendix M. And I will go into greater detail in chapter 11.

The Church Planter's Profile
Strengths and weaknesses
Spiritual and emotional maturity
Character qualifications
Divine design

The Design Question

The information in this section answers the question, Who designs and builds new cultures? The design question for the lead church planter is, Does this describe you? If not, then God may be directing you into another area of ministry or to minister under the lead of someone else. Note that I've worded the above very carefully. I want to underline the truth that this is descriptive of the *lead* church planter, not necessarily others who would make up the team.

God will lead leaders into church planting who don't necessarily fit the profile, but they are exceptions, not the norm. And the people who don't fit the profile will likely be part of the team that ministers and leads under the direction of the lead culture architect. Therefore, if God has let you know that he wants you to plant church cultures, yet you don't fit the lead profile, find a lead culture architect and become an important part of his team. Look at your design and ask, What will I contribute to the team as a support person? Without support people, the plant likely won't survive beyond a year or two.

It's important to note that leadership in general and leadership skills can be learned. Some leaders may not be wired like a point person but may be able to learn to function like one in some contexts. They simply need a person with good leadership skills whom they can emulate. Does this describe you? Do you simply need some exposure to lead culture architects to learn how to function like one?

What Kind of Culture?

Once the culture creator has affirmed that he is a church planter—that the church planter's profile is his profile—next we ask, What kind of culture will he create? As it takes shape, what will it look like? The answer involves both observation and interpretation. Observation addresses what you will see when the new church begins its meetings. Interpretation surfaces the creator's cultural beliefs and values.

Apple	Culture	Exegesis
Peel	Behavior	Observation
Flesh	Values	Interpretation
Core	Beliefs	Application

Observation

The first step as you move from the peel to the core is observation. As we have seen, discovering a church's culture involves asking what you see, hear, or feel. When you visit a church, what behavior do you observe or experience? However, church planters are building a culture, so the question changes and becomes, What do you want people to see or experience when they visit your church? What should they observe? What for you would be the ideal church?

Earlier I encouraged you to take the Behaviors Audit in appendix A. The instructions ask you to circle the response that best describes an existing culture. When you are creating a culture, you should circle the responses that you want to describe your future church—not what is but what could or should be. For example, perhaps you have a passion for reaching those who live in the inner city and are poor and disenfranchised. That would dictate what or whom you want visitors to see on a visit. Perhaps you want to minister to a mixed ethnicity. Then you would want a visitor to see, for example, Asian, Hispanic, Anglo, and African Americans. If you want to plant a church among a mixed ethnicity, you may want visitors to hear a multiplicity of languages as well.

You would benefit most in this first step by retaking the Behaviors Audit in appendix A, choosing options based on what you want people to observe in the planted church. Several that may be important when creating a culture are the following:

1. *Different ethnicities.* People of different ethnicities who accept and show love for one another.
2. *Diverse languages.* People who speak different languages that reflect the church's cultural diversity.
3. *Adequate parking.* You may have invited a lost or unchurched person to visit who may be looking for an excuse to turn around and go home. Don't give him or her that excuse.
4. *Clean facilities.* Cleanliness—especially for women and those with children—is next to godliness. You will need to pay attention to the

cleanliness of bathrooms and kitchens when looking for a place to hold services.

5. *Good signage.* While those who regularly attend a church know their way around the facilities, visitors don't. Place signs and volunteers in strategic locations in and around your facilities to guide visitors to Bible studies, Sunday school classes, small group meetings on the premises, and worship services.

6. *Parking attendants.* Some of the first contacts that visitors make are those people they encounter in the parking lots. You would be wise to draft a team of volunteers who would be available to greet and help guests find a place to park and direct them to the classrooms or worship areas.

7. *Greeters.* I can't emphasize enough the importance of having the right people in the right places to greet not only regular attenders but guests. Think through how people navigate your facilities and place greeters appropriately.

8. *Warm and inviting people.* Placing greeters in the right places isn't enough. They need to be the right people. Some people are friendly and inviting and some aren't. Most often the best greeters are extraverts and people people. Guests know when and where they're wanted.

9. *Good communication.* When The Malphurs Group works with a church, we ask how well the church communicates with its people. The answer is usually not well. Rick Warren says that people tend to be down on what they're not up on. Good communication leads to trust. Poor communication leads to mistrust, because people think you're trying to hide something from them, whether you are or not.

10. *Good follow-up.* Many church starters put much effort into the things I've already listed, which are up-front and worship-day activities. Just as important is good follow-up. This can vary anywhere from a phone call from the pastor to a gift from the church delivered to the home of the visitor. My church, which is located in Texas, provides all its visitors with a basket of salsa and chips, a Texas tradition.

11. *Good, quality worship.* Usually the first staff hire is the worship person. Don't cut corners when it comes to the person or persons who lead your worship time. Worship is just as important to people as the sermon.

12. *Good phone etiquette.* Another area that may be overlooked is phone etiquette. When a person calls a church, what do they hear? This may be the person's first contact with the church, and how well they're treated can make the difference as to whether they show up to a service.

13. *Good, in-depth Bible teaching.* The church needs to emphasize good Bible teaching in general and its application in particular.

14. *Happy, excited children.* The church needs to have a strong ministry to children. Visitors with children will want to know what the church offers their children.

15. *Happy, excited youth.* The needs of young people need to be met as well.

Interpretation

When you start at the culture's peel and work your way into the core, the second step is to interpret the church planter's culture. This is critical, because in most situations the creator's culture will become the church's culture. How can we know what that culture will be? As we learned in the preceding chapter, his culture entails both his core beliefs and his values.

THE PLANTER'S CORE VALUES

If the culture creator hasn't already taken the Core Values Audit in appendix B, now is the time to do so. Every church is values-driven. As we learned in chapter 4, one's core values will empower and guide his culture. Values explain why a leader does what he does. Therefore unearthing one's core values is essential to culture starters. I believe that the leader benefits in several ways by using appendix B to discover his core values. First, the leader will have a good read on all that he truly values in addition to his core values, as the list contains twenty values and a space at the end to add others. Also he will discover what he doesn't value and what he should value.

In addressing the question as to whether the church planter has the best values for planting a church, we learned that the Jerusalem Church's core values, given in Acts 2:41–47, are a good yardstick, because this was a biblically based, spiritually strong church.

Jerusalem Church

Five Essential Core Values

1. Evangelism (Acts 2:41, 47)
2. Biblical instruction (Acts 2:42)
3. Fellowship (Acts 2:42, 44–46)
4. Worship (Acts 2:42–43, 46–47)
5. Service (Acts 2:45)

It would be ideal if the culture planter holds all five as his actual core values. Our experience in working with established church leaders at The Malphurs Group is that many don't value evangelism and service or ministry. While all are important, evangelism stands out as extremely important if one is to pursue church planting. Currently among established churches from coast to coast and border to border, evangelism is a dying value in the American church. Thus I come very close to saying that evangelism should be mandatory for the church starter. And if it isn't an actual core value, it needs to be an aspirational value, and the leader needs to work hard at seeing it become an actual value. However, my experience in training culture starters is that most do value evangelism.

The Planter's Core Beliefs

If the church planter hasn't taken the congregational Beliefs Audit in appendix D, he should do so before reading any further. As you recall, a culture is values-driven but beliefs-based. All the beliefs listed in the congregational Beliefs Audit are important. But now you will use the audit to discover your core beliefs and other important beliefs that impact the church.

The Beliefs Audit isn't meant to be exhaustive. If you are aware of any beliefs that you feel are important to the culture of the church that aren't listed here, then add them to the list. The observation question is, What are your core beliefs, and what beliefs did you mark as important to your culture development?

Application

The third step for the culture architect is application. We discovered in chapters 7 and 8 that the application step addresses commonalities and uniqueness, strengths and weaknesses, spiritual maturity and immaturity, and effectiveness.

Commonalities and Uniqueness

The culture planter will need to answer the question, What will the new ministry have in common with other cultures, and what will be unique? In general, the new culture will not hold much in common with struggling, established churches, outside of the basics such as mission, vision, values, and strategy. Every church, whether a new start or established, must address these. (I'll say more about them and their importance in chapter 12.)

Often a culture planter will start a church in reaction to the practices and programs of established churches. This is especially true in response to Builder and Boomer ministries. The culture planter is dissatisfied with what's happening in these churches and yearns for something new and different, and what he comes up with is often most unique. Again I use the example of Ed Young Jr., who planted Fellowship Bible Church in Grapevine, Texas. He and his core team were most concerned about what they sensed was a lack of creativity in church ministry. They observed that far too many churches were creativity starved. Consequently, they started a culture that focused on being most creative in making disciples.

Strengths and Weaknesses

What will be the new culture's strengths, and what weaknesses will it need to avoid? Most likely, the church will mirror the planter's strengths and weaknesses that I addressed above. Often the strengths will be the planting pastor's preaching and personality. The weaknesses may be found in the areas of administration, coordination, programming, and others. Wise planters will seek help in these areas, recruiting those who are good at them.

Spiritual Maturity or Immaturity

While the leader should be mature, the church that he plants won't be mature out of the starting blocks. This isn't necessarily bad, as it takes time for a congregation to grow up and become mature. A great example is the Jerusalem Church in the first century. In the early chapters of Acts, we can observe a church that is biblically strong and spiritually vibrant but not yet mature. Maturity doesn't happen overnight.

Leader Effectiveness

You as a leader must determine where you will be most effective. Assuming that you are gifted as a church starter, your first task is to recruit a church-planting team. There are at least two reasons for this. One is that New Testament ministry is team ministry. For example, look at the various teams the apostle Paul ministered with throughout the Pastoral Epistles and Acts. The other is that the planter needs people who complement him in terms of their gifts in ministry to the new culture. There is no room for loners in ministry in general and church planting in particular.

How Will the New Culture Be Implemented?

At this point we should have a good read on the planting person or culture architect. We know if he is wired to be a church planter. We have also unearthed the cultural product—his beliefs and values—and what he wants new people to observe about the new culture and how that applies to the new work. Finally, we want to implement what we have learned. Where do we go from here? What is the process for starting a new culture? The answer is the five stages of culture implementation.

I find it helpful to teach church planters the five stages of planting a culture that parallel birthing a child. They are the conception, development, birth, growth, and reproduction stages.[4] Planters and others find that this analogy provides them with a structure to bring clarity to the planting process. It provides a skeleton that they flesh out with "how-to" information. The following focuses briefly on each stage.

Five Stages of Church Planting

Conception
Development
Birth
Growth
Reproduction

The Conception Stage

Typically the conception stage begins with a leader—the culture architect—to whom God has given a vision for starting a church. To summarize what I've already said: most often these leaders are strong visionary people with an entrepreneurial spirit who love the challenge of creating a culture.

CULTURE ISSUES AND OTHER MATTERS

Early on, culture architects are wise to address a number of issues, such as the future culture's direction, consisting of its articulated mission and vision. He must consider the culture's discovered values that provide its identity along with what will empower and guide it. The church planter will also design a strategy—the how-to—that he believes will best accomplish the mission and vision.

I also advise that church planters accomplish the following in the conception stage: recruit an intercessory prayer team, find a location where they'll meet initially, establish a budget and begin to raise funding, develop a doctrinal statement, write mini bios to introduce those on the planting team, investigate possible denominational or a network affiliation, determine the church's polity, anticipate contingencies, and write up the church's constitution and bylaws.

A STRONG FOUNDATION

The culture architect is basically laying a foundation in the conception stage on which he'll erect the culture superstructure or church. The importance of this stage is underlined by the fact that a superstructure will not survive on a weak foundation. I advise seminary students to work on the conception stage while in seminary, because they can use the academic environment to raise and answer certain questions—especially those that address theology. I advise others to work on the conception stage while on the staff of an existing church where they can find practical answers to their questions. In essence, the conception stage takes place behind the scenes well before the new culture goes public.

The Development Stage

RECRUIT A TEAM

Next the architect will recruit a staff and core group of people who share his vision blueprint for the new church culture he has conceived. They are people who so believe in the vision that they are willing to invest their time, money, and energy in getting the church up and running. If the culture architect is in seminary, he would be wise to look for other students to be part of his team. I encourage our seminarian church planters to be on the lookout on campus for potential church plant team members. They will need to cast their vision regularly among the other students, perhaps over lunch or coffee. If they see a light come on, it may mean they've found a potential team member who shares the vision.

Church planters who are not in seminary will need to be part of a denomination or network that supports church creators and connects like-minded planters to form teams. The culture creator will also need to gather a core group during the development stage. They, in turn, will get the word out to others and invite them to come and be a significant part of the new work.

MATTERS TO ADDRESS

In the process of recruiting a staff and the core group, the leader will knowingly or unknowingly inaugurate the culture formation process with the early group. There are several matters that need to be addressed.

1. During this time it is important that the team align with the leader's mission, vision, core values, and strategy that were conceived in the conception stage. The strategy would include the community they hope to reach (their Jerusalem—Acts 1:8), how they plan to reach them, how they'll make disciples (small groups, Bible teaching, and so forth), where they'll locate, funding, and most of what was included under the conception stage.
2. The leader will need to understand and communicate the importance of measuring and evaluating certain aspects of ministry that include what they're doing and who's doing it. As someone has said, "What gets measured is what gets done."

3. The leader needs to realize that how he responds to a crisis signals what
   he believes is important. There will likely be a number of crises early
   in the development stage and many more later in the process. A crisis
   serves to tear off the mask of inauthenticity. When crises hit, don't give
   up—this is often God's way of showing you who you really are and
   what you really believe.
4. As the team raises funds, decisions will need to be made about resource
   allocation. What gets funded and what doesn't? Where the ministry
   spends its money speaks volumes about what is important to the culture.

The Birth Stage

REACH CRITICAL MASS

The birth stage is when the new culture goes public. The mistake that too
many culture leaders make is they launch too soon, with the result that they
get stuck at the two-hundred-people barrier and eventually begin to decline.
Critical mass is essential. To avoid the two-hundred barrier, the critical mass
at the launch must be no less than fifty to one hundred committed people. In
other words, in terms of future healthy growth, the bigger the better at the
beginning. These people will be meeting together for planning and worship
during the development stage. And they may call themselves a church among
themselves and with other believers who might be interested in joining them.
But they don't publically announce themselves as a church to the community
until they commence the birth stage.

SPREAD THE WORD

To get the word out about the new plant, the culture needs to take two
steps: market the church and locate the church.

Market the Church

The culture will need to market itself. Word needs to get out that a birth is
taking place. Some church planters go so far as to send out birth announcements and provide birth certificates. Good birthing times continue to be Eas-
ter Sunday, Christmas, Mother's Day, or a special Sunday designated for the
launch, such as a Spring Celebration. Bad birthing times are Super Bowl Sunday,
holiday weekends, and similar times, when people in general and unchurched
seekers in particular will not show. Be alert to such special events and holidays.

By this time the church will have chosen a name. Younger people seem
to be turned off by denominational titles. I attend a large Southern Baptist
megachurch in Rockwall, Texas. You wouldn't know that it is Baptist because
it has dropped the designation *Baptist* from its name and is known as Lake

Pointe Church. Some adopt the name of the community where they're located and include community in the name, such as Rush Creek Community Church and Willow Creek Community Church. The planter needs to be careful here because often new churches relocate several times and may move out of the community where they started.

Find a Location

The new culture will also need to locate a place to meet. So far the two most popular locations have been schools and movie theaters. Willow Creek Community Church began in a theater in Palatine, Illinois. One of my friends started a church in an older, well-known fine arts theater located near the University of North Texas in Denton, Texas. They named the church Sunday Morning on the Square. To market the church, they sent out clever mailers into the community that were shaped like a piece of film that said: "If life has you feeling like a rebel without a cause [the title of a popular 1950s movie starring James Dean], check out the new feature at the Fine Arts Theater." Another said, "If your life's dreams seem to be gone with the wind, check out the new feature at the Fine Arts Center."

Other new churches have met in hotels, bank buildings, YMCAs, community centers, abandoned churches, storefronts, and even funeral homes with chapels. The church I planted in Miami, Florida, met in a Seventh-day Adventist Church that was available on Sunday because they meet on Saturdays. Several features to consider in locating a place to meet are the following: visibility, accessibility, size, cleanliness, location, cost, storage, signage, parking, and reputation.

The Growth Stage

The goal of the growth stage is spiritual and numerical growth. If the church doesn't grow, something is seriously wrong, and it will begin to die.

CHURCH GROWTH FACTORS

There are a number of growth factors that will help new cultures grow.

1. *Leadership.* As mentioned above, many culture builders who lead growing churches are strong visionary entrepreneurs with a compelling biblical vision that excites and challenges their followers.
2. *Vision.* There must be a single, clear vision that addresses small group ministries, evangelism, and Bible study and develops leaders all along the way.
3. *Congregational mobilization.* Leaders must see that their people understand that, according to Scripture, it's the congregation that is to

do the ministry (Eph. 4:11–13). If this doesn't happen, the church will not mature (v. 13).

4. *Assimilation.* Some churches plateau because the same number of people coming in the front door are going out the back door. The church must implement ministries, such as small group ministries, application Bible studies, men's groups that feature special events accentuating biblical manhood, and family ministries to help assimilate the people who come to the church.

RESULTS OF GROWTH

As the church begins to grow, it forms a common shared history that ingrains the culture into the soil of the church. And those who attend and basically agree with the culture will stay while those who differ will either move on to a more favorable culture or stay and attempt to change the current culture. This isn't likely to happen as long as the founder is at the ministry helm. Over time the church's culture will not likely change much, because the beliefs have become assumptions and seem to work in solving most of the major and minor issues or problems the church faces throughout its life.

THE IMPORTANCE OF CHANGE

The fact that the church culture is unlikely to change doesn't mean that it can't change. There are certain things it can and must do to promote change so the culture does not grow stale, cease to minister well, and stop attracting people. Thus the pastors must function as culture overseers and sculptors regularly assessing, changing, and shaping what needs to be a shifting culture. This is the topic of chapters 11 and 12.

The Reproduction Stage

It's not enough that you establish a new culture. It's imperative for church health that the new culture focus outward and reproduce itself. Thus the church becomes not just another church, but a church-planting church. There are a number of advantages that such a sponsoring church brings to a culture.

1. *Finances.* One characteristic of failed church plants is a lack of finances. It takes money to do ministry, and the planting or mother church can help the new church with its finances. For example, they might assist with a culture starter's salary for three years. The first year he receives a full salary. Then the support decreases proportionately over the next two or three years as the new church takes responsibility for meeting its needs.

2. *A core group*. The sponsoring church can supply people who will make up the initial core group of the church plant. For example, there may be several people in a church who live near each other at quite a distance from the church. This makes the area where they live fertile soil for a church plant. The established, sponsoring church would alert these people to the potential for a church plant and encourage them to commit to being a part of it.

3. *Accountability*. Lone-wolf church planters have little if any accountability. There will always be temptations in the areas of finances, sexual promiscuity, integrity, and so on. The pastor and/or ministry staff of a sponsoring church can provide the needed accountability for the new church's pastor and staff.

4. *Encouragement*. All ministries have their ups and downs emotionally, and the new church plant is susceptible to them. This is when the established culture can come alongside the leader, the staff, and the core and provide encouragement to counter their times of discouragement.

5. *Prayer*. While the newly planted culture needs to recruit an intercessory prayer team, prayer is also a responsibility of the planting church. Their responsibility isn't simply that of providing physical resources. Since the new church will face a spiritual battle, fought in the spiritual realm, according to Ephesians 6:12, it will need spiritual reinforcement. Satan doesn't want to see new culture plants. And, according to Ephesians 6:18–19, the primary weapon in this spiritual battle is prayer.

6. *Counsel*. A problem that all church planters face is the knowledge problem—knowing what to do when facing various situations or decisions that need to be made. This is where the counsel of a seasoned senior pastor or ministry staff person can be of much benefit to the new work.

7. *Credibility*. When the church goes public, some people will be asking, Is this new church legitimate? Who's behind it? How does the community know it's not a fly-by-night operation? The answer is for the planting church to identify with and endorse the new culture and thus lend to it the church's credibility. This can be most effective, especially when the sponsoring church is known and has a good reputation in the community.

8. *Shared talent*. The established culture will have talented people whom it has attracted over time. And it could help the new start by loaning it some of this talent. For example, at the first birth event, it could provide musicians, vocalists, or even a drama team to lead in quality worship.

Though this book emphasizes church revitalization and even church adoption as potential solutions to the dying American church dilemma, I'm convinced that planting cultures is the best option. Therefore my challenge to established church cultures, denominations, and networks is to maximize their church-planting efforts.

Questions for Reflection and Discussion

1. Before reading this chapter, were you aware that the church in America is struggling? If so, how did you know? How is your church doing? What does the fact that many churches are struggling tell you about how we've been doing church?
2. The author has given you a number of ways to determine the culture or cultures that have had the greatest impact on you that you bring with you to a new venture and what that means in terms of culture formation. What have you learned?
3. As a church planter, what are your strengths and weaknesses? Are you a mature or immature Christian? How do you know? Are you a person of good character? Have you taken the Character Assessment for Leadership Audit in appendix H?
4. Is your divine design that of a church planter? What are your natural and spiritual gifts? What or whom are you passionate about? What is your temperament?
5. What do you want people to observe when they visit your church?
6. What are your core beliefs or assumptions? What are some other important though not core beliefs?
7. What are your core values? What are some other important values besides your core values?
8. As a culture creator, what will your church have in common with other churches? How will it be unique?
9. What strengths will you display, and what are some potential weaknesses?
10. Do you agree with the author that it takes time for a new church to mature?
11. In which of the five church-planting stages is your church? What have you learned about this stage in this chapter?

10

The Church Pastor as Culture Sculptor

Part 1 Preparation

In chapter 9 we discovered that the church in America is struggling and in serious decline. One solution is to plant a new church or culture. That was the focus of chapter 9. Another solution is to revitalize existing church cultures, which involves skillfully guiding them to embrace life-giving change. This is the focus of this and the next two chapters. As in the last chapter, I will use various terms to refer to the pastor who is revitalizing a church culture, such as *culture architect*, *leader of change*, *leader of transition*, plus others. I do this for stylistic purposes only. These terms refer to the same person, not to different roles at different steps in the change process.

When we consider church revitalization, we must ask a critical question: How does a culture architect lead an established church to change its culture, even in a minor way? In a sense, every pastor of an established church, whether a new pastor or one who has been there for years, must be a culture architect. As we discovered in chapter 9, this is because the majority of churches in North America are immature and unhealthy and in desperate need of change. The amount of change will depend on where the church is in terms of the three views found in chapter 6: isolation, accommodation, and contextualization.

So all church pastors will have to address how to lead their church in regularly adjusting their culture. In fact, this should be a major aspect of what pastors do. I would go so far as to say it should be in the job description. How do pastors go about bringing change to established church cultures? This chapter and the two that follow will provide the answer to this question. I have written this chapter to equip pastors in preparing an established culture for change. Chapter 11 will address the personnel for shaping the culture, and chapter 12 will provide the process that the church pastor needs as a culture sculptor to accomplish a culture turnaround.

There is a myth about change that has destroyed many leaders' careers in both the business and the church world. They assume that preparing their culture for change is a waste of time. They believe that they will be better off if they jump right into change and implement it as quickly as possible. Then after several weeks or months into the process, they realize that their failure to prepare the culture for change has left them without any support from the very culture they are attempting to change. Without that support, it won't happen. The lesson learned is that if you don't take time to prepare your culture for change, you won't have the basic support required to accomplish the change you so desperately need. The culture architect, like a farmer, must prepare the soil for change. Preparation always precedes planting. This preparation consists of six steps: pray for change, do a church analysis, read the church's culture, learn why people resist change, know how churches and their leaders respond to change, and use the tools that facilitate God-honoring, spiritually healthy change.

Pray for Change

Not enough can be said about the importance of prayer to the change process. Leaders must constantly remind themselves of the critical role prayer plays in revitalizing people. The battle over change is ultimately a spiritual not a physical battle, and it is being fought on spiritual ground, not between personalities in earthly church facilities. In Ephesians 6:10–20 Paul reminds us that we are involved in spiritual warfare against evil spiritual forces. A vital piece of the armor that God provides for every Christian is prayer. Paul writes, "And pray in the Spirit on all occasions with all kinds of prayers and requests. With this in mind, be alert and always keep on praying for all the Lord's people" (v. 18). I believe that there's a direct relationship between the prayer life of the culture sculptor and successful change.

A reason that prayer is so important is that it reminds us of our insufficiency without Christ. The culture farmer can become so involved in the physical details that he forgets the spiritual dynamic of what he's doing. In John 15:5 the Savior reminds us that without him we can accomplish nothing of spiritual significance: "I am the vine; you are the branches. If you remain in me and I in you, you will bear much fruit; apart from me you can do nothing."

To attempt church revitalization without these words emblazoned across the walls of our minds is to invite failure. Many wise change agents have a worn, ragged page where John 15 appears in their Bibles. Others have mounted this verse on a plaque and hung it on their office wall as a regular reminder of their insufficiency outside of Christ. What reminders do you have in place?

Do a Church Analysis

Since they know the church best, invite the key leaders of the church to do the church analysis. Besides the pastor, key leaders are any ministry staff, the elders or board, Sunday school teachers, Bible teachers, small group leaders, deacons, and others of influence. The analysis is vital because it will give you an idea of where the church is in terms of its health, which will in turn determine what you do and your approach to it. In addition, it has a shock effect; it will likely silence those vocal congregants who object to change when they're faced with the facts. The church analysis consists of four vital signs: average worship attendance, average giving, the church's strengths, and the church's weaknesses.

The Church's Annual Average Worship Attendance

Track the church's annual average worship attendance. Be sure to go as far back as the church has records. You want to see the big picture. (Note that you're looking for actual worship attendance, not church membership. The latter tells you nothing.) In addition to spiritual growth, God wants his churches to grow numerically, because that's a sign of health (Acts 2:41, 47; 4:4; 5:14; 6:1, 7; 9:31, 35, 42; 11:21, 24; 14:1, 21; 16:5). Spiritual and numerical growth normally work together.

So where is the church currently? Is the church growing, plateaued, or experiencing a decline? If it's in decline, what is the rate or percentage of decline? Create visuals or graphs to help communicate this information. If the church continues to decline at this rate, when will it have to shut the doors? This is what has shock effect! Should you even attempt to revitalize the culture, or should you let it die? If you decide to breathe new life into the culture, how fast do you need to move? The state of the church's attendance will help you answer these questions.

The Church's Annual Average Giving

Track the church's annual average giving. As with the worship attendance, go as far back as the church has records. As a church grows numerically, God wants its people to increase their giving. This involves congregational giving as a whole. The larger the church, the greater the offering. This also includes people's individual giving to God. As people mature in the faith, in most cases their individual giving will increase, depending on their situations in life. Thus you need to determine if the offering is growing, plateaued, or declining. Again create visuals to communicate what is happening with the offering. If it's declining, what is that rate of decline, and when might the church run out of money to operate? This too has shock effect! Also it's important to think about what a decline in giving says about people's confidence in the church.

The Church's Strengths

What are the church's strengths? What has it done well? What is it doing well? The experience of The Malphurs Group, which has conducted many church analyses, is that churches tend to be strong in worship, fellowship, women's ministries, children's ministries, and biblical instruction. In some of the older churches, the pastor gets high marks if he has performed well as a chaplain. This includes much visitation in homes and hospitals, as well as performing weddings and funerals and attending meetings.

The Church's Weaknesses

What are the church's weaknesses? Where has it been weak, and where is it weak today? The experience of The Malphurs Group is that churches tend to be weak in evangelism, lay involvement in ministry, communication in general, strategic planning, vision casting, leadership, and leadership development.

Read the Church's Culture

The pastor who is planning or attempting to bring change to a church culture must not attempt to do so blindly, though most do. As much as possible he needs to read and understand the ministry's culture before attempting to introduce change. How does he do this? Since I covered how to read the church's culture in chapter 7, I will review it only briefly here. Recall that reading or exegeting a church's culture moves from outside (the peel) to inside the Culture Apple (the flesh and core). This involves observing the culture, interpreting the culture, and then making application to the culture.

Culture	Exegesis
Behavior	Observation
Values	Interpretation
Beliefs	Application

Observe the Culture

The first layer or peel is visual or observable. On a typical Sunday or whenever your church meets, put on your visitor's glasses and attempt to observe what visitors see or experience when they visit your church or when they interact with your church during activities in the community. Walk around your facilities or the community—what does a visitor hear, see, or feel?

Interpret the Culture

Next we move from outside the Culture Apple to inside—the flesh and core—and we ask, What does all that we have observed mean? It is time to interpret what we have experienced. This involves discerning the church's values and beliefs.

READ THE VALUES

Based on what you have experienced, what are the church values in general and core values in particular? Values explain why people do what they do, what we observe them doing. Churches are values-driven.

READ THE BELIEFS

Next we continue to probe inside the Culture Apple as we move from the flesh (values) to its inner core (beliefs). This involves surfacing the culture's beliefs and assumptions that undergird its values. Churches are values-driven but beliefs-based. Here the question to ask is, What does the church believe or assume is true of itself?

Make Application to the Culture

At this point in the process, you will have a good grasp of the church's culture. Now you need to apply this to the church's situation. The question is, What do you do with this information? The following application exercises will give you the answer.

1. *Determine the church's commonalities and uniqueness.* What does the church share in common with other ministries, and in what ways is its culture unique?
2. *Discover the church's strengths and weaknesses.* Where is the church strong, and where is it weak? Do the strengths outnumber the weaknesses?

3. *Discern whether the culture is spiritually mature or immature or some-where in between.* Use the Spiritual Maturity Audit in appendix G to help with this.
4. *Determine where you as a leader will be most effective.*

Learn Why People Resist Change

People, even Christian people, are allergic to change! They break out in hives at the mention of the word. But this is not a new lesson for an experienced veteran of culture change. Experience teaches that there are multiple reasons for people resisting change. And the astute change agent better be aware of the more common reasons if he is to lead a church successfully through the change process. The following are just a few of the reasons people resist change.

Felt Needs

WHAT IS THE PROBLEM?

Every man, woman, and child passes through this life with certain basic needs. However, it is their felt needs that demand action. Felt needs are the key that unlocks the closed mind and touches even the most calloused heart. In most typical churches there are people who resist change because they do not feel a need for change. Some of these people are not aware of all the change that is taking place around them. They do not realize that more change has taken place in the last twenty years than in the last two thousand years.

Others are aware that something is happening but are not sure what it is. They do not like what is going on and long for a return to the past. They yearn for the good old days when life was a lot simpler and hold the church captive to the past.

WHAT IS THE SOLUTION?

The solution is to help these people and their churches discover that every-thing is not all right. This may be difficult with churched people who are in their fifties, sixties, and seventies. The alert culture architect of change will capture their attention and fuel a desire for change by pointing to the need for the kind of church that will reach their children and their grandchildren. He touches a felt need by asking, What would you be willing to do—what would you be willing to change—to reach your kids and your grandkids for the Savior? Or if the children and grandchildren are already believers, he should ask, What would you be willing to change to have them sitting next to you in church? In addition, he would call their attention to the results of the church analysis and the signs of church decline. It's hard to deny the facts.

The Status Quo

WHAT IS THE PROBLEM?

Many people in typical churches refuse to change because they prefer the status quo. Someone has said that their slogan is: "Come weal or come woe, our status is quo."

The status quo represents "what is" or "the way things are" in our churches. For most churches in the twenty-first century, it is still the forms and practices of the churches of the 1940s through the 1960s. However, the world of the 1940s, '50s, and '60s is not the world of the twenty-first century. Consequently, as the culture changes and the people within each culture change, so the church must change how it puts into practice the eternal principles of Scripture.

WHAT IS THE SOLUTION?

The solution is to cast a new vision for the church. The status quo represents "what is." The culture change agent begins by pointing out the various discrepancies in or what is wrong with "what is." But he must not stop there or he behaves like the fireman who runs around yelling, "Fire!" but never bothers to reach for a water bucket. The culture change agent must cast a clear, compelling vision of "what could be." A viable solution must be offered for every problem. The visionary change agent has the responsibility as leader to point his people to a better way.

Vested Interests

WHAT IS THE PROBLEM?

People in traditional churches may resist change because they cling to various vested interests. They make a strong commitment to Christ, which results in the investment of their time, talents, and treasure in the church and its programs. It is most important that Christians commit to various avenues of ministry and remain faithful to them. Over time, however, certain benefits to the individual accrue, such as position, power, and prestige. As the organization grows, the power and prestige expand with it. Through this subtle process, people begin to feel the need to protect their investments, whatever they may be.

Change may involve the loss of power and prestige. Whenever a church transitions from an old to a new paradigm, everyone goes back to zero. Whatever leverage one had because of the old paradigm is dramatically diminished with the emergence of the new. The result, on the part of many people, is a strong resistance to change, based on the potential loss of power.

WHAT IS THE SOLUTION?

The solution is to make every effort to win these people over to the new vision. The culture change agent needs to identify those in the church with vested interests and spend some one-on-one time with them, ministering and communicating the new vision for the church. Communication and overcoming the problems of miscommunication are half the battle! By focusing on these people, the change agent has an opportunity to make certain that the new direction is fairly represented and gets a proper hearing. The pastor of change takes the time necessary to cultivate and recruit each of these people individually for his team so that they share ownership in the new paradigm.

Distrust of Leadership

WHAT IS THE PROBLEM?

Some people dislike change because they distrust those who would lead them through the change process. For example, older people, on the one hand, prefer leaders who have some experience and maturity under their belts. They find it most difficult to follow a leader who they suspect is a novice—a recent seminary graduate, a pastor with little or no experience, a pastor without credentials, and so on. On the other hand, younger people may possess an antiauthority sentiment. They are not sure if they trust anyone in a position of leadership, whether experienced or inexperienced. They have witnessed what they believe is a generation of leaders who have been inauthentic and seriously lacking in integrity. In addition, they believe that they know as much about leadership as anyone else; therefore they come across as unteachable.

WHAT IS THE SOLUTION?

The solution is for leaders to realize that people today, both young and old, are asking two essential questions. The first is, Can you be trusted? Those who, in the future, successfully lead the church through the culture revitalization process will be people who model Christlike character. The second question is, Do you know where you are going? This involves ministry direction or vision. Astute church members want to know the leader's vision before they climb on board the ministry train. If they agree to involve themselves in the change process, they have a right to know the direction of that change. Therefore change agents who combine godly character with ministry direction offer ministry credibility, which attracts ministry followers.

The Stress of Change

WHAT IS THE PROBLEM?

Another reason people struggle with transition is stress. Much change has taken place in the early twenty-first century. All the evidence indicates that the pace will only increase. The problem for Americans in general and churched people in particular is a change overload. People can handle only so much over a short period of time. Actually the rapidity of change makes people sick. They no longer feel certain of anything—job, spouse, beliefs, morality—everything seems to be changing all the time. A pervasive uncertainty hangs like a fog over everything in the modern world.

In light of the dizzying pace of rapid change taking place in the world out there, people look to the church as a place of safety and protection from the shattering stress of change. When the church is the only entity in their lives that does not change, this provides them a certain amount of stability. The problem is that the church that fails to change fails to impact the culture of change. It becomes a cultural dinosaur—a memorial to a world that no longer exists.

WHAT IS THE SOLUTION?

How can a church implement planned, positive change and remain a bright light and savory salt in the community? There are several steps that an architect of change can take to alleviate some of the stress.

1. *Communication.* As much as possible people should be kept informed of what is taking place. People resent most of all not being informed of change. They believe the leadership is trying to hide something from them.
2. *Assurance.* Members who are followers of change agents and generally agree with them and the need for change still need assurances from trusted people that the proposed changes are in the best interests of the church. Thus, for example, a word of testimony from a credible source who experienced a similar change in another situation provides the encouragement and assurance necessary to calm troubled spirits.
3. *Participation in the change process.* Architects of change should attempt to involve their people, wherever possible, as active agents in the program of change. The key to people accepting change is the mobilization of a lay army of fully devoted disciples.

Sacred Cows

WHAT IS THE PROBLEM?

Churched people resist change of what they consider sacrosanct. We tend to make sacred what's not intrinsically sacred, making it a "sacred cow." Whatever is considered sacred becomes relatively immune to change. Over the years churches nurture and milk their own sacred cows. In the process of "fleshing out" various biblical principles, they elevate the forms of those principles to a position of special stature. Eventually the form is confused with the principle and the former is valued more highly than the latter. The typical church is replete with examples: the church's music, a particular version of the Bible, having three meetings a week—Sunday morning, Sunday evening, and the Wednesday evening prayer meeting.

WHAT IS THE SOLUTION?

A solution to the problem is sound biblical teaching. The leader of change who is an expositor of the Scriptures should take great pains to make a clear distinction between the eternal, unchanging principles of the Bible and the various forms those principles take that must change if the church is to remain or be relevant.

When some people have a herd of sacred cows grazing on the church's front lawn, the solution is to challenge them politely and lovingly and in private. For example, the change agent could get together with a person and invite him to justify his view from the Scriptures. The goal is that this person on his own sees that he is wrong and changes his mind. This is the ideal. If this doesn't work, the change agent will need to explain how he is wrong. While the resistant person may not change his opinion overnight, chances are good that he will not express it in public with the culture change agent present, knowing that the latter might challenge him.

The Complexity of Change

WHAT IS THE PROBLEM?

We can be sure of many things, one of which is that life itself will only become more complex. In fact, many old-timers complain and express a desire to return to the good old days when life was a lot simpler. If only they had a time machine that could transport them back to those days! It's true that life was much simpler then, but there is no time machine.

Strong biblical leadership in the American church will also produce significant positive change, which may result in much complexity for the members of the church. For example, a church may add small group ministries to its curriculum (change by addition). Those in the church who are familiar with a Sunday school program but not small groups may not understand all that is involved in small group ministries. They view them as complex and daunting rather than taking the time to understand them. The natural tendency of many church attenders is to resist the complexity by opposing the change. Here is the logic: complexity can be confusing and disruptive; therefore resist the change and eliminate the source of complexity. However, if enough people follow this logic, they will stifle effective leadership and dull ministry momentum.

WHAT IS THE SOLUTION?

The solution is to balance good leadership with good management. Then as leaders implement the various changes necessary for effective ministry, the managers of change work with them to bring order out of complexity. This is what good managers do. Effective ministry requires an individual or team of individuals with both leadership and management capabilities and gifts. The church must take responsibility to recruit and enlist them.

Self-Centeredness

WHAT IS THE PROBLEM?

I have observed that discussions about why people refuse to change seldom mention self-centeredness. When I ask certain church members the reason they refuse to entertain a proposal for change, none has ever given selfishness as the reason. But the reality is that most people are looking out for number one. Most people have a "meet my needs" mentality, not only in the world out there, but in the church (the world in here) as well. Far too many people probe the church and its programs with the question, What can you do for me? They suffer from Christian nearsightedness. Thus a final reason for resistance to change is the sin of self-centeredness.

WHAT IS THE SOLUTION?

The solution is for God's people everywhere to examine their hearts regularly (2 Cor. 13:5). They must examine the motives of their heart. Why are they resisting a particular change? Is it based on their love for the Savior, their concern for the church and its vision, or their own personal agenda? The answer lies more in how they disagree rather than in what the disagreement is about. Does the one who is disagreeing express care and concern for the leader who proposed the change initially as well as others who follow his lead? Is the resistant person being supportive and loving or only showing concern for himself?

The Change Resistors

Felt needs
Status quo
Vested interests
Distrust of leadership
Stress of change
Sacred cows
Complexity of change
Self-centeredness

Know How People Respond to Change

Who votes for and against change? The answer is the congregation. And the pastor who hopes to lead his congregational culture through change needs to know and understand this. To accomplish change, he needs to look at his people from two vantage points. The first is the people who make up his congregation in general, and the second is the lay leadership in particular.

Congregations

When a leader introduces change into a church's culture, the people will fit into one of four categories, depending on how they respond: early adopters, middle adopters, late adopters, and those who never adopt, as represented on the continuum in the figure below.

Continuum of the Change Response

Open to Change   Resistant to Change

Early Adopters	Middle Adopters	Late Adopters	Never Adopters

EARLY ADOPTERS

Veteran change agents have discovered that when they introduce a new idea or proposal for change, there will be those in the ministry who jump on board almost immediately. These are early adopters who fall into two groups: early innovators and early adapters.

The early innovators make up only 2 to 3 percent of most established congregations. They are people who exist at the outer fringe of change. Early innovators are the real pioneers or original thinkers in terms of new ideas.

They are highly innovative dreamers who see all kinds of creative possibilities for the ministries of the church. Their tendency is to focus more on the cognitive than the practical aspects of the ministry. Thus they talk a lot about innovation but are not good at implementing it. They enjoy exploring various theories and ideas for ministry but are found toward the rear if the ministry ever becomes a reality.

Early innovators are one of the most frustrated groups in the church. They thrive on creativity and love to innovate. They see lots of potential for the church in America but feel that it may never be realized unless something unusual happens. The problem is that they find themselves in churches that are much the opposite. They have suggested numerous ideas for change only to hear: "We've never done it that way."

In general the church has turned a cold shoulder to them. It views them as different and has grown tired of entertaining all their "weird" ideas. If these early innovators have been in the church for any length of time, they have probably given up and become quiet attenders or inactives. But this response has served only to damage their credibility in the eyes of the active members, so they have little clout.

The other group of early adopters are the early adapters who make up 8 to 18 percent of the church. They have grown tired of the status quo because they have watched it sap the church of its vitality. Thus they are open to change and are looking for new ideas for the church and are especially willing to try a change that signals progress. They are not necessarily impetuous but are sensitized to the idea of change and respond to an opportunity quickly. They are quick to spot a good idea when they see one and often get credit for the ideas of the early innovators. Finally, they tend to be young, well educated, well traveled, more likely to participate in numerous activities, and less rooted in the existing system.

Early adapters tend to be frustrated in the typical, traditional church. But they are optimistic and dream of a better tomorrow. In general, most congregations like them and get along with them—it has to do with their youthful enthusiasm. In fact, they are active in the life of the church and usually gravitate toward various leadership positions in the ministry. Even though the congregation respects them, they are slow to adopt their ideas and implement the changes they suggest.

A key church revitalization principle is for a leader to identify and recruit as many active, vocal allies as possible for a program of change before it is introduced to the congregation. Thus the change agent should seek out the early adapters and rally them behind his programs and proposals. They are the people who will be his allies and join his team.

Actually it will not be too difficult to find them because early adopters gravitate quickly toward the leader of change. The strategy is to move these people who are spiritually qualified into positions of strong leadership in the church, such as the board and various influential committees. This may prove difficult because they may be the younger members of the church who have not yet attained the necessary credibility and seniority. Still there is hope, because usually major changes are initiated by a tiny minority, not a majority.

NEVER ADOPTERS

Using the continuum in the figure above, note that the early adopters who are most open to change are on the far left. On the far right are the never adopters. The two groups serve as bookends or the two extremes that represent the contrasting attitudes toward change in a typical congregation. Each bookend exerts influence for or against change from their end of the shelf.

The people who never adopt change are the laggards or strongest resistors and make up anywhere from 2 to 20 percent of the long-established church. A typical never adopter is the deacon who walks into a meeting late, realizes that a vote is taking place, and says, "I don't know what you're voting on, but whatever it is I'm against it!" Chances are very good that he will never vote for change and will openly resist new ideas and proposals. These people are solidly committed to the status quo and sincerely believe that they can re-create yesterday if they only hang on to *what is* long enough.

These people can be persistent, negative, and obstinate. At their worst they may be divisive or even attempt to split the church (1 Cor. 1:11–17). Often they exert more clout in the church than the early adopters. There are several reasons for this: they are usually older and their age and experience grant them seniority on boards and committees, and they are the church's "squeaky wheels" who attract all the attention and exert an influence far out of proportion to their numbers.

MIDDLE ADOPTERS

The middle adopters are between the two extremes of the continuum. Clearly they are in the majority, for they make up 60 to 80 percent of the church. They are key because their response to the leadership of the change agent will determine whether the church is revitalized.

These people are ambivalent toward change. More inclined toward the status quo, they do not actively pursue change, nor will they automatically reject it. When confronted with new ideas and proposals, they prove to be cautious, skeptical, and full of questions. While the change agent views them as overly cautious, they prefer to be thought of as conservative.

In general, they want to go along with the pastor and withhold a verdict until more of the evidence is in. They need time to adjust to any new ideas or proposals, so they tend to sit back and watch what happens. They will not accept change today but may tomorrow.

The change agent must be patient and make sure that tomorrow becomes today. In the process of leading middle adopters through change, leaders need to maximize communication. They must clearly and carefully confront middle adopters with all of the facts behind their reasons for change.

LATE ADOPTERS

The late adopters are between the middle adopters and the never adopters and represent as much as 18 percent of the congregation. The late adopters are the last in the church to endorse a new idea or program of change. Like the never adopters, they are often articulate and can be expected to speak out against anything new or innovative. In general they are indistinguishable from the never adopters, and this will give the impression that there are more never adopters than there are.

In time the late adopters go along with the new idea or proposal. While they may never acknowledge it verbally, they will fall in line with the direction of the majority or middle adopters—as the majority goes, so go the late adopters. This shows again the reason the middle adopters are so important to the ultimate revitalization of the church.

The problem with the late adopters is that they go along with change but are not necessarily convinced of its value. The fact that they reluctantly raise their hand in favor or quietly say yes at the final vote does not translate into a changed heart. It only means that they have resigned themselves to the fact that some change in the church is inevitable. Consequently, they may take the place of the recently departed never adopters as the church's guardians of the status quo and serve as its squeaky wheels.

Lay Leaders

Churches have levels of leadership and lay leaders can, either formally or informally, exert influence that can be used to accomplish change. They are members of the governing board, ministry staff and other board and committee members, Sunday school teachers and small group leaders, support ministry leaders, and a patriarch and/or matriarch. The job of the change architect is to identify and persuade these primary leaders that the change is good; they will influence and convince everyone else.

THE GOVERNING BOARD

The members of the church governing board are located at the top level of leadership. Right or wrong. most long-established churches have a group of part-time voluntary lay leaders who sit on a board and serve the church primarily by making decisions about anything from the relocation of the facility to the color of the daffodils outside the nursery or whose turn it is to mow the lawn. Often the pastor is also on the board.

The people on this board represent the formal leadership of the church and may include the informal leadership as well. The number of people serving on a board will vary from one or two to as many as twenty or thirty people, depending on the size of the church.

The wise leader should initiate the change process by determining where each board person is on the change response continuum. Chances are excellent that they will be sprinkled through all four categories—the largest number being middle adopters. The change agent, even before he accepts a call to the church, can use the board as a gauge to gain an early reading of how the congregation will handle change. He could ask individual board members innocent questions related to the potential for implementing change. A question might be, Has anyone ever attempted to change the order of worship? Or he could call or correspond with the former pastor, inquiring as to why he left the church and asking if he has any advice or words of wisdom for its next pastor—especially if he is a change agent.

MINISTRY STAFF AND OTHER BOARD AND COMMITTEE MEMBERS

If the leader of change determines that the majority of the lay governing board are open or behind his taking the church in a new direction, then he is ready to approach any ministry staff members and members of other boards and committees.

Actually the new change agent should interact with any full- or part-time ministry staff while consulting with the board. The staff people are a vital part of the team. If they are not on board with the new vision, they will need to be replaced. This possible option must be an item for discussion at board level. The same principle applies in situations where the present pastor catches a new vision for the church that is not in accord with that of any of the existing ministry staff. In an attempt to keep all the members happy all the time, most lay boards are reluctant to let any staff person go for any reason. They seldom see the wisdom in releasing those with another vision, and the results have proved disastrous.

Except in the smallest churches, there will be additional boards and committees, such as finance committee, personnel committee, missions committee, Christian education board, and building committee. The change agent who overlooks these boards—especially the finance and personnel committees and their leadership—makes a fatal error in judgment. In light of their public positions and the fact that some are in elected places of leadership, they are, as someone once said, "a force to be reckoned with." Several will be future governing board members. Without their support, the ministry will fragment into various disparate pieces.

Sunday School Teachers and Small Group Leaders

The next or third level of leadership is made up of Sunday school teachers, Bible study teachers and leaders of growth groups, youth groups, and other small groups in the church. These ministries touch people's lives directly and intimately. Perhaps more than any other people in the congregation, these teachers and leaders occupy positions of significant influence in the lives and opinions of others. Often it is these behind-the-scenes people who are doing much of the actual hands-on ministry of the church and form the very leadership backbone of the entire local body.

Support Ministry Leaders

The leaders of the church's support ministries are a level of leadership that should not be overlooked. These ministries consist of the usher team who seat people, those who collect and count the offering, parking lot attendants, volunteer cooks, and others. Though not as influential as those at other levels, these ministries will have leaders who exercise influence over their people and are not to be ignored.

The Patriarch or Matriarch

Finally, it is vitally important that change agents recognize the church's patriarch and/or matriarch. Usually these are older people who have been at the church a long time, if not from the founding or planting of the church, and they have or have had positions of leadership. They wield much power over the other leaders in general and especially over a board. Governing board members will look to them for the major decisions that a church faces. I advise pastors to find out who these people are and spend time with them, possibly over breakfast or lunch, trying to determine if they will support or resist taking the church in a new direction. It is doubtful that change will happen without their support.

Five Levels of Leadership

1. Governing board
2. Ministry staff and members of other boards and committees
3. Sunday school teachers and small group leaders
4. Leaders of support ministries
5. A patriarch and/or matriarch

Use the Tools That Facilitate Change

Every catalyst of intentional culture change needs a change agent's toolbox filled with various tools for accomplishing revitalization. He views the process of change much as an auto mechanic views the engine of a car. An automobile engine needs periodic adjustment and fine-tuning throughout its life to run smoothly and efficiently. The change process requires the same, but the tools do not consist of screwdrivers, a socket set, or special diagnostic equipment but of various principles of change. As the change agent leads the church through the change process, he will apply these principles at various times in various places to keep the process running smoothly. The tools that the change agent must put to use are faith, insightful questions, change language, good communication, implementation teams and ad hoc committees, and an understanding of the different kinds and levels of change.

A Tough Faith

In a decade of megachange, near the beginning of the third millennium, God uses men and women of faith to breathe new life into plateaued and dying churches. At the dawn of the first millennium, the Savior was impressed by men and women of faith, as illustrated by the centurion in Matthew 8:8–10 and the Canaanite woman in Matthew 15:21–28. The Gentile centurion was a commander of one hundred men. When he uttered a command, his soldiers jumped to comply. He came to Jesus to request healing for his paralyzed servant, yet he felt totally undeserving of the Savior's presence in his house. When Jesus heard this, he was "astonished" and said, "I have not found anyone in Israel with such great faith" (8:10). The Canaanite woman had to push through all kinds of obstacles to get to the Savior. He identified her faith as a "great faith" (15:28). By way of stark contrast, his constant complaint with his so-called faithful Jewish disciples was their lack of faith. Numerous times the words "O ye of little faith!" echo through the pages of the Gospels.

How important is faith? According to the writer of Hebrews, "without faith it is impossible to please God" (11:6). A "tough faith" is required, not an "easy faith." It is tough because it makes such irrational, high-risk demands on the human intellect, which has grown accustomed to acting on the assurance of prior vision and knowledge. But leaders of change must learn to operate with the eyes of a Noah or an Abraham if they expect God to bless their ministries with life changes, which, in turn, bring culture changes.

Insightful Questions

The wise leader encourages change more by asking insightful questions than by offering directions or giving ultimatums. Like carbon on a spark plug, directions and ultimatums invite resistance. Questions serve leaders of intentional change as a tool to blow the carbon away for greater engine life and mileage. People who resist change and innovation are not thinking clearly. Questions serve to catalyze and challenge the thinking process and can encourage change in several ways.

1. The new pastor in a church is allowed some naïveté. Consequently he can ask numerous "dumb" questions about the status quo that most people will find inoffensive yet enlightening and convicting. A new pastor could ask, "Why is the paint peeling off the outside of the church's facility?" or "How long has the plumbing been clogged in the men's bathroom?" Like a three-year-old child just discovering the world, he has permission to ask repeatedly, "Why?"
2. By skillfully asking the right questions, the change agent can challenge people to think along the same lines and come up with similar ideas or new ideas on their own. As long as the change agent does not mind who gets the credit, this grants people ownership of new, innovative ideas.
3. Questions point people in the right direction. The Savior used this technique in the Garden of Gethsemane when he asked Peter and the disciples, "Could you men not keep watch with me for one hour?" (Matt. 26:40); and later, "Are you still sleeping and resting?" (v. 45). His point was they needed to watch and pray so they would not fall into temptation (v. 41).

The Language of Change

Language is one of the most powerful tools for expressing new and innovative ideas concerning change. Successful leaders use language in general and certain terms in particular that excite and motivate people. Therefore those who lead their churches through the change process must pay particular attention to the terms they use. Deserving special attention is the word *change*.

The term *change* means different things to different people. It may conjure up good feelings or bad depending on the prior experience of the listener. Insightful pastors who lead those with a negative view toward change would be wise to use other words and various synonyms for *change*: nouns such as *alteration, diversification, variation, modification, substitution, modulation,* and *innovation,* and verbs such as *alter, vary, temper, modulate, diversify, qualify, turn the corner, modify, transform, innovate, recast, revamp, transpose,* and *reorganize.* In a potentially explosive change situation, these terms can be used to avoid needlessly offending the congregational hardliners.

Good Communication

Good communication is a tool that is critical to church revitalization no matter if the congregation is at the very beginning or well into the process. Good communication is as important to the change process in the church body as the circulatory system is to the human body. Change in itself is such a threatening experience that it guarantees misinformation, some of which is intentional and some unintentional. Also, normal people want to know what is happening or else they become suspicious. By working hard at communicating well, the leader of transition not only builds vital trust but keeps open the channels of communication and corrects any miscommunication between himself, other leaders, and the membership.

The problem is that the typical congregation communicates poorly if at all. And when a church is going through the change process, the lack of communication will result in lots of resistance to the process. Most in the church, including the pastor, are unaware of this.

Leaders can accomplish good communication in several ways.

1. First, they must listen as well as talk.
2. They must be available and take advantage of every opportunity to communicate the vision and the plan. Writing letters, hosting desserts, and meeting one-on-one with people are good ways to communicate.
3. They must be alert to any misinformation in general and false rumors in particular.
4. They must communicate through periodic progress reports. People respond negatively when surprised. Periodic progress reports minimize congregational surprises.

5. Along with formal progress reports, leaders of change may want to leak information informally as well. This too gives people time to talk themselves into supporting new ideas and backing changes before they are announced publicly.
6. Any communication of change must be positive. Find the plus in every change no matter how difficult the situation.

Implementation Teams and Ad Hoc Committees

In some churches the responsibility to plan and initiate change falls to standing committees. These committees are notorious for resisting change and opting for a maintenance mentality that results in a maintenance ministry. According to change expert Lyle Schaller, a solution is to create an ad hoc special futures committee that studies any proposed changes. He argues that the ad hoc study committee is a completely different breed of institutional creature than a standing committee and provides several advantages that accomplish change. One is that the pastor could chair a special ad hoc futures committee. The advantage is that the two different committees might work together as a team.

Another way to avoid maintenance ministry is to form implementation teams and task them with culture change. While most committees are characterized by talk, implementation teams by name and nature are characterized by action. For example, a communication implementation team could be tasked with improving the church's overall communication.

Knowing the Kinds of Change

Catalytic change agents lead congregations through the transition process more effectively when they understand the different kinds of change and how each affects people. There are three kinds of change that implement revitalization strategies: change by addition, subtraction, and replacement.

Three Kinds of Change

Change by addition
Change by subtraction
Change by replacement

CHANGE BY ADDITION

Change by addition creates a new situation by adding to the present church programs, schedules, and so on. It is a vital tool in the strategy of pastors who attempt to implement change in plateaued congregations. An example is the church that desires to center its prayer in a new, robust network of small groups rather than the current traditional Sunday or Wednesday night prayer meeting. Instead of subtracting the sparsely attended Wednesday prayer meeting from the schedule, keep it, treat it as a small group, and get on with the new small groups program. The problem with this strategy is that it is comparable to the accumulation of barnacles on the hull of the ministry ship. Eventually, some will have to be scraped off if the boat is to float.

CHANGE BY SUBTRACTION

Change by subtraction is a tool that creates a new situation by scrapping the old one. It seldom occurs by itself and usually combines with change by addition. It is helpful periodically to scrape the barnacles off the side of the ministry ship if you want it to move through the water faster.

CHANGE BY REPLACEMENT

Change by subtraction and replacement is key to revitalizing churches that are in decline. However, it is much more disruptive to congregational life than change by addition and will incur the greatest resistance. For example, to disband a traditional, declining Sunday school class that has been meeting since the birth of the church can devastate the handful who remain faithful in attendance. This doesn't mean you shouldn't do it; just be aware of and prepared for the consequences.

Knowing the Levels of Change

Change takes place at different levels in people's lives. An awareness of each level serves as a tool to measure the effectiveness of change and to insure quality control. There are three levels of change.

Levels of Change

Change through compliance
Change through identification
Change through internalization

CHANGE THROUGH COMPLIANCE

The first level is compliance. Change through compliance is forced change. People change because they feel they have to, not because they want to. Compliance change is caused by someone in authority or by an event beyond a person's control. The change takes place on the surface, not in the heart of the people; therefore its results are minimal and largely ineffective.

CHANGE THROUGH IDENTIFICATION

The second level of change is identification, which involves both individual initiative and the efforts of others. We identify our own wants and need for change and then discover attractive models (cultures) that exhibit the change in which we're interested. An example is the pastor who attends a pastors' conference put on by a successful megachurch in a different part of the country. The megachurch provides the pastor with an attractive model of change, something that identifies what could happen in his church. When he returns home, he attempts to apply to his own church what he has learned from the particular megachurch model.

This seldom works. Instead, pastors should attempt to learn from these models but not ape them. If you insist on adopting a megachurch model, then take other key, influential people with you to the conference. Often they will climb on the bandwagon with you. Better, work through the strategic planning process that will help you design a model that is more authentic to who you are, when you are, and where you are. For more information in this, see my book *Advanced Strategic Planning*.

CHANGE THROUGH INTERNALIZATION

The third level of change is internalization. It takes place below the surface—in the heart. Internalization accomplishes maximum change and takes place because people want it and incorporate it into their lives. While the Holy Spirit can use all kinds of change to accomplish cultural transformation, usually he does so at this third level. And when you see this happening, it's a good sign that the Holy Spirit is involved.

As leaders of intentional change lead their ministries through the transformation process, a knowledge of these levels of change will help them determine if they are accomplishing their desired results and can serve as tools of quality control.

Tools for Change

Tools for Change
A tough faith
Insightful questions
The language of change
Good communication
Implementation teams
Ad hoc committees
Knowing the kinds of change
Knowing the levels of change

Change Application Worksheet

The following worksheet can help you determine the kinds of changes that your church may be ready to handle. First, work your way through the following on your own. Then do the same with a change team or a strategic leadership team or any other group that you believe would benefit from this exercise, such as your board, elders, deacons, or other people of influence.

1. Identify and write out the specific changes you are attempting to implement in your ministry.
2. What kind of resistance are you experiencing to these changes? Which of the eight reasons listed in this chapter might explain this resistance? Circle them.

   Felt needs
   Status quo
   Vested interests
   Distrust of leadership
   The stress of change
   Sacred cows
   The complexity of change
   Self-centeredness
   Other reasons

3. How might the author's suggested solutions to each of these types of resistance apply to your situation?
4. Estimate the percentage of people in your church who fall within each of the four categories of change response. Write the percentages in the spaces below. Where is the largest percentage of people located? What does this tell you about accomplishing change in the church?

   Early adopters ___
      Early innovators ___
      Early adapters ___
   Middle adopters ___
   Late adopters ___
   Never adopters ___

5. Evaluate each layer of leadership in your church in terms of whether they are predominantly early, middle, late, or never adopters. Assign them a percentage and/or a grade from A to F. Place that percentage and/or grade beside each layer and write any helpful comments under them.

Level 1 The board ____
Level 2 Staff and other boards and committees ____
Level 3 Sunday school teachers and small group leaders ____
Level 4 Leaders of support ministries ____
Level 5 Patriarch and/or matriarch ____

6. What conclusions would you draw about possible changes in your church based on your answers to questions 4 and 5?
7. In light of the information gained in questions 4, 5, and 6, should you attempt to introduce change in this church? If you're candidating for a position in this church, should you withdraw your name?
8. Would the Savior be impressed with your faith? Why or why not? Could your faith be described as an "easy" or a "tough" faith?
9. In your conversations with people in your ministry, do you offer ultimatums or ask insightful questions? What are some of the changes that are needed in your ministry? What kinds of questions could you ask that might promote these changes?
10. Do the people under your leadership react negatively to the use of the term *change*? What other terms might you adopt that are less inflammatory? Write them down, memorize them, and begin to use them intentionally.
11. How would you rate your ministry's ability to communicate—good, average, or poor? How would you rate your ability to communicate? Are you a good listener? (You might want to ask your spouse or a close friend.) What are some of the opportunities in your ministry to communicate more directly with your people?
12. If your church has a governing board, what role does it play in the decision-making process in your church? Are the board members advocates of the status quo or of meaningful, significant Christ-honoring change? Have you ever established an implementation team or an ad hoc committee for change? Why or why not? Who might serve well in such a capacity?
13. How would you characterize the changes you are attempting to make? Are they changes of addition, subtraction, replacement, or a combination? Are you in a plateaued or declining situation? Which is the best kind of change for your situation? Why?
14. What level is the majority of change that takes place in your ministry—compliance, identification, or internalization? What percentage would you assign to each level? What does this tell you about the quality of change in your church?

11

The Church Pastor as Culture Sculptor

Part 2 Personnel

Who are you? Are you a culture sculptor? The bad news for the church is that most pastors aren't sculptors. This could be true of as many as 80 percent of pastors, because 80 to 85 percent of churches are in decline. These are small, struggling churches where basically the pastor functions as chaplain or culture maintenance man who does the ministry for the people. Typically such pastors preach, visit, marry, and bury. These culture custodians and a dwindling number of older church members are the glue that holds many of these churches together. The good news, however, is that to some degree such pastors can learn and embrace the characteristics of a culture sculptor. This is the purpose of this chapter.

Throughout much of the twentieth century, leadership was critical to pastoral ministry, but the focus was on preaching. Of course preaching is important; now due to the decline in churches, that focus has shifted to include leadership as well. This means that we're paying more attention than in the past to such matters as what leadership is, who leaders are, and how one leads as well as preaches. We've discovered that certain leaders who lead well and have been blessed by God in the process are well wired for what they do. For example, I mentioned in chapter 9 that most denominations and networks ask prospective church planters to go through a rather rigorous assessment that surfaces their divine design to see if they're church planters. That's because we've observed that those Christ-followers whom God has used to plant godly, spiritually dynamic churches are designed much alike. The same is true for church or culture revitalizers. They too have many similar characteristics. This chapter will address what we've learned about those whom God has used to turn around churches.

Before we move in that direction, it is imperative that I address a popular viewpoint that on the one hand has encouraged many to become pastors but on the other hand has resulted in discouragement, a sense of failure, burnout, and pastoral ministry dropouts. And it is very possible that you may unwittingly embrace this false view.

It is the idea that anyone can do anything or be anyone he or she wants to be. I have heard this view espoused in the culture in general and in the church in particular. Once I heard President Bill Clinton tell a group of ghetto kids that they can do whatever they want to do in life. His purpose—to encourage them—was noble. The problem is, this isn't true.

In the church world the idea is that if anyone wants to be a pastor and lead a church, then he should go for it, and it will happen. The biblical truth is that we cannot be or do whatever we want to do. God has bestowed on each of us a wonderful, unique divine design that consists of many of the things that we will look at in this chapter (including gifts, passion, and temperament). We cannot do anything we want, because God has designed us in a wonderful way to accomplish his ministry or what he wants. Only as we discover how he has wired us will we be able to understand what specifically he wants us to accomplish for him in this life, whether it's through pastoring a church or some other important ministry.

Now with this biblical truth or correction in mind, we are ready to examine the unique divine design or makeup of turnaround pastors. I wrote chapter 10 to equip pastors in how to prepare an established culture for change. In this chapter I will address the personnel for shaping the culture. In particular we will explore the character qualifications, spiritual qualifications, spiritual gifts, passion, temperament, and natural characteristics of culture revitalizers, along with must-read applications.

You're thinking, *Wait a minute, didn't we cover some of this material in chapter 9 on church planting?* Though I covered *some* of this material in chapter 9, my plan here is to go into much greater depth and apply the concepts specifically to renewing cultures.

Character Qualifications

Personal character qualifications are essential to the culture sculptor's ministry. The apostles required first-century church leaders to have these characteristics (see Acts 6:3–5). No one leader has the exact same design—some are strikingly similar and some are vastly different. Regardless, their lives are to be characterized by the same spiritual qualities. If God has designed a leader to revitalize churches but the leader does not demonstrate these qualities, then he does not meet the character qualifications to lead any church. Therefore the profile of one who shapes cultures begins with the person's character. In 1 Timothy 3:1–13 and Titus 1:5–9, Paul articulates the character qualifications for leaders, and these are the same for church pastors.

The early church existed at two levels—one was the house church and the other was the city church that consisted of all the house churches in the city. In these passages the apostle is addressing first-century house church pastors (elders) whose churches made up a citywide church, such as the church of Jerusalem, Corinth, and Ephesus.

Appendix H, "Character Assessment for Leadership," gives the twenty-two character qualities and an explanation of each one. It is a tool to help you determine if your character qualifies you for leadership at the pastoral level.

The leader who believes that God has uniquely designed him for church revitalization must be sure that he meets and maintains the qualifications outlined in this text. As we have seen, many people in churches perceive change as an enemy. They resist it and often react adversely whenever and wherever it occurs. Therefore they carefully study the character of their leaders to see if they are men of integrity. Any discrepancies found in those who attempt to lead them through the change process may encourage harsh criticism and much resistance. Consequently, cultural change agents must not only meet these qualifications initially but work hard at maintaining them consistently throughout their lives.

Spiritual Qualifications

Just as the character qualifications are essential to the change architect's ministry, so are the spiritual qualifications. A spiritual person, according to Paul in Galatians 5:25, is one who lives by or keeps in step with the Spirit. In verses 22–23 Paul provides us with the following list that characterizes those who live in this way. They possess love, joy, peace, patience, kindness, goodness, faithfulness, gentleness, and self-control.

I believe that it is the fruit of the Spirit that Paul is talking about in Galatians 4:19 when he tells the Galatian believers of the need for Christ to be "formed" in them. Just as the Holy Spirit produced his fruit in the Savior's life on earth, he does the same in our lives. When people see this fruit in our lives, they observe what people saw in the Savior's life in the first century. The application question is: Does this fruit characterize your life? If so, how? If not, why not? The wise leader will constantly monitor his steps to assess whether or not he is a spiritual person who meets the spiritual qualifications of the culture sculptor. The good news is that if he doesn't now meet these qualifications, he can grow to a point in his spiritual life where he does keep in step with the Spirit and Christ is being formed in him.

Spiritual Gifts

God has sovereignly chosen to bestow spiritual gifts on all those who are his spiritual children (1 Cor. 12:7, 11; Eph. 4:7). This fact alone should motivate us to discover our unique gift-mix and how we best fit into his service. Spiritual gifts are certain divine competencies or special abilities that God bestows on all his children for service. Knowing our gifts contributes to the discovery of our ministry niche. They are some of the tools that make up the culture navigator's tool kit. The Spiritual Gifts Inventory in appendix I will help you discover your gifts. You may wonder if some gifts have proved unique to change agents. How might a leader know if he has been spiritually gifted to lead a typical culture through a turnaround?

In his doctoral dissertation on the characteristics of turnaround pastors, Pastor Gordon Penfold concluded that spiritual gifts were not a deciding factor in a turnaround situation. In his research, non-turnaround pastors had many of the same gifts as turnaround pastors with different results. For example, 43 percent of non-turnaround pastors had the gift of leadership and 62 percent of turnaround pastors possessed it. Much the same proved to be the case for teaching. Penfold asked both turnaround and non-turnaround pastors to identify their top four gifts, and leadership and teaching were high in both groups.[1] However, the fact that non-turnaround pastors placed the gifts of teaching and leadership high on their lists does not mean that they are not important to turnaround pastors and revitalization. Others such as Lyle Schaller offer research that certain spiritual gifts are important to turnarounds, as we will see below. If revitalizers did not have these gifts at all, I doubt that much turnaround would happen.

Regardless, there are several spiritual gifts that may not be mandatory for revitalization but that would naturally go with change and revitalization and should aid in the implementation of significant cultural change in established churches. While the change agent should not expect to have all these gifts, the more he has, the better.

Leadership

The gift of leadership is identified in Romans 12:8. It is found in people who have a clear, focused vision and are able to communicate that vision to others in a way that influences them to become their followers. This gift is important for anyone who desires to transition cultures—it takes gifted leaders to move churches off plateaus or turn around declining churches. Usually such churches are without vision and need a leader who can create dissatisfaction with what is (the status quo) and cast a vision for what could be. Leadership is not the same as the gift of administration and should not be confused with it. Penfold concludes, "There were more pastors who list the gift of leadership among turnaround pastors (61.9 percent) compared to the non-turnaround pastors (42.8 percent)."[2] Leadership can certainly be a key ingredient to turnaround.

Teaching

The gift of teaching is found in Romans 12:7; 1 Corinthians 12:28; and Ephesians 4:11. It is the ability to comprehend and communicate Scripture so that people clearly understand it and their lives change as a result. Many go into pastoral ministry because of their love for Scripture and the desire to communicate God's truths to others. The problem is that some are excellent teachers but they aren't leaders, and this is a formula that leads to culture decline. These teachers would make a far greater contribution to the body of Christ if they assumed a teaching position in a church alongside a senior pastor who has the leadership gift. Though teaching is not a required gift for turnaround pastors, it is important to them and their ministries. Penfold notes that it was the first gift listed by both turnaround and non-turnaround pastors.[3] Thus it is not unique to revitalizers but nonetheless is important to their ministries.

Faith

The gift of faith is found in 1 Corinthians 12:9. It is the ability to envision what needs to be done and to trust God to accomplish it even though it seems impossible to the average Christian. Often it clusters with the gift of leadership and is found in visionary leaders who ask, dream, and attempt big things for God (see Eph. 3:20). This gift may be confused with vision but it is not the same, though faith enhances the visionary capacity of the leader. The gift of faith helps pastors want to revitalize their churches and believe that change is possible. It aids in overcoming the fear of failure and convinces pastors to take risks for Christ's kingdom.

Encouragement

The gift of encouragement is listed by Paul in Romans 12:8. It is the ministry of encouraging and consoling. This gift is in high demand in churches enmeshed in the change process. Cultures that are dying need daily encouragement and consolation. In Penfold's research the gift of exhortation scored in the top four gifts of turnaround and non-turnaround pastors.[4]

Preaching

The gift of preaching is not found in the three lists of gifts in the New Testament (Romans 12; 1 Corinthians 12; Ephesians 4). However, it is closely associated with the gift of apostle, given in 1 Timothy 2:7 and the gifts of apostle and teacher in 2 Timothy 1:11.

Preaching is the God-given ability to communicate God's Word relevantly and persuasively with clarity and power so that it impacts the lives of its hearers. Some equate the gift of preaching with prophecy.

This gift involves more than a good sermon every Sunday. It has more to do with casting vision. Schaller writes, "One of the more highly visible methods of intervention in congregational life is the appearance of the skilled, persuasive, respected, influential, and effective leader who (a) has a vision of a new and different tomorrow, (b) can persuasively communicate that vision to others."[5] Pastors as change agents must be able to communicate effectively with their people. Therefore the casting of a significant, compelling vision from the pulpit is important in transitioning established cultures. If leaders cannot communicate their dreams for a better tomorrow, their ministries will likely not see a better tomorrow.

Evangelism

The gift of evangelism is mentioned in Ephesians 4:11. It is the ability to communicate clearly the gospel of Jesus Christ to unbelievers either individually or corporately so that they come to faith in Christ. A Christian who strongly desires to see lost people come to faith and pursues them will have an impact on struggling churches. It can go either way. On the one hand, some churches are inspired by the efforts of those with evangelism gifts to implement a Great Commission vision. Their example is infectious! On the other, some churches become irate. They are not happy with all the new people coming to the church and think they pose a threat because "they are not like us." They prefer the status quo.

In Penfold's research, evangelism was not a prominent gift among either turnaround or non-turnaround pastors and thus is not a requirement for a turnaround. However, the potential contribution of the gift of evangelism or a passion to win souls for Christ can be seen in the ministries of men like Bill Hybels, Rick Warren, and Andy Stanley. The problem is that evangelism seems to be a dying gift in the American church.

Spiritual Gifts and Turnaround

| Leadership |
| Teaching |
| Faith |
| Encouragement |
| Preaching |
| Evangelism |

Passion

Spiritual gifts supply change agents with the tools or special abilities for their trade. Passion serves to focus and motivate these spiritual gifts. Some would equate passion with a call to ministry. It is somewhat subjective because it is basically an emotion. It is a feeling word and may be described as a burning, gut feeling that a certain ministry is the most important place that God would have you. In Romans 15:20 Paul uses the term "ambition" to describe his passion to proclaim the gospel to the Gentiles (vv. 15–16). The leader must be careful to discern between passion and passing interests. Passion "sticks to the bones" in the sense that it is long term. Passing interests come and go like strangers in the night. They are here today and gone tomorrow. Passion stays with you for an extended period of time. Paul writes, "It has always been my ambition to preach the gospel." Some church planters acknowledge that they have wanted to plant churches for as long as they can remember. The very thought excites them. That is passion.

The Importance of Passion

Passion becomes critical in helping pastors determine if they are designed to pursue church revitalization. For example, men with and without significant pastoral experience who catch the vision for a Great Commission church are not sure whether to pursue church planting or church revitalization. The question is: Where is your heart? What does your heart whisper in your ear? What does the burning deep in your soul tell you? I have known several seminarians who had a passion for church planting but opted instead for a pastoral ministry in an established church because of various pressures, such as finances, to do so.

Later they have confessed to me that all they think about in their ministries is planting a church.

Passion and Culture Builders

Leaders who are change agents for church renewal situations have a passion for Christ's church in general and to minister to people in plateaued or declining churches in particular. They know it won't be easy but have a special place in their heart for people who have become disillusioned with the typical church and are going nowhere in their spiritual lives. They feel much like the Savior who "when he saw the crowds . . . had compassion on them, because they were harassed and helpless, like sheep without a shepherd" (Matt. 9:36). They believe that in these situations they can make a difference and can hardly wait for the opportunity to prove it. They love Christ's church and believe that it is the hope of the world—the vehicle through which he desires to win the world to himself.

Temperament

God-given spiritual gifts provide the special abilities for ministry, and a God-given passion supplies long-term direction and motivation for those abilities. However, God-given temperament provides unique personal behavior patterns for one's ministry. As with spiritual gifts and passion, certain temperament types are found in pastors who are good at leading churches through change. Peter Wagner observes this when he writes:

> The fifth and final limitation on how strong a given pastor's role can be is highly personal. It depends on the temperament of the pastor himself or herself. Some pastors are take-charge people, and some could never bring themselves to take charge. . . . I myself feel that each of us needs to regard ourselves as a product of God the Creator. He has not created every pastor for pastoring a large, growing church.[6]

The Importance of Temperament

Culture renewal pastors in the point position tend to display certain consistent behavior patterns on both the *Personal Profile* (or the *Biblical Personal Profile*)[7] and the *Myers-Briggs Temperament Indicator* (*MBTI*) or the *Keirsey Temperament Sorter II*. These patterns can help distinguish turnaround from non-turnaround leaders. When pastors, coaches, or seminary professors observe these patterns in a leader, they can challenge him to consider culture revitalization.

The Personal Profile

In his doctor of ministry dissertation, Pastor Robert Thomas used the *Biblical Personal Profile* to discover specific personality characteristics of effective revitalization pastors. He surveyed twenty Baptist General Conference pastors who, according to their various districts, "could turn a church around."

Thomas described the ministries of these pastors as small, passive Baptist General Conference churches. He used the term *small* because the churches were under two hundred people. He used the term *passive* because they experienced an average annual growth rate of less than 10 percent over a three-year period before the new pastor arrived. The evidence that "they could turn a church around" was greater than the 10 percent average annual growth rate these churches experienced over a period of time after the arrival of the change agent.

Thomas's Results

Upon the completion of the pilot study, Thomas discovered that these effective revitalization pastors fell within the profile of the Persuader Pattern.[8] If you have not taken the *Personal Profile*, you will need to do so for this research to make sense. A similar tool, Temperament Indicator 1 in appendix J, can also be of help.

The Persuader Pattern is characterized by a high I (influence) in combination with a secondary D (dominance). What does this mean? I-type persons are natural-born leaders who like to be around people and are articulate and motivational. They tend to generate lots of enthusiasm, enjoy participating in a group, and genuinely desire to help other people. They are very people-oriented and are risk takers who do not like the status quo and are up-front, "out on the point" kinds of people.

D-type persons want immediate results, love a challenge, and are catalytic. They tend to be quick decision makers who question the status quo, usually take authority, and are good at managing trouble and solving problems. They, like I-types, are risk takers who are task oriented and are up-front, "out on the point" kinds of people. The Persuader Pattern results from bringing the high I temperament together with a secondary D. The high I predominates, but the D also influences the temperament. For more information on the Persuader Pattern, see appendix K. I should also mention that since Thomas's research was done, the tool has been changed by the addition of a seventh grid. However, the effect on the Persuader Pattern is minimal.

Thomas's Application

The value of Thomas's research is that either the *Personal* or *Biblical Personal Profile* can be used in the assessment process to help pastors determine if their design is conducive to church revitalization. Ken Voges writes, "The Biblical Personal Profile (BPP) measures behavioral tendencies. It is not meant to be a prescriptive tool. You and others do not 'have to behave' like your profile. However, it is a fairly accurate predictive tool. You will 'tend' to behave as described."[9]

Penfold's Research

Similar to Robert Thomas's research, Pastor Gordon Penfold used the *DiSC Classic* version of the *Personal Profile* in his doctor of ministry dissertation to determine whether turnaround and non-turnaround pastors were similar or distinct in their temperaments. He gathered his information from evangelical pastors in the Rocky Mountain States (Colorado, Utah, Wyoming, Montana, and Idaho). His research question sought to discover whether there are identifiable characteristics of turnaround pastors in these churches. An important part of the study focused on their temperament. Penfold secured the names of forty-nine pastors and sent all a packet that included the *DiSC Profile*. Twenty-eight responded, completed, and returned the results of the profile. To distinguish turnaround from non-turnaround pastors, Penfold used an average annual growth rate of 2.5 percent (the expected biological growth rate of a typical church) in worship attendance for five years regardless of the church's size.[10]

Penfold's Results

In comparing the profiles, two strong trends emerged. First, the turnaround pastors, with the exception of one, scored a mid to high D and/or I range but low on the S and C range, much as in Thomas's study. The non-turnaround pastors scored in the high S and C range, but low on the D and I range. The high D and/or I range corresponds with five *Personal Profile* styles (the Promoter, Inspirational, Creative, Developer, and Practitioner styles), the two highest being the Promoter (high I) and Inspirational profiles (high D and I). (It is surprising that, though some were close, no one fell within the Persuader Profile.) The high S and C correspond with the Perfectionistic (high S and C) and Objective Thinker (high C) styles. These styles are not conducive to change but are more prone to preserve the status quo.[11]

Penfold's Application

Penfold's research would indicate that those with a high D and/or high I on the *DiSC Profile* could potentially be good turnaround pastors. There was one pastor whose profile did not meet this criterion. However, he was an exception to the norm. (It would be interesting to see if this person's church was located in a high population-growth context, which often promotes a church's numerical growth even when the church doesn't necessarily want to grow.) While I believe that it would be a mistake to tell anyone who aspires to be a pastor that the high D and/or high I profile means he can be used by God to turn around a church, this information would lead us to ask the kinds of questions that would help determine if this is the case. For example, a typical question for such a pastor could be, Has there ever been a time in your life when you have gone into a situation where an organization such as a business was in decline, and, under your leadership, it turned around and is now experiencing healthy growth? Another is, Do you admire and find yourself strongly attracted to the ministries of turnaround pastors?

A Critique

Though based on somewhat small samples of pastors, Thomas's and Penfold's research serves as a starting place or a reference point for discovering leaders whom God has designed for church revitalization. The farther one moves from this point in terms of temperament, the less likely the person will function well as a culture change agent in the point position. I believe that a person who is a primary high I and/or high D could lead a church as a change agent. Those, however, with a primary high S or a primary high C would serve better on a team with the high I or high D person in the point position. The person who is a high S or C may find it difficult to lead a turnaround. Should he take a church, chances are it would plateau or go into decline.

The Myers-Briggs Temperament Indicator

I am not aware of any studies using the *Myers-Briggs Temperament Indicator* comparable to Thomas's or Penfold's work with the *DiSC*. The *MBTI* is different from the *DiSC* and works with four sets of preferences: E-I, S-N, T-F, and J-P. The first preference set (E-I) relates to where leaders focus their attention and derive their energy. The second set (S-N) looks at how people find out about things and how they prefer to take in and process information. The third set (T-F) relates to what people do with the information they take in or how they make decisions. The fourth set (J-P) reflects how people orient to the outer world in terms of structure and the time it takes to make decisions. If you've never taken the *MBTI*, then do so at your earliest convenience. It should be administered by a professional such as a counselor or someone else who has been trained to administer and interpret it. You can locate copies online. (I would also recommend the *Keirsey Temperament Sorter II*. It is practically the same tool as the *Myers-Briggs* but much simpler to take and evaluate. It doesn't have to be administered or interpreted by a professional, but you might find it helpful to work with such a person. It too can be found online.) In addition, I have placed a similar tool (Temperament Indicator 2) in appendix L, which you may find helpful.

Working with type theory while at the University of California, David Keirsey and Marilyn Bates discovered that certain letters of the *Myers-Briggs Temperament Indicator* combined to form four basic temperaments: NF, SJ, NT, and SP. This proves most helpful in discovering change agents. These four combinations can be placed along a continuum of change ranging from the most open to change on the left to the most resistant to change on the right. The NTs are on the far left while the SJs are on the far right.

The SJ combination is the temperament most opposed to change. SJs are the traditionalists who are the conservators and protectors of past values. They resist change and attempt to preserve the status quo. They make up 50 to 75 percent of most congregations, and their motto is, "If it ain't broke, don't fix it!"[12] SJ clergy function best in a maintenance role.

The NT combination is the temperament best designed for change. NT pastors are strong, visionary leaders who are agents of change. The N represents people who take in information holistically, preferring the world of ideas, possibilities, and relationships. They are the world's visionaries who thrive on change and new ideas. For them "believing is seeing." The T represents leaders who make their decisions on the basis of logic and objective analysis. They prefer to win people over by their logic. They take a more impersonal approach to decision making and can come across at times as insensitive.

Culture changers are clearly Ns. Change agents must be strong visionary leaders who prefer change and innovation, which encourages growth in plateaued and declining cultures. For more information on the *MBTI* turn to appendix M.

If a person's temperament is not the NT combination, that doesn't mean he can't function in a different way on a revitalization team or learn to behave more like an NT. Key here is the person's knowledge of himself.

Natural Characteristics and Abilities

Leaders who desire to revitalize churches are wise to examine their natural characteristics and abilities. This section will focus on the characteristics, abilities, and circumstances of a biblical change agent, Nehemiah, and on Pastor Gordon Penfold's research into the leadership characteristics of turnaround pastors. I have chosen Nehemiah because God used him to lead the Jews who survived the exile in Jerusalem through the difficult task of rebuilding the city walls. He models the skills and abilities of a superb culture revitalizer in a most difficult situation. I have used Penfold's research because it focuses specifically on turnaround pastors. The list of characteristics that follows is not exhaustive, and rarely do culture change agents have all of them, but they should identify with some of them. I will begin by covering Nehemiah's characteristics and abilities, note any overlap with Penfold's list, and end, where applicable, with Penfold's characteristics.

An Outsider

Nehemiah was an outsider. When he heard about the desperate situation of the Jews in Jerusalem who had escaped and survived the captivity, he was living in Susa, located about 250 miles east of Babylon (Neh. 1:1). He came to Jerusalem from the outside and brought a fresh perspective to their situation. They had become immersed in their difficulties and accepted them as the status quo. Nehemiah viewed the situation from a different perspective and arrived in time to shake them out of their lethargy.

Author Joel Barker asks, "What kind of person is a paradigm shifter?" He writes, "The short answer is simple: an outsider."[13] He explains that those leaders who come in from outside the present organization or situation lack investment in the old paradigm and thus have little to lose by creating a new set of rules.[14] This demonstrates the advantage in most cases of bringing in a new pastor as change agent from outside the church as opposed to promoting an assistant from within the ranks. It also encourages the use of a godly, skilled consultant in the revitalization process. We at The Malphurs Group have found that people in a church do not see us as caught up in the church's politics or having an axe to grind. Therefore, as we walk them through a turnaround, churches are more willing to follow our direction than they would that of an inside person.

A Motivator

Nehemiah knew how to motivate people. In Nehemiah 2:17–18a he cast a strong vision in which he exhorted the Jews to rebuild the walls. In verse 18b they responded, "Let us start rebuilding." Change agents should look for the ability not only to cast vision but to motivate their followers toward the accomplishment of the vision. This becomes a never-ending process, because the status quo is like a powerful magnet that attracts people to it. Once the change agent initiates the change process, he must naturally motivate his people to continue the process, or they will slip back into a status-quo mentality.

A Persuader

Nehemiah knew how to both motivate and persuade people. In Nehemiah 2:1–8 Artaxerxes, after inquiring about Nehemiah's sad disposition, asked what he might want from him. Nehemiah's response in verses 3–8 is a masterful example of how with God's help (v. 8b) he was able to persuade a pagan in a high position to be sympathetic to his cause. His persuasion was accomplished not by manipulation but by his godly example and history of service.

This ability to persuade, which I discussed above in the section on temperament, is the Persuader Pattern. In fact, Robert Thomas's research with the *Biblical Personal Profile* revealed that the Persuader Pattern best characterized pastors who had successfully led small, passive Baptist General Conference churches through revitalization.

A Risk Taker

There is no question that Nehemiah was a risk taker. When he appeared before the king with a sad face due to his mourning (Neh. 2:1–2), he was possibly risking his life, because in the ancient Near Eastern culture you simply didn't do so (Esther 4:1–4). He also took a tremendous risk when he challenged the Jews in Jerusalem to rebuild the city walls (vv. 16–17). There was no assurance that they would respond to his vision or follow his leadership. Why should they follow this outsider who materialized from nowhere? But he took the risk, and God blessed the results with rebuilt walls and revitalized people.

In his chapter on paradigm pioneers, Joel Barker writes:

> Non-rational decision-making and courage: those are the two hallmarks of a leader. And can you think of anyplace where leadership is required more than the changing of paradigms? Leaders are willing to take a risk. This great risk, however, is balanced with tremendous opportunity: if it turns out that the new paradigm is one with depth and breadth, those who change early have the first crack at all the territory.[15]

So while the change agent faces tremendous risk in challenging a culture to change, there is a trade-off. Today there is the tremendous potential for being a part of something new and exciting that God is initiating across America in the early twenty-first century.

A Recruiter

Nehemiah had the ability to recruit the allies necessary to implement his plan for Jerusalem (Neh. 2:17–20). He was successful because he was a vision caster (v. 17), motivator (v. 18), and encourager (v. 20). Without the help of the people, he realized there would be no rebuilding of the walls or gates of the city.

Revitalization pastors cannot do it alone. They are dependent on the abilities of other leaders and workers to accomplish the task of rebuilding the church. Therefore they must make a regular effort to recruit allies to come on board and be a part of their team. This would also have an impact on critical mass. The more you have on board who support culture change, the more likely the culture will change in time.

A Catalyst

Nehemiah was a catalyst for change in his leadership of the Jews in Jerusalem during a dark period in Israel's history. He not only led them through change but also initiated much of that change. He was not a spectator but an initiator. He proved to be proactive, not passive. For example, he took the initiative to speak with King Artaxerxes about the tragic conditions in Jerusalem (Neh. 2:1–3), and he initiated the first contact with the Jews in Jerusalem (v. 11). Penfold includes this as one of his characteristics, writing that turnaround leaders are direct or proactive, not passive.[16]

In *Discovering the Future* Joel Barker discusses the characteristics of paradigm shifters (change agents) and writes, "The paradigm shifter is a catalyst, a change agent, and part of the role of a catalyst is to stir things up."[17] Someone has to catalyze the change process, and change agents are designed expressly for this purpose.

Not a Quitter

Nehemiah displays throughout the book an insatiable desire to persevere in spite of overwhelming odds. His ability to hang tough is most clearly demonstrated in Nehemiah 4:1–6:14 when he responds to the opposition party in Jerusalem who would greatly benefit if Nehemiah cast aside his vision. Most of the opposition came from Israel's unbelieving enemies (Sanballat, Tobiah, and Geshem) in the form of such devices as ridicule (2:19; 4:1–5), conspiracy (vv. 7–10), and rumor (4:11–12).

An ever-present distraction for change agents can be the temptation to quit. Some view opposition as a part of the challenge. The challenge to change minds and hearts is what pulls them into the situation to begin with. Others struggle more with opposition. The regular presence of unreasonable, misguided resistance from people within as well as outside the ministry (whom I refer to as vision vampires and vision vultures) can eventually cause change agents great damage emotionally and spiritually. There will be times when they want desperately to quit. In their mind they may offer their resignation numerous times each day. However, they must not be quick to quit.

This does not mean that eventually leaders of change do not come to a point where they may resign. Some status-quo situations are set in concrete. But resignation should not be an option until they have given the situation their best over a reasonable period of time. The average tenure of pastors among Protestant denominations in America is 3.7 years. Yet it takes a minimum of five years for a pastor to gain the credibility to become the leader of a congregation.

While it could mean other things, the culture molder's emphasis on finishing the course may be what Penfold is alluding to when he notes that turnaround pastors are focused and determined.[18]

A Problem Solver

Nehemiah was obviously a problem solver, but the problems he faced were overwhelming. The walls to the city were broken down, and the gates were burned to the ground. Even more important was the Jews' emotional and spiritual response to their circumstances—they were in great distress and disgrace (Neh. 1:3). Nevertheless, Nehemiah did not back away from the difficult situation. Instead, he attacked it and led these people in solving their problems. Barker in his discussion of a change agent (a paradigm pioneer) writes, "This person can best be described as a tinkerer. The key characteristic of tinkerers is that they fix problems that have become important to them."[19] Penfold's research also found that turnaround pastors are good problem solvers.[20]

A Visionary

I have no doubt that Nehemiah carried a picture of the rebuilt walls and gates of Jerusalem in his mental wallet from the time God gave him the vision until all were in place (see Neh. 2:17). Visionaries have the innate ability to see what others do not or cannot see. While they see needs, they have the natural capacity to see beyond those needs to the unique, exciting opportunities the needs present.

It is critical that leaders as change agents be visionaries. The visionary carries within his mind a snapshot of what the church will look like after it has progressed through the change process. Therefore the leader knows where he is going and communicates a clear direction for the church. This enables him to cast a concise, focused vision to motivate his people to pursue the changes necessary to accomplish the vision. Lyle Schaller writes that a leader as change agent "(a) has a vision of a new and different tomorrow, (b) can persuasively communicate that vision to others, and (c) is able and willing to make the effort to win allies who will help translate that vision into reality."[21]

Penfold notes that there is a distinct difference between turnaround and non-turnaround pastors in the area of leading with vision. Turnaround pastors communicate vision vividly and have a clear picture of a preferred future.[22]

A Delegator

Even the most careful reader of the book of Nehemiah could miss it the first time through the book. In fact, if you were not specifically looking for it, you might miss it altogether. I am talking about the fact that Nehemiah did not rebuild Jerusalem's walls and gates. He was instrumental in the accomplishment of the project but did not do it by himself. Chapter 3 and the following chapters of Nehemiah give the names of people who actually accomplished the work. Nehemiah was a delegator, not a doer. He was a team player rather than a soloist.

Penfold agrees about the importance of being a delegator. He writes: "Turnaround pastors are good at delegation. Non-turnaround pastors are less adept at this. Delegation is essential as no single person or small group can carry the load required for a turnaround."[23]

Leaders of change in the twenty-first century cannot accomplish change on their own. It is critical that they develop a team of runners to whom they regularly hand off the baton of responsibility. Leaders who develop a plan must delegate its implementation to others or attempt it on their own. Those who choose the latter are destined for frustration and eventual failure.

Outgoing

While the high S temperament in the *DiSC* profile is outgoing, the high C is not. This is critical, as Penfold notes: "Turnaround pastors are significantly more outgoing than their non-turnaround counterparts. This is extremely important in order for a church to grow with new people."[24] This also favors extraverts over introverts. Turnaround pastors are extraverts.

Innovative

Turnaround leaders are more innovative than traditional. Penfold writes, "Turnaround pastors are not afraid to break the mold and try new things; non-turnaround pastors are more reserved. This fits well with non-turnaround pastors being high S and high C in the *DiSC* profile. They like stability."[25]

Energetic

There is something about revitalization that can sap the strength and energy of a culture shifter. Penfold writes, "Turnaround pastors are more energetic and turnaround requires a tremendous amount of energy."[26]

A Team Player

Pastors who revitalize cultures know they cannot do it by themselves. This is the trap that high C pastors fall into, especially those who are perfectionistic. They do it themselves because they do not trust anyone else to do it as well. This characteristic walks arm in arm with delegation, which a revitalizer also does well. Penfold writes, "Turnaround pastors appear to be better team players. Teamwork is essential in a growing church."[27]

Leader Trainer

Turnaround pastors are better at training leaders than most other pastors. Penfold writes, "New leadership opens new doors for ministry. . . . Pastors must increase their leadership base if a church is to grow."[28]

Relational

Culture builders must be relational. People expect them to be people-people. Penfold says, "Both groups (turnaround and non-turnaround pastors) have strong relational capabilities. Turnaround leaders have the edge in this regard as well. It is difficult for any church to grow without a relational pastor. Relational pastors tend to produce relational people."[29]

Communicator

Turnaround pastors are better-than-average communicators. Penfold comments, "Good communication is necessary for life. It is no less true in the church. The turnaround pastors have a significant lead in this category."[30] Based on this, you might think he is talking about their ability to preach. He is, but this also includes communication in general.

Conflict Resolver

Culture navigators will face conflict. Thus Penfold says, "TAP (turnaround pastors) have the edge when it comes to conflict resolution skills. Change produces conflict and good conflict managers will help move the church further faster."[31]

The Application

According to the material presented in this chapter, you are either a turnaround or a non-turnaround pastor or leader. The following questions will help you apply the information to your life and ministry.

What If I'm Not a Turnaround Pastor?

Your answer to the following question will affect the rest of your ministry life. What if you discover that you are not a turnaround pastor? What does this mean? In most cases, it means that as a senior or lead pastor, your church most likely will plateau or be in decline. Yes, there are exceptions to the norm that may be explained by looking at the church's context. (It's hard not to grow when a church is located in a high-growth area.) Do you find this to be the case in your situation? Let's face it, God is God, and he can use anyone to revitalize a church, regardless of his divine design. But we have to wonder why he would create us one way and not use us according to that design. Normally he does. The norm is that he uses people to be turnaround pastors whom he has purposely wired that way.

Can a Non-turnaround Pastor Become a Turnaround Pastor?

The answer to the first question raises a second question: Can a non-turnaround pastor become a turnaround pastor? Of the possible questions you could ask, this one is the most difficult to answer. It walks us back to the old nature-versus-nurture debate in leadership circles. Does a person have to be born a leader, or can one learn to be a leader? My intuitive read on this is that it is not one or the other but that both are true. A person can be born with a unique leadership gift, and in addition the Christian may be given the spiritual gift of leadership (Rom. 12:8). However, a person without the gift can also grow and develop as a leader. This is the reason we attempt to develop leaders in our churches and seminaries.

I have mentioned a number of characteristics above of turnaround pastors. These are skills that can be learned and honed. The problem is more with temperament. Temperament is God-given and not subject to change. However, I do believe that while a person cannot change his temperament, he can adapt to another temperament with varying results. Adaptation is a bigger adjustment for some than for others. I have found in my ministry that I can adapt to the temperament that is expected of me in a ministry situation. One of the reasons is that I am a student of the temperaments and know them well.

Because it is not natural to adapt our temperament, it can prove somewhat difficult and uncomfortable for many leaders to do so. Also, in a pressure or stressful situation, the natural response is to default to your God-given temperament, which may not be the best for that situation. Thus the answer to the question is that it depends on the person and how comfortable he is adapting to another, different temperament. Some can do it, and some cannot and should not.

Should a Non-turnaround Pastor Try to Become a Turnaround Pastor?

Now a third question is raised: Should a non-turnaround pastor try to become a turnaround pastor? As I look back over the material presented in this chapter, I can see where it might seem a little overwhelming. While the studies cited in this chapter are most helpful, understand that no one has all or must have all these qualities and characteristics to be involved in changing a church's culture. So don't walk away from this chapter feeling overwhelmed or disillusioned. Someone said that when eating a fish, eat the meat and leave the bones. Yes, we do need turnaround pastors. The studies I have seen estimate that anywhere from 5 to 25 percent (the latter seems a little high) of pastors are wired to turn around churches.

An important question here is, What does your situation call for? If your church needs a turnaround, should you attempt to become a turnaround pastor or should you move on to another ministry? As I've said, I believe it is possible for a non-turnaround pastor to learn to some degree how to be a turnaround pastor. To be most effective, however, you need to discover your divine design and minister accordingly.

Early in the chapter we learned that you cannot be or do anything you want. More important, God made you the way you are for a purpose, and that is vital to any and all ministry that you pursue. You will be most effective at what he has wired you to do, whether it's a high- or low-profile position. In addition, those who aren't wired as a lead culture shaper but are convinced that God would have them involved in leading a culture through change could pursue the following. Consider working alongside a culture shaper as a staff person or volunteer, helping him in every way possible to renew the culture. Bring who you are to the situation. That is where you will be at your best. It is also possible that his behavior and thinking may provide you with a model that will teach you how to lead change. Remember, you are a leader, and leaders are learners.

Questions for Reflection and Discussion

1. The author argues that regardless of one's role or divine design in leading a culture, character is critical. Would you agree? Why or why not?

2. Have you taken the Character Assessment for Leadership in appendix H? If not, why not? If so, what did you learn about your character? Where did you do well, and where do you have some work to pursue?

3. Do you meet the spiritual qualifications to lead a ministry? Does your life reflect the fruit of the Spirit in Galatians 5:22–23? Why or why not?

4. Have you discovered your spiritual gifts? Why or why not? If not, stop and take the Spiritual Gifts Inventory (appendix I) right now. Do you have any of the gifts that characterize culture shapers? Which ones?

5. What are you passionate about? What do you feel strongly and care deeply about? Is it Christ's churches? How might your passion direct the ministry of your gifts? Do you believe in a call to ministry? If so, could it be the same as your passion?

6. Did you find the information on temperament helpful? Why or why not? Have you taken the *Personal Profile (DiSC)* or the *Myers-Briggs Temperament Indicator (MBTI)* or the *Keirsey Temperament Sorter II*? Have you taken Temperament Indictors 1 and 2 in the appendixes? If so, what is your temperament? Do you have the temperament of a culture shaper? Why or why not?

7. Like Nehemiah, you have certain natural characteristics and abilities for leadership and ministry. What are yours? How do they compare with those of Nehemiah and those in Penfold's research?

8. According to the material presented in this chapter, are you a turnaround or a non-turnaround pastor or leader? Why or why not? What specifically leads you to this conclusion? If you are not a turnaround pastor but you need or want to be one, can you operate comfortably outside your natural design to revitalize a church?

12

The Church Pastor as Culture Sculptor

Part 3 The Process

In chapter 10 I asked, How might culture sculptors go about bringing change to established church cultures? I began answering this question in chapter 10 on equipping pastors to prepare an established culture for change and in chapter 11 on the personnel who are able to shape a culture. Now this chapter will provide the process that the church pastor needs as a culture sculptor to accomplish a culture turnaround.

To accomplish change in today's cultures, we need a dynamic model that walks the culture through the change process. Kurt Lewin—a German-American psychologist who in the 1950s did research on organizations—has developed the best model for understanding organizational change.[1] His model involves a three-stage process that consists of unfreezing a culture, changing the culture, and then refreezing it. He explains and illustrates this process by using the analogy of changing the shape of a block of ice. If you have a block of ice but prefer to have a cone of ice (I would prefer a Popsicle), what would you do? First you would melt the ice (unfreeze) so that it becomes water. Second, you would put the water in the cone mold (change), and finally you would freeze the water in the shape of a cone—or Popsicle—(refreeze).

In this chapter I will walk you through a similar process and apply it to the church culture. My process consists of four steps: first, you read the current culture, next you unfreeze it, then you transition the culture to a new level, and finally you form or re-form it at the new level.

Shaping an Established Culture

Step 1 Read the current culture.

Step 2 Thaw out the current culture.

Step 3 Transition the culture to a new level.

Step 4 Re-form the new culture at the new level.

Read the Current Culture

How to Read the Culture

I have addressed how to read or discover a church's culture in chapter 7 and how to read a pastor's culture in chapter 8. They are similar processes that are vital and lead to shaping or reshaping existing church cultures. In both cases, you begin outside the Culture Apple with the peel and work your way into the apple's inner core. You accomplish this by exegeting the current culture that involves three steps: observation, interpretation, and application. The result is that you better understand the established church's culture and are in the best position to shape or change it for the better.

Apple	Culture	Exegesis
Peel	Behavior	Observation
Flesh	Values	Interpretation
Core	Beliefs	Application

In chapter 9 we moved from reading the culture to shaping or creating it. We went from exegeting an established culture to creating a brand-new culture. While the exegetical process was the same, the questions changed. They are in the chart below.

Reading and Shaping Congregational Culture

	Reading the Culture	Shaping the Culture
Observation	What do you see?	What should you see?
Interpretation	What does it mean?	What should it mean?
Application	What difference does it make?	What difference should it make?

In this chapter, unlike the others, we'll bring the two processes together. We'll both read and shape an established church's culture. At this point in the process, you have before you an established church that you may know little about unless you're its current pastor. Whether you are the current pastor or a person who is candidating to be the lead pastor or in some other role, you need to understand what you're getting yourself into and whether or not you have the knowledge and abilities as well as the design to reshape this culture by leading it through change. So how do you read the current culture?

As we learned in chapter 7, reading a culture involves the three-step exegetical process of observation, interpretation, and application. The following serves as a quick review.

OBSERVATION

Observation asks, What do you see? When a prospective pastor, a believer looking for a church, or an unchurched, lost visitor attends a church meeting, what does he or she see? Are people carrying their Bibles, hugging one another, weeping with one another, praying over one another, and so on?

INTERPRETATION

Interpretation asks, What does it mean? Here you move from what you've observed to interpreting your observations. The key to explaining the church's actions is discovering both its values and its beliefs. Churches are values-driven and beliefs-based.

APPLICATION

Application asks, What difference does it make? Taking the application step will help you know the culture's commonalities and uniqueness, its strengths and weaknesses, whether it's spiritually mature or immature, and whether you as a leader of this culture would be effective or ineffective.

The Results

CHURCHES FROZEN IN STATUS QUO

Once you have worked through the exegetical process and read the culture, you will know whether it's healthy, unhealthy, or somewhere in between. Since 80 to 85 percent of the churches in America are plateaued or declining, we know that most are unhealthy. They are frozen in the status quo. Therefore to lead them and breathe new life into their cultures, their leaders and followers must become discontent with that status quo. But this is easier said than done because most congregants in general seek a context where they feel safe from any possible harm and somewhat in control of their circumstances. And the latter leads to the former. This provides them with a false sense of comfort and well-being that does much to preserve the status quo. Thus any suggestion of a change may be greeted with a polite—sometimes not so polite—"No thanks!" This is illustrated well in the Pentateuch when the Israelites faced difficulties in the desert. All they could think about was returning to captivity in Egypt, rather than pushing through to freedom in the Promised Land. Status quo has the same blinding effect on churches.

Church Leaders Frozen in Status Quo

As we saw in chapter 10, some church leaders resist change because they're clinging to certain vested interests. They have been in the church for a while and over time have accrued certain benefits, such as position, power, prestige, and prominence. This is the status quo for these people, and for them, change means the potential loss of these benefits. With change everyone goes back to zero in terms of influence. Whatever leverage they had under the old culture paradigm is nullified by the new. Such leaders will put up strong resistance to change, based on the potential loss of benefits.

So in the first step of reading the current culture, you see how the church is doing. And since most are doing poorly, it presents the problem you face and the reasons change is needed. Continue through steps 2–4 to bring about change.

Shaping an Established Culture

Step 1 Read the current culture.

Step 2 Thaw out the current culture.

Step 3 Transition the culture to a new level.

Step 4 Re-form the new culture at the new level.

Thaw Out the Current Culture

When I was a child, about once a month my mom thawed out the freezer in our refrigerator. If she failed to do so, the ice buildup would take away necessary storage space, would interfere with freezing the contents, and could prove to be a mess to clean up later. Today refrigerators have a process whereby they defrost themselves, and most everyone has a frost-free refrigerator. Wouldn't it be wonderful if church cultures came with the same feature? But that's simply not the case with the majority of cultures. Therefore we need a process that thaws out the church's status-quo freezer before the culture gets frostbite.

What can change agents do to unfreeze the culture? What can they do to move people out of the status quo or to consider giving up the status quo? The good news is that there are a number of things they can do. While all may or may not apply in every context, I would suggest one or a combination of the following.

Inflict Pain

One way to initiate change is to inflict emotional pain. Often medical doctors have to hurt people to heal them. The same is true of culture doctors. What does this mean? The change agent may have to make the present state or the status quo significantly uncomfortable before change comes about. Lyle Schaller refers to this as rubbing raw the wounds of discontent. Bill Hybels articulates the same when he says: "Leaders move people from here to there. . . . The first play is not to make 'there' sound wonderful. The first play is to make 'here' sound awful."[2] If you make "there" look good and don't make "now" seem awful, "now" will hang around to compete constantly with "there" for people's allegiance.

So what can we possibly do to inflict pain? How does one rub raw the wounds of discontent or make "now" look ugly? The answer is to tell churches the truth! And that answer applies particularly to the 80 percent of churches in America that are plateaued or declining. Change agents inflict pain by calling attention to the struggling state of their churches. Most of these churches know something is wrong but are ignoring it, much like the proverbial ostrich who at the first sign of trouble buries his head in the sand. It's simply too painful to face reality. Others simply don't know what to do so they do nothing, hoping against hope that the situation will self-correct. For them the "now" is the church's decline and eventual death. Thus the ministry of the culture defroster is to cause pain by regularly and loudly calling the church's attention to its frostbitten condition. He makes this information public so that it can't be ignored, all the while realizing that there could be an angry backlash that could cost him his job.

For example, we at TMG do much the same when we work with declining churches. We ask the church to provide us with their average annual worship attendance and offerings, going back as far as it has kept records. Most often we discover that the church's attendance and giving are in serious decline. We can even figure out the rate of decline so that we can predict when the church will have to close its doors. Our experience is that the probability of death and closure grabs people's attention and causes extreme mental anguish. And it can't be ignored. Something has to be done and it has to happen now. It cannot wait. Later won't do. If the church has to close its doors, there will be no more status quo. In addition, we ask the sobering but potentially painful question, Do you want to be remembered as the generation who let the church die? Will people point to you and say, "It happened on their watch"?

At the same time, we ask the church to recruit a strategic leadership team (SLT) made up of their leaders who, in turn, take our TMG Church Analysis. This analysis has a section on strengths and weaknesses, and we ask the strategic leadership team—some of whom may be change resistant—to identify those strengths and weaknesses. As I've said, the most common weaknesses that keep surfacing over the years are evangelism, lay ministry or service, communication, planning, vision, leadership, and leadership development. These plus other weaknesses issue a congregational wake-up call. They have an eye-opening impact because they have largely been ignored or overlooked and are vital to the life of the church. Also, we point out that by ignoring them, they are in disobedience to God's plan and will for their church. In effect, they are out of God's will for their culture. Though it may be greeted with silence, this too gets their attention.

Another example is the decline in attendance of a church's youth and young adults. Barna has pointed out that the typical church is not keeping its young people. We at TMG use these facts to cause emotional pain. Here is how we do it. Since usually a number of the people on the strategic leadership team are older saints, we ask them what they would be willing to give up—what they would be willing to change—to have their son or daughter sitting next to them at church on Sunday mornings. After a significant pause, we repeat the statement but substitute their grandchildren in place of their son or daughter. You can hear a pin drop.

We and many others have observed that people make decisions based not on the facts but on their emotions. Even after considering the facts that should inform their decision, people go with their emotions and against the facts. Should you inquire, they respond with either "It felt right" or "It didn't feel right!" As in the examples above, we at TMG employ the facts but use them to touch the emotions. And this is the key in causing pain that brings God-honoring change in the life of a culture.

Ask the Sixteen Make-or-Break Questions

Another tool that TMG uses is the Sixteen Make-or-Break Questions. They are make-or-break because if a church can't answer all positively, they are headed for failure if not there already. We use these with churches that are still growing but are not hitting on all cylinders. A plateau is just around the corner, or they are plateaued and decline is just around the corner. These churches are different from the former struggling churches. When you point out to them the need for change, often the response is, "Attendance is up; we're doing just fine" or, "If it ain't broke, don't fix it!"

Your job in this situation is to point out that something *is* broken and then help the people see it—to see what they do not want to see. So how can you get the attention of church leaders when on the surface all seems well? How can you get them to see the need for change now and not wait until it is obvious to all that the church is broken? Our tool Sixteen Make-or-Break Questions has been used successfully with such churches.

1. Do you know what the church's four critical vital signs are (the church's worship attendance, offerings, strengths, and weaknesses)? Can you name them? Do you have your finger on your church's pulse so that you can regularly read your four critical vital signs?
2. Do you have a contagious, biblical mission statement that serves as a compass to navigate your church through whitewater change? Does it roll off your tongue with clarity and conviction?
3. Do you habitually consult your mission statement when making any and all decisions that affect the future direction of your church? Do you ask how these decisions will affect the accomplishment of the church's mission?
4. Have you carefully identified your actual core values so that you understand what truly empowers and guides your church and explains why you do what you do or do not do what you should do?
5. Has your church's impact in your community been such that if you were to suddenly disappear, it would leave a serious hole in your community?
6. Do your people view themselves merely as the church's members or Christ's missionaries?
7. Do you have a clear, simple pathway for making disciples that most in your church understand and are actively pursuing?
8. Do you have an intentional lay-mobilization process for increasing and empowering lay volunteers to lead and do the church's ministries?
9. Is your ministry staff team being developed while developing others as authentic, servant leaders?
10. If you have a governing board, have they been equipped to use the groundbreaking policy governance model to direct their leadership of the church? (This is a new model for church governance that sets policies that govern the senior pastor, the board, and the senior pastor–board relationships. To learn more see Aubrey Malphurs, *Leading Leaders* [Baker, 2005].)
11. Do your facilities contribute functionally to the realization of your vision in the community?

12. Do you have a biblical strategy in place for raising finances that has resulted in an increase in giving in spite of any recession?
13. Is your church's vision vibrant and alive, and does it cast a clear, exciting picture of your future? In the last thirty days have you overheard a church member articulate or discuss your vision?
14. Do you have an intentional process for developing key leaders at every level in your church? Can you outline it on a napkin over a cup of coffee?
15. Have you crafted a personal, individualized leader development plan for your own growth as a leader in your church?
16. Have you or anyone on the ministry staff identified and enlisted a coach or mentor to help you and/or your team members grow and stay fresh as leaders?

After asking these questions, the change agent would ask, How are you doing in response to these make-or-break questions? We've not had a church yet that scored well on these questions! After articulating them to a leader or leadership team, we are greeted with silence. When you dip below the surface, you discover that what's at the surface isn't an accurate read of where the church is headed.

Develop Opportunity Eyes

A third way to unfreeze the current culture is to develop opportunity eyes. Often people confuse the church with its building. According to Scripture, the church is people, and just as people have a life cycle, every church has a life cycle. It consists of birth, growth, decline, and eventually death. However, there are certain times in the history of the typical church when its life cycle can be interrupted. These "interventions" interrupt the status quo and present opportunities for the implementation of Christ-honoring change. While change does not necessarily occur after an intervention, the likelihood that it will increases.

The alert culture shaper views these interruptions or interventions in the church's life as open windows for potential change, while realizing that the church's windows open periodically and then close within a short period of time. God may use the change agent to open some of the windows, but others only God can open. Regardless, the skillful culture architect must be alert to the various windows that are open and be ready to use them to accomplish biblical change before they close and the opportunity is lost. I will discuss six such windows.

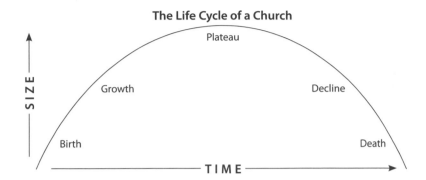

The Life Cycle of a Church

A WIDELY PERCEIVED CRISIS

A crisis event has the greatest potential to initiate change in the typical church. Scripture is replete with examples of how God raised up strong leaders of change to lead his people in a crisis situation. God used Joseph and the evil intentions of his brothers to save many lives in crisis (Gen. 50:19–20). God raised up Moses to lead Israel out of a crisis situation in Egypt (Exod. 3:7–10). God touched the life of Nehemiah and used him in the lives of the Jews who had escaped the captivity in Jerusalem (Neh. 1:2–11).

For a crisis to be an opportunity, as many people as possible must become aware of it. If there is a crisis and no one recognizes it, then not much will happen. People have to know something is seriously wrong so they will move to remedy the situation. This is the major problem facing the church in the early twenty-first century. Approximately 80 to 85 percent are in a crisis situation, and many people are not aware of it. Others suspect something might be wrong, but they are afraid to go to the doctor because he might confirm their worst fears.

A crisis can take many forms. One is when the senior citizens in the church far outnumber the younger people. Another is a plateau or decline in attendance. This captures people's attention and may catalyze a positive commitment toward change. A third is the retirement or resignation of the pastor and staff. A fourth is a natural disaster that damages or destroys the church facility, such as a fire or flood. Other crises are a church split, the moral lapse of a pastor or staff person, the firing of a pastor, a lawsuit, and an obsolete facility. The key is for leaders to develop "crisis-sensitive eyes." They must be quick to spot a potential crisis and use it to point the church in a new direction.

The power of a crisis to accomplish change is the pain associated with it, which we noted earlier. Crises interrupt the status quo in an emotionally painful way. And pain has a way of gaining everyone's attention. No one enjoys pain, whether it is physical, emotional, or spiritual. Consequently, at the onset of a particular crisis, most begin the quest for pain relief. Like a physician, the wise, loving leader of change faces the congregation with its pain and proposes God's viable solutions as remedy.

A CHANGE OF PASTORS

A pastoral change can motivate the revitalization of a congregation. Often God uses this window-opening event to implement a new vision for the church. The advantage is the church grants the new pastor a certain amount of leverage. The resignation or removal of the former pastor disrupts the congregational status quo. Next, people realize the new pastor is not aware of their cultural politics or "how we do things around here." They also want to make a good first impression—they want the pastor to like them. Third, the board is relieved to have someone fill the pastoral office—they were not aware of how much the former pastor accomplished until he left. The result is an initial willingness to flex.

Churches that are in decline and aware of it may respond favorably to significant change during the honeymoon with the new pastor. They have a sense that if they don't act now, there may be no tomorrow. More likely, however, the new pastor in a plateaued church will have to earn the right to lead the ministry through the change process. It may take some time to build necessary credibility with a plateaued congregation. My research indicates that the years five through eight of an average leader's tenure are the most effective. So a leader must stay around long enough to gain the right to lead the culture in a new direction.

RENEWAL OF THE PASTOR

Most students of change acknowledge that the primary catalytic factor for a church culture's change and growth is the pastor. As the pastor of the church goes, so goes the church. Perhaps a better expression is—as the pastor of the church grows, so grows the church. The problem is that many pastors in plateaued or declining churches become discouraged and drop out. They may take another, more promising church, but an alarming number drop out of the ministry entirely.

At some point in his ministry, every pastor struggles with discouragement. If it happened to Paul (2 Tim. 4:9–18), it will happen to the best of us. Therefore wise pastors will develop strong friendships and connect with people who are gifted encouragers. A most important step is to find a mentor or coach who will work with the pastor on renewal. Penfold notes in his dissertation that turn-around pastors, unlike non-turnaround pastors, have had and still have a coach or mentor who works with them regularly. Also there are some good seminars and conferences that will encourage leaders. One is the annual Global Leadership Summit put on by the Willow Creek Association. The most readily available help is good books, articles, and research by those knowledgeable in their fields that provide helpful insight and encouragement. In fact, there are more books that have been written to instruct and encourage pastors today than ever before.

Renewal of the Lay Leadership

An overlooked open window of change is a renewal of the church's leaders, such as a governing board, elders, and deacons. Not only can pastors experience renewal, but lay leaders may also go through the same experience. Helping lay leadership rediscover the church's mission can provide an intervention event that leads to possible change.

There are several ways to accomplish lay-leader renewal in a culture. One is to educate the board as much as possible in biblical principles of change and renewal. They could read current books together on leadership or the spiritual life. Attending a visionary, cutting-edge church conference or seminar together can go a long way in renewing leadership. Andy McQuitty is the pastor of Irving Bible Church, located northwest of Dallas, Texas. He took his elder board to hear Rick Warren at a conference center in the mountains of scenic Colorado. This conference heavily influenced these leaders toward a new vision for the church. Consequently, while Andy cast a new vision for Irving Bible Church, the Rick Warren conference aided him in the process.

Another way is to ask your leaders to listen to or view audio and video recordings from new paradigm churches that God is blessing. And you would be wise to listen to or view them together, followed by a discussion of their contents. Another source of leadership renewal is a consultant whose expertise is in lay renewal, change, and leader development.

The Expertise of a Church Consultant

Often churches do not value or have confidence in the leadership of the pastor. There are a multitude of reasons—both good and bad. In far too many cases pastors simply don't know what to do. Regardless of the situation, in any culture where the pastor does not have the allegiance of the board and/or the congregation or he simply doesn't know what to do to bring renewal to the culture, a church consultant can serve effectively. Qualified, skilled consultants bring a certain objectivity to a situation that instills confidence. They can spot problems and suggest solutions that could translate into change. And the congregation views them positively because they realize that consultants are not involved in the church's politics nor do they have an axe to grind. They will "tell it like it is."

Some pastors may have the people's confidence in their leadership knowledge and abilities but may find themselves in a situation where they need the wisdom and advice of a specialist. It may be a building program, church planting, church revitalization, fund-raising, capital campaigns, strategic planning, or leader development that would benefit from the expertise of a consultant.

Churches without pastors would be wise to seek the advice of a consultant before pursuing any new ventures. Many are convinced that they know as much about leadership and the ministry as a pastor (and some do). The result is that these earnest laypeople make numerous mistakes that have a deep impact on the ministry. A respected consultant can provide them with the expertise to facilitate the ministries of the church and influence them to make needed critical changes.

PLANTING A CHURCH

Not only should churches be birthing other churches, but one means for encouraging change in established church cultures is the open window of church planting. Church planting is an exciting option for dying churches. Some congregations are beginning to view their death as an opportunity to give life. One congregation disbanded several years ago and entrusted their property to a ministry that sold the building to a new Hispanic congregation at a greatly reduced price. Income from the sale was used for the retirement of three missionaries from the former church and other church-planting work. A Baptist church in Dallas had declined to around thirty members. The future looked grim. So the congregation decided to sell the facility and pour the resources into a church plant in a nearby growing community. Some of the congregation joined the planted church while others dispersed into various churches in the community. Approximately two years later, the growing church plant has two to three thousand people in worship each Sunday and is renting a sizable space in a strip mall where they can meet.

OTHER WINDOWS/OPPORTUNITIES

There are additional open windows for change. Calling attention to the church's poor image in the community gives most members the push they need to address it. Nehemiah did something similar to this in Nehemiah 2:15–17.

Reminding people of the church's better days and encouraging them to embrace what made those days better, such as evangelism, lay ministry involvement, and strong Bible instruction should be the challenge they need to make the future their best days.

Other ways to thaw out the culture are to show how the status quo works against the church's best interests, as discussed above; present change and innovation as opportunities rather than threats; challenge the church to become the best it can be; and perhaps the most extreme is to close the church. This involves pronouncing the last rites for a dying church. Then after six to nine months, a new or renewed pastor starts over with a new group of people and/ or those in the old church who have the same vision.

Wise molders who desire to lead their churches through the change process are constantly sensitive to the various windows of opportunity—they develop "opportunity eyes." As opportunities open, change agents are quick to spot them and use them to cast a new vision for their ministry. When several windows open at the same time, they realize the chances for change increase proportionately.

How to Thaw Out the Current Culture

Inflict pain.
Ask the sixteen make-or-break questions.
Develop opportunity eyes.
Recruit a strategic leadership team.

Recruit a Strategic Leadership Team

All of the above should be helpful in unfreezing the status quo. We at TMG have found, however, that recruiting a strategic leadership team has been most effective. This team is made up of the church's key leaders, and they are the ones who go through the change process. The primary reason for recruiting this team is that leaders are more open to change when they have some say or involvement in the process. Right or wrong, because they're involved, they perceive initially that any change is under their control—they have a say—and they do. Then the rest of the congregation see their leaders, the people they've grown to trust, heavily involved in the change process and feel more confident about it because of their involvement.

The team will consist of anywhere from ten to no more than twenty-five people, depending on the church's size. They need to be the core leaders of the church, such as the pastor himself, any ministry staff, the members of a governing board, Sunday school or Bible teachers, and small groups leaders.

The change architect will be the primary person to select these leaders with some or much input from others, such as a board, board chairman, and ministry staff. The general qualifications are the following: godly, Christlike character (Gal. 5:22–23), a servant mentality (Matt. 20:28), positive people (known for what they're for—not for what they're against!), peacemakers not troublemakers, people who pursue church unity, and leaders who are respected people in the culture. What if a board member does not have these qualities? You may choose to include this person and deal with any problems as they come up. Perhaps a better choice is to use this as an opportunity to confront that person or simply explain why they were not chosen. Should there be a problem, now is likely the best time to address it.

The SLT will operate primarily by consensus decision making that may at times call for a vote of the team. I would encourage the team to meet at least once a month for the sake of momentum as well as goals accomplishment. Friday evenings and Saturday mornings seem to be good times for laypersons to meet. Finally, it's most important that the team communicate with the congregation, letting them know what is taking place. There are to be no secrets or surprises. When SLTs communicate constantly, the congregation will learn to trust them if they don't already, as they lead the church through the culture change process.

Shaping an Established Culture

Step 1 Read the current culture.

Step 2 Thaw out the current culture.

Step 3 Transition the culture to a new level.

Step 4 Re-form the new culture at the new level.

Transition the Culture to a New Level

As we discovered in chapter 10, people respond differently to change. Some are early adopters, while some are late adopters, and still others are never adopters. The architect of culture change must be sensitive to where his people are as they begin to thaw out of the status quo. What he will learn is that there's no clear line of demarcation between the thawed stage and that of moving to a new level. The transition from thawing to changing the culture doesn't happen overnight.

Regardless, the culture shaper and his team (SLT) must move ahead. They must press on. There's no time to pause to catch your breath. To stall now would prove disastrous. They must move the church to a new level. This involves asking and answering two questions: What kind of culture should you shape? How will you implement it?

What Kind of Culture?

To answer the first question, we must return to the Culture Apple and the exegetical process that moves us from the peel to the core. Step 1 involved reading the current culture by asking and answering the questions in the column on the left in the chart on page 189. With this information in mind, the culture shaper moves to asking and answering the questions in the column on the right that address shaping the culture.

Reading and Shaping Congregational Culture

Reading the Culture	Shaping the Culture
What do you see?	What should you see?
What does it mean?	What should it mean?
What difference does it make?	What difference should it make?

WHAT SHOULD YOU SEE?

The observation question when reading the culture of the established church is, What kind of culture do you see? When we answered this question, we found that in far too many churches it's not good. When shaping or reshaping the established church we ask, What should you see, what do you want to see, or what could you see? And the answer is a spiritually healthy, biblically based, Christ-honoring culture.

WHAT SHOULD IT MEAN?

The interpretation question when reading the established culture is, What does it mean? The answer unearths the culture's core values and beliefs, which for the majority of churches fall far short of what God wants them to be. When reshaping the established culture, the question is, What should it mean? And the answer is that what we observe should mean that the church has biblically based core values, such as those found in Acts 2:41–47, and biblically based beliefs that form the foundation for these values.

WHAT DIFFERENCE SHOULD IT MAKE?

The application question when discovering the culture of an established work is, What difference does it make? And the answer is that with few exceptions, it's not making much of a difference. Whereas the application question for shaping or forming the established work is, What difference should it make? God has chosen to use the church to spread the gospel of Christ throughout the world. And the answer to the question is that Christ's church should make all the difference in the world.

Having asked and answered these three shaping questions, next we move to the implementation question.

How to Implement the Culture

The answer to the implementation question is a process that all churches must work through if they are to be biblically based, spiritually strong cultures that are true to who they are (their identity), when they are (their time), and where they are (their location).

As the culture shaper works on unfreezing the status quo and moving to a new level, he also needs to be ready to answer the following questions that his people will surely pose.

- The mission questions: What is the new direction for this change? Where do you want to take us?
- The strategy question: How will we get there?
- The vision question: What will it look like when we do get there?

It's not enough for the change agent to say, "We need to change." People will want to know where they are going with this change and how they will get there, which consists of the following four steps. (Should you want more information on these steps or a process that takes you through them in more detail, see my book *Advanced Strategic Planning*).

SELECT THE STRATEGIC LEADERSHIP TEAM

In the section above, "Thaw Out the Current Culture," I advised the selection of a strategic leadership team. These people will be the primary ones who feel the pain, face the sixteen questions, and address crises and other potential opportunities for change. If you have not already selected this team, you need to do so as the first step in moving the thawed-out culture to the next level. The culture shaper will work primarily with and through these leaders because they will play a most critical role in moving the church through the transition to the new level.

DEVELOP A MISSION STATEMENT

The culture shaper will work with the SLT in developing a biblical mission statement for the church. According to Scripture, the church's mission is the Great Commission that involves making disciples (Matt. 28:19–20; Mark 16:15; Luke 24:46–48; Acts 1:8). Our experience at TMG is that most churches have a mission statement. However, they don't know or have forgotten what it is. Most often the unarticulated mission is to take care of people, especially the older saints. And the pastor's role is to be the chaplain or primary caregiver. But this is not Christ's mission for his church nor his role for pastors. So we work at developing a broad, brief, biblical mandate that provides the church with its ministry direction or what it's supposed to be doing. The mandate or will of God for the church according to Matthew 28:19 is "make disciples." Two of my favorite expressions of this mission are "To know Christ and make him known" and "To present Christ as Savior and to pursue Christ as Lord." Regardless of the mission statement, it's the pastor's role to see that the culture embraces Christ's mission.

DEVELOP A VISION STATEMENT

Next the change agent and the team will work together in developing a biblical vision statement for the church. Whereas most churches have some sort of mission statement, most don't have a clear, common (shared), passionate picture of God's future for their church as they believe it can and must be. This lack is a major contributor to a status-quo mentality. Earlier in this chapter, we discovered that our first focus should not be on "there"—the vision for the future—making it sound wonderful. Our focus now must be to make "here" sound awful.

If you have followed the process so far, you've done much to make "here" sound awful or painful, and people will be looking for pain relief. Now we're ready to make "there" sound wonderful. Both the mission and the vision provide the church with its "there" or its direction.

The purpose of the mission is to articulate the direction, while the purpose of the vision is to paint a picture of what that will look like. The vision is a picture of what could be that should not only instill hope for a future but should also excite people about moving toward that future. Thus the culture shaper and others must articulate, communicate, and implement a clear, compelling vision.

DISCOVER THE CORE VALUES

The culture may have already taken the step earlier (discussed in chapter 4) of discovering its core values. If not, the SLT will need to do this. As you recall, the church's core values explain what powerfully guides and directs the church. I like to compare them to the rudder and engine of a ship. The engine empowers or moves the ship forward toward its destination, and the rudder guides it so that it arrives at that destination. The problem is that just as the rudder and engine are below the waterline of the ship and not noticeable, so are the church's values. Thus a church will need to discover them if it wants to know what is driving it and where it is going. If you have already taken this step, use this as an opportunity to check up on the accuracy of your work. Review the values-discovery process and the results, and ask, Did we get it right?

In chapter 4 we looked at the Jerusalem Church's core values: evangelism (Acts 2:41, 47), biblical instruction (v. 42), fellowship (vv. 42, 44–46), worship (vv. 42–43, 46–47), and service (v. 45). These are strong, biblical core values that were driving this church. At TMG we ask churches to compare their values to these, because the Jerusalem Church was a biblically based, Spirit-led church. When a church does not embrace all of these, as is often the case (for example, many churches are not involved in evangelism and service), the missing values should become its stated aspirational values, which it seeks to turn into actual values over time.

DEVELOP A STRATEGY

Finally, the church must develop a strategy that will accomplish the mission and vision. The church's strategy consists of six items.

1. *Community outreach*. This involves the church in missional evangelism with a focus on reaching out to and being involved in the church's ministry community or its Jerusalem (Acts 1:8), as well as in international missions. In most cases the church's ministry community includes about a one-mile radius from the church's geographical location.
2. *Disciple making*. The goal is to develop a clear, simple, memorable pathway for making disciples. Everyone in the church should understand the process and know where they are along the pathway. Not only do I address disciple making in chapter 9 of *Advanced Strategic Planning*, but I have written an entire book on making mature disciples, *Strategic Disciple Making* (Baker, 2009).
3. *Congregational involvement*. The SLT develops a process for mobilizing its people and involving them in doing the ministry of the church rather than expecting or insisting that the pastor and/or staff do the ministry.
4. *Staffing*. We at TMG suggest that the church's ministry staff spend more time and focus on training leaders in their areas of expertise. For example, the staff person who is responsible for worship will develop worship leaders among those who work with him or her on a voluntary basis. Leadership is the hope of the church in the sense that everything rises or falls with leadership.
5. *Setting*. The team evaluates the facilities in terms of strategic location and functionality. Is the facility located in the best place to reach its community while ministering to its membership? Does the church have a plan or strategy for accommodating its people and providing parking should there be lots of growth over a short period of time? Looking at the facilities from a visitor's perspective, do they enhance the ministry or detract from it?
6. *Funding*. The culture shaper should stand out as a leader in directing the church's finances and take responsibility for determining the church's operational and ministry funding needs. He also must know how to

raise the necessary funds to accomplish the ministry and be involved in the process of fund-raising.

Accomplishing the strategy cannot be the responsibility of the ministry staff. This would simply overwhelm them, especially in a smaller church. Instead, we at TMG challenge churches to recruit lay implementation teams (ITs) that take responsibility for implementing the strategy. I'll say more about this in step 4.

Shaping an Established Culture

Step 1 Read the current culture.

Step 2 Thaw out the current culture.

Step 3 Transition the culture to a new level.

Step 4 Re-form the new culture at the new level.

Re-form the New Culture at the New Level

At this point in the process, the congregation in general and the strategic leadership team in particular should be somewhat discontent with the status quo and be working through the changes inaugurated in the third step, such as the development of a congregational mission, vision, and strategy. It's not necessary that they have completed all of them, but they should be well on their way.

The concern at this stage is twofold. First is how to preserve the gains of the first three steps so that the gains made won't fall through the cracks and be lost, while, second, not getting stuck or frozen at the new level. At this point the church might be compared to a stretched rubber band that could quickly and easily snap back to its former shape. The concern is to preserve the progress and yet maintain momentum without simply becoming frozen again in the new status quo, which is the problem with Lewin's refreezing at the new level. Using the earlier block-of-ice illustration, is there a way to avoid refreezing the water into the shape of a cone or a Popsicle as Lewin suggests? How do you avoid creating Popsicles? I believe there is a way, and it involves re-forming, or in this case forming a slushy or milkshake—choose your favorite—rather than a frozen Popsicle. Accomplishing this involves the concurrent use of the environmental scan and implementation teams. The purpose of the environmental scan is for leaders to stay current, not to fall behind the culture. The purpose for the involvement of the strategic leadership team is to make sure the culture perpetually implements the changes that were made in transitioning to the new level and renews itself rather than returns to its old ways.

The Environmental Scan

How does the culture shaper as a leader keep up with all the changes that are taking place in the world outside the church and the world of the church that could affect the church positively or negatively? This problem isn't new; the men of Issachar faced and responded to it in 1 Chronicles 12:32 where the writer says that they "understood the times and knew what Israel should do." The obvious question is, How do culture leaders understand their times so they know what's going on and what their church should do? The answer is to conduct regular environmental scans. The environmental scan focuses on two worlds. The first is the world outside the church, and the second is the world of the church.

THE WORLD OUTSIDE THE CHURCH

The world outside the church is the world you read about in the newspaper and online or hear about on the evening news. It comprises what is taking place locally, statewide, nationally, and internationally. Knowing this information serves to keep you current with the culture.

Study the Five Sectors

You will find it helpful to break the important information you encounter into at least five sectors: the social sector (lifestyle issues, people movements, crime, race, and so forth), the technological sector (computers, the internet), the economic sector (the economy, Social Security, taxes, employment, and so on), the political/legal sector (church and state issues, preferential tax treatment for churches, and other issues), and the philosophical sector that would include religion in general and churches in particular. These sectors may be viewed separately or together. For example, what is happening to the economy will affect the social sector, as well as others.

You will need to ask: What if anything is taking place in these sectors locally and around the world? What's making the news, and how will it affect people and the church's response to them? A poignant example is Hurricane Katrina, which has changed the entire way of life for many people in New Orleans, Louisiana. In addition, we must keep in mind that ultimately everything that happens reflects the sovereignty of God and that he's using these events to accomplish his will (1 Chron. 29:10–13).

Watch for Shifting Paradigms

In addition to recognizing that what is currently happening in the world is the future of that world, we must consider where it is all taking us. How might we anticipate the future? This involves our following and understanding of fads, trends, megatrends, and paradigms. Fads reflect short changes that exert little influence. Trends last longer and exert greater influence. More important are megatrends that last even longer and exert greater influence. The most important, however, are paradigms because they have the greatest impact.

A paradigm is a shared set of assumptions—about what people believe is the right way to do something, such as how we "do church." Like a pair of glasses, it's the way people view their world in general and their church in particular. As one old-timer said, "It's the way we do things around here!" Our various church models or cultures are themselves paradigms made up of various paradigms. For example, we have a worship paradigm, a pastoral performance paradigm, a preaching paradigm, a stewardship paradigm, a Sunday school paradigm, a small groups paradigm, and so forth. While not always evident, look for new megatrends in general and shifting paradigms in particular.

Recruit a Contemporary Culture Team

You may want to recruit a contemporary culture team whose job is to keep you and the leadership in general informed and up-to-date on culture. Ask this team to "scan and clip" various sources (newspapers, websites, the internet, magazines, and others) and be on the lookout for megatrends and paradigm shifts. When they find something they deem important, they are to copy or even clip the articles and save them. The culture team could meet monthly or quarterly for breakfast and narrow their findings down to what's most important and then pass this information on to the culture shaper.

THE WORLD OF THE CHURCH

The environmental scan must also focus on the world of the church. What churches out there are accomplishing their disciple-making mission and how are they doing it? What is taking place in the church world locally, statewide, nationally, and internationally? What can we learn from others about being the church and doing church well? What can we learn from them about what God is doing? The answer is to scan the church environment, which involves studying local, area, state, national, and international churches. Look for trends, megatrends, and paradigm shifts. Look in particular at newly planted churches, because they often represent what is new and happening at the "edges" of the church world.

To focus on the world of the church, you need to read voraciously. There is more information than ever before on churches, both in print and on the internet (websites in particular). One example is a book by Christian A. Schwarz, *Natural Church Development: A Guide to Eight Essential Qualities of Healthy*

Churches (Church Smart Resources, 1996). Basing his research on more than one thousand churches in thirty-two countries on five continents, Schwarz believes that growing, healthy churches exhibit eight characteristics: empowering leadership, gift-oriented ministry, passionate spirituality, functional structures, inspiring worship, holistic small groups, need-oriented evangelism, and loving relationships.

Through surfing church and parachurch websites, we can learn much about churches. They can provide us with a gold mine of information as to what God is doing in and through his churches. In addition, take time out of your busy schedule to attend some of the so-called stellar ministries around the country, arranging to visit with the pastors and members of the staff.

The information you gain through the environmental scan can be used by implementation teams to help you and your church make needed changes.

Implementation Teams

The milkshake or slushy is a figure for implementation. The culture shaper and the SLT need to form implementation teams (ITs) whose responsibility is to regularly update and implement the changes that were made and the new direction of the church. Those who make up the SLT would be part of and lead an implementation team that would also include members of the congregation. We at TMG recommend that you recruit ten teams: the lead implementation team, the intercessory prayer team, the congregational communication team, the community outreach team, the disciple-making team, the congregational mobilization team, the staffing team, the location and facilities team, the finance team, and a creativity and innovation team.

IMPLEMENTATION TEAM GOALS

With the aid of the change architect and possibly a consultant, each team would set goals that serve to help it put into practice in its area the new direction of the church. One of the most important goals will be to evaluate and update regularly its area of ministry. Consequently, the teams will never cease to function, even when they've accomplished a number of their ministry goals. They'll always be asking what I refer to as the "slushy question," How are we doing and what do we need to tweak or change to make this culture more effective? As noted above, the culture could include a creativity and innovation implementation team with the sole function of assisting the other ITs in remaining a soft slushy and not a frozen Popsicle. You will find an Implementation Team Worksheet in appendix N, an example of what this process looks like.

The key to all of this is the culture sculptor. He will need to be outspoken in his support of these teams and serve as their cheerleader, especially when the novelty wears off and implementation impediments surface.

A WARNING

Finally, as they work through the overall change process, change architects need to heed a warning. There will always be people (the late and never adopters) who will want to return to the "good old days," that is, the status quo. Whenever something goes wrong, and things will go wrong, they will say, "I told you so!" While the late adopters will come around eventually, the never adopters will not. Though not easy to do, the church may want to encourage these people to find a culture where they can be happy, if such a church exists.

The problem is, most leaders hate to see people leave the church. However, the truth is that someone will be leaving the church regardless of the situation. Would you rather have the never adopters leave or the movers and shakers, who will leave if the church remains in the status quo?

Questions for Reflection and Discussion

1. Is your church's worship attendance plateaued or in decline? Is the same true for its giving? If so, how might you use these truths to lead your culture to accept a new direction? Would these truths inflict some pain on your people? Is this good or bad? How might you use it for good?

2. How would your congregation respond to the sixteen questions? If your church is growing numerically and thus resistant to change, would the sixteen questions help get their attention and address reality? How might you use the sixteen questions with them in encouraging a new direction for your culture?

3. Is your church experiencing a crisis or has it experienced some crises recently? Identify it/them. How might you use this seeming difficulty to bring needed change to your culture?

4. If you are a pastor, are you thinking about leaving your church? Why? Have you been there longer than five to eight years? Could your thoughts be premature? Do you need to experience personal renewal? Do you regularly expose yourself to new paradigm ideas through books, tapes, and so on? Have you attended a good pastors' conference within the last year? What can you do right now to correct the problem you are encountering?

5. Has your church ever planted another church? Why not? Are these reasons valid or simply excuses not to change? (Most fall in the latter category—really!).

6. Have you or the church ever used the expertise of a consultant? Why or why not? How might a consultant be of help in your present situation? If you are in a denominational church, does the denomination offer consultation?

7. Have you ever worked with a coach or mentor? Why or why not? Do you have people around you who are encouragers? If not, how can you draw some encouragers into your inner circle?

8. Have you and your board ever attended a cutting-edge pastors' conference together? Why not? What would it take for this to happen? How might you encourage your board to accompany you? Would it be worth going even if all the board cannot attend? Would it be worth your time if only one or two board members caught your vision?

9. Is your church in a serious decline? Is death fairly certain? Would it be wise for you to lead the church to close and use this as an opportunity to bring new life out of the old situation? What is stopping you?

10. Have you formed a strategic leadership team? If not, why not? Do you see the wisdom in working through such a team of leaders? Why or why not? Who in your church should be on this team?

11. Do you have a strategic process to help guide your church through the culture change process? What are your mission and vision? What are your driving and guiding core values? What is your strategy for accomplishing your mission and vision?

12. Do you believe that the environmental scan would help not only to keep you current but to look to the future? Why or why not? Would it be wise to recruit implementation teams to help keep plans and goals from falling through the cracks? Why or why not?

13

The Church Pastor as Culture Blender

Adopting Established Church Cultures

The primary objective of this book is to shape or form cultures that honor Christ and spread the gospel. One way to accomplish this is to plant a new culture (chapter 9). Another is to revitalize a struggling established church (chapters 10–12). A third possibility that's begun to receive some notice of late is merging two or more cultures together to form a new culture. This chapter addresses this third option with seven questions: What is the state of the American church? What are some options for the church? What is the thinking behind a merger? Do church mergers work? Why don't mergers work? Is there a way to make them work? What is the future for church mergers?

The State of the American Church

Every year the president gives the State of the Union address. The purpose is to answer the question, How are we as a nation doing? In the same way we should address the state of the American church. How is it doing? As mentioned above and throughout this work, the church in America is struggling. But what does this mean? Let's look at some significant telltale signs of this struggle.

1. *The number of unchurched people is growing.* Depending on whom you read, the number of churched people in the United States is somewhere

between 17 and 40 percent, whereas twenty years ago it was between 50 to 60 percent. Thus an increasingly large percentage of America is anywhere but in church on Sunday morning. This is sobering, especially when you realize that many of those who are unchurched are young people—the future of the church.

2. *The number of cults and other religions is growing.* While Christianity is declining, certain cults (Jehovah's Witnesses and Mormons in particular) are growing, along with other religious groups, such as Muslims, Buddhists, Hindus, and Wiccans. Some have argued that people today simply aren't interested in spiritual matters, but the reality is that many are interested but are seeking alternatives to the Christian church.

3. *Approximately 80 to 85 percent of churches are plateaued or in decline.* These churches that are plateaued or in decline would be classified as immature and unhealthy on the culture continuum. For this chapter the most important fact to note about the state of the church is that most of these plateaued churches are small. The majority, as many as 80 percent of them, have no more than two hundred people. They are stuck at what church growth research refers to as the "two hundred barrier."

Some Options for the Church

When a small church is plateaued or in decline, there are a limited number of options they can consider for their survival.

A Revitalization

One option is for the declining church to pursue revitalization. The pastor could read a book or even take a course on church renewal and then attempt to apply the principles to his struggling culture. A better option would be to bring in an outside ministry that specializes in turning church cultures around, such as my ministry (The Malphurs Group). The advantage is we've been down this road many times and know where all the cultural "road bumps" are. Also congregants trust people who are from the outside, who aren't involved in their church's politics. In general, the success of a potential turnaround is deeply impacted by the depth of decline or decay and how long the culture has been in decline.

A Funeral

If the group has been in deep decline for an extended period of time, it should entertain a second option—the "last rites." While this may sound simple, it's anything but. Many church people, especially older ones, react emotionally, not logically, to such a step. They will likely resist these efforts. So don't be surprised when they do. The key here is to prepare them for the death of their culture. Regardless of the resistance, at some point the church will die through attrition, and the pastor will need to treat these individuals as grieving relatives and help them work through the grief process.

A Merger

A third option is to merge churches. Since the majority of churches in America are small cultures, merging some of them is a good solution to the problem of decline.

I define *church merger* as *two or more congregations attempting to blend together to form one larger, legal entity*. Thus a merger has to involve at least two churches; it could include three or even more. They blend by meeting together, sharing the same facilities, and participating in the same programs. They also may incorporate and adopt a constitution and bylaws. On the surface, the concept sounds great, but underneath the surface, it's fraught with problems.

The Thinking behind a Church Merger

Here's the thinking behind church mergers. Currently the majority of churches in America are small, struggling churches. Rather than let them struggle and die, two, three, or more of them could be blended together, forming one larger church. It is assumed that a single, larger church could better address the problems that many of the smaller churches face separately. There would be several benefits of such a culture blend.

> *Hope.* The aging congregants hope against hope that somehow a new, merged church will make it. And talk of a merger, whether it actually happens, supplies that hope. People can hope that the church body will survive and continue to live and breathe on its own.
>
> *More cash.* Another benefit when two or more churches merge is that there is more cash available to pay the bills, repair the roof, pay the pastor a full-time wage, and so forth. The thinking is that two or more can pay the bills better than one.
>
> *"Fresh hands."* One characteristic of most of these smaller churches is the 20-80 principle. Translated this means that 20 percent of the people

SHAPING CONGREGATIONAL CULTURE

(sometimes even less) are doing 80 percent of the ministry. More people working together means they could do more ministry. (The problem with this reasoning is that it's a non sequitur argument. More people doesn't automatically mean more ministry.)

Stronger leadership. Another benefit could be stronger leadership. A merged or larger church could provide the funds to call a full-time pastor and pay him a decent salary. And if things really go well, the church might be able to recruit a youth pastor.

A place to meet. Finally, in some situations these small cultures are without a facility. They may be failing church plants that quickly plateaued before they became large enough to pursue and purchase facilities. Thus a merger could bring together a church without facilities with one that has them.

Do Church Mergers Work?

On the surface, the merger scenario sounds like a wonderful win-win solution. According to some research, around 2 percent of American Protestant churches have participated in a merger in the last two years. And should you peek below the surface, you would probably find that blending smaller struggling churches often results in one larger struggling church, not necessarily a spiritually healthy church.

A typical example is an older Evangelical Free Church in the Dallas–Ft. Worth Metroplex that merged with a younger, independent Bible church. The older people of the smaller church brought to the merger their property, facility, and traditional church culture. The younger group—a failed church plant—was larger and brought with them a more contemporary church culture. However, both were in serious numerical decline. The newly merged culture, though larger in size, lasted another year and then closed its doors. Unfortunately this is the autobiography of many small American church mergers. But that raises the question, Why didn't it work?

Why Church Mergers Don't Work

There are numerous reasons that culture blending doesn't work. Here are three.

1. *A survival mentality*. For most churches the primary motivation for a merger is survival—to keep the doors open and thus maintain the status

quo. This rarely if ever works. The key motivation must be mission- or vision-driven, and that mission or vision focuses on the Great Commission, which involves revival not survival.

2. *Non-turnaround leadership.* The newly blended church may keep one of the two pastors of the previous two declining churches, but if he continues to do what he did that resulted in decline in the first place, the merger will not work. Some churches attempt a co-pastorate, with the pastors of the churches attempting to work together to colead the church. This simply doesn't work. No one is quite sure who's in charge and who does what. And people's loyalties remain with "my pastor." The merged churches would be wise to bring in a visionary from the outside who has the gifts of leadership, evangelism, and good preaching. If this isn't an option, then they should choose the pastor who is closest to this ideal and is willing to pursue the kind of training that will help him close the gap between where he is and where he needs to be to lead and revitalize the culture.

3. *Disparate cultures.* A third problem arises from attempting to blend two disparate cultures. It's imperative that a merger be viewed from a cultural perspective. The groups in the example above attempted to unite two cultures that had little in common. There was no alignment between their beliefs and values. It was doomed from the start, but they didn't know it. It sounded like a great idea and the answer to their prayers. The fact is, the majority of mergers don't work, and the churches eventually close their doors, which may not be bad if it frees people up to find and be involved in a healthier church culture.

Making Church Mergers Work

Some mergers do work. Some churches have certain assets that make a successful merger more likely. Here are five that are important.

1. *A revival mentality.* One essential characteristic is merging for the right reasons. For too many the one primary reason is survival. The legitimate reason is a biblical mission and vision that leads to revival, not just survival.

2. *Turnaround leadership.* The ministry rises or falls with leadership. The pastor must be more than a chaplain or "hired hand" who by himself attempts to do the ministry for the people. Most likely he'll be a younger person—possibly a recent graduate from seminary—with

little experience. Regardless, he could be a turnaround pastor who is a gifted leader with a clear, challenging vision. If not, look for a pastor who is.

3. *Similar cultures.* Read or exegete the cultures of both the churches (chapter 7) involved and the pastors (chapter 8) to determine how culturally diverse or similar they are. Here's the principle: the more two congregations share the same culture, the greater the likelihood that a merger will work. The less culture they share, the greater the likelihood of failure.

4. *Adopt, don't merge.* Another better solution is a church adoption where a healthy church blends with a smaller, struggling church. The latter joins the former with few if any concessions; they simply attempt to cooperate and blend in. Of the various approaches to accomplishing a merger, adoption has proved to be the most successful.

5. *Look for a merger-to-multisite opportunity.* An adoption that is part of the multisite movement has a good opportunity for success. This is a merger-to-multisite strategy that seems to be infusing struggling churches with new life. The way it works is a multisite church adopts a declining or dying church as one of its sites. Often it includes an infusion of cash and energy that result in a fresh, new vision for the struggling church and succeeds in impacting the neighboring communities for Christ.

An example is Fort McKinley United Methodist Church located in Dayton, Ohio. Fort McKinley was a one-hundred-year-old church that had declined to forty attenders. Then God spoke to them and another Methodist church—Ginghamsburg Church—about a merger. (The latter is a healthy, thriving United Methodist congregation located just north of Dayton.) They merged with the understanding that Fort McKinley would be one of the sites of the Ginghamsburg Church, and today Fort McKinley has become a vibrant church of four hundred congregants who are serving three to four hundred people per month who live in its at-risk community.

Another example is Church of the Resurrection in Leawood, Kansas, a suburb of Kansas City. They merged with Grand Avenue Temple, a 145-year-old church, with a facility that had been turned over to a ministry for the homeless. Along with a multisite approach, Church of the Resurrection infused Grand Avenue Temple with capital funds, new energy, and fresh hands to get the ministry done. The new church merger—Resurrection Downtown—is now averaging 240 attenders per week who are active in evangelism, worship, and a developing small group ministry.

The Future for Church Mergers

In the next two years, 8 percent of churches will consider a merger. If you combine the number of Protestant churches that have blended in the last two years with these, the two groups represent as many as thirty thousand churches in America. (It's interesting that we see similar trends in other parts of the world, such as Europe and Australia, which indicates it may indeed be a movement.)

However, the future for merging two or three small, struggling churches is bleak, so bleak that I would not recommend they even attempt it. Yet the prospects for success increase significantly when a healthy church intentionally adopts or absorbs a smaller church and even more so when a multisite church is the adopter. In fact, I view the latter as playing a most important role in a new movement of God toward producing healthy churches all across America. America isn't lacking for churches with facilities. What is lacking is spiritually healthy churches with facilities. But God appears to be using church adoptions and the multisite-merger movement to breathe new life into many of these churches that have given up on ministry in and to their at-risk communities.

Questions for Reflection and Discussion

1. How many churches in your community would you estimate are small and struggling? How many have closed or are in the process of closing their doors? (If you don't know, see if you can find the answers.)
2. How many churches in your community have attempted a merger? If so, did it work? Why or why not?
3. Are you aware of any larger churches in your area that have adopted a smaller, struggling church? If so, identify them. Is the adoption working? Why or why not?
4. Is there any good reason why the larger, healthy churches in your community or denomination shouldn't attempt to adopt struggling churches? Could this start a movement that will spiritually revitalize your community and others for Christ?
5. What might hinder a successful multisite merger? What might stop you from attempting such a merger whether you're the adopting church or the adoptee church?
6. Do you believe that God could be using the multisite-to-merger approach as a movement to see numerous cultures revitalized so as to reach rather than give up on their communities? If so, what will you do about it?

APPENDIXES

Appendix A

Behaviors Audit

Directions: Circle the response that best describes what a visitor to your church might see.

1. Neighborhood or community

   Is the neighborhood new, old, or in between?
   - Is the church located in an urban, suburban, or rural area?
   - Does it consist of apartments, houses, businesses, or a combination?
   - Are the people who live in the community Anglo, Hispanic, Black, Asian, other, or a combination (multiethnic)?
   - Are the people in the community of the same ethnicity as those who attend the church or are they different?
   - Does the neighborhood seem to be declining or growing in numbers?
   - Do you feel safe?
   - Do the neighbors appear to be at home on Sundays (unchurched)?
   - Are there any signs that the community is interested in spiritual matters?
   - Do the church's attenders park on the street in the neighborhood or on the church parking lot?

   COMMENTS: _____

   _____

2. Demographics
   - Is the congregation made up of Anglos, Blacks, Hispanics, Asian, other, or a combination (multiethnic)?

- Are the people poor, affluent, or somewhere between?
- Does the congregation appear to be undergoing some kind of transition?
- What is the congregation's collar color: white collar, blue collar, a combination?
- Are people mostly young, middle-aged, or elderly?
- Are there young families with kids?
- Does the congregation's observed demographics align or not align with the neighborhood's demographics?

COMMENTS: _____

_____

3. Language
- What do you hear?
- What languages do people speak: English, Spanish, other?
- Is the church mono- or multilingual?
- Do people speak "temple talk" or "churchese"?
- Do you understand what's being said?
- What languages are spoken as part of the service?
- Are there translators or translation available?
- Is one language spoken predominately?

COMMENTS: _____

_____

4. Facilities
- Do the facilities include educational space, a worship center or sanctuary, offices, other?
- Is the style of architecture unique or common?
- Does the facility "look" like a church?
- Do the buildings have "drive-by appeal"?
- Are the facilities clean and well maintained, especially the nursery, the bathrooms, and the kitchen?
- Are the facilities clean and well maintained but don't look their best due to age?
- Are the facilities safe? For example, is there any exposed electrical wiring? Are there any steps that need to be repaired?
- During worship do people sit in pews, chairs, or both?
- Does the church have adequate seating for all attenders?
- Is any paint peeling off the facilities?
- Are there areas that need paint?

- Is there a lot of clutter?

COMMENTS: _____

_____

5. Parking
   - Is there plenty of available parking?
   - Does the church provide visitor and handicapped parking?
   - Is there special parking for the elderly and expectant moms?
   - Are parking places reserved for the pastor and staff and their spouses?
   - Are security or police vehicles present?
   - Do people park out on neighborhood streets?
   - If people park out in the neighborhood, does this appear to be a problem?

COMMENTS: _____

_____

6. Grounds
   - Are the grounds clean and well kept (clear of trash)?
   - Is the lawn mowed and edged in the summer and leaves raked in the fall?
   - Are the grounds attractive, with adequate grass, bushes, and flowers?

COMMENTS: _____

_____

7. Signage
   - Is there signage at the entryway to announce where to turn in to the church?
   - Is there adequate signage so that visitors know where to park?
   - Is there signage that tells visitors where to go to find information about the church?
   - Is there signage for the bathrooms, nursery, auditorium, and classes?

COMMENTS: _____

_____

8. Attendants
   - Are there friendly, helpful attendants located in the parking lots to direct people where to park their cars?
   - Are there attendants to direct visitors where to get help in finding their way around the facilities?

- Are there people available to direct visitors to the nursery or Sunday school classes?
- Are all of these people present in inclement weather?

COMMENTS: _____

_____

9. Vehicles
- Are the vehicles people drive new, old, or somewhere between?
- Are they expensive, inexpensive, or in between?
- Do they appear to be well maintained or not?
- Are there any trucks?
- Does the church use any church vehicles, such as a church van or bus?

COMMENTS: _____

_____

10. Clothing
- Are people wearing casual dress, business casual, or business formal?
- Are they stylish, wearing the latest styles?
- Is there a particular style of clothing (for example, Texas has a growing number of cowboy churches where most people wear blue jeans, cowboy hats, and cowboy boots)?
- Is there a particular style of clothing that reflects a certain ethnicity?
- Do clergy wear special clothing (robes or vestments) or do they dress like those in attendance?

COMMENTS: _____

_____

11. Friendliness
- Are people friendly? For example, do they greet you?
- Do people answer your questions and offer to help visitors find their way around the church?
- Are people friendly to one another?
- Do people seem to care about one another?

COMMENTS: _____

_____

12. Emotions
- Do people show their emotions? For example, are they emotionally expressive during worship time (wave their hands) or unemotional (pocket their hands)?
- Do people sometimes respond to a sermon with tears?

COMMENTS: _____

_____

13. Security
    • Are there police or security people in the parking lots, patrolling the facilities, present during the offering, and available at other times?
    • Are there security cameras?
    • Are the facility and grounds well lighted?
    • Do people seem to feel safe visiting this church night or day?
    • Do women feel safe—especially at night?

COMMENTS: _____

_____

14. Manner of address
    • Do people call one another by their first names?
    • Do people use titles, such as Mr., Brother, Mrs., Miss, Sister, and so on?
    • How do people address the pastor? Do they use Pastor, Rev., Dr., or Rev. Dr., or do they use his first name?

COMMENTS: _____

_____

15. Technology
    • Is the church technologically astute? Is it high-tech or low-tech?
    • Does it have front- or rear-screen projection?
    • Does the church use their projection for announcements, teaching, other?
    • Is there a soundboard?
    • Is there a sound booth?
    • Do they show film clips during the sermon?
    • Does the church have a website?
    • Do people have and use iPads or other electronic devices during the service?

COMMENTS: _____

_____

16. Communication
    • How does the church communicate with people? (Does it use bulletins, make announcements, email, send U.S. Postal Service, or other?)
    • Does it seem to communicate well or poorly?

COMMENTS: _____

_____

BEHAVIORS AUDIT

17. Ordinances
    • Does the church practice the ordinances (baptism and the Lord's Supper)?
    • How often are they observed (weekly, monthly, quarterly, annually)?
    • Does the church immerse or sprinkle when they baptize people?
    • Do they use wine or grape juice, cracker or matzo for communion?
    • Do they observe foot washing as an ordinance?

    COMMENTS: _____

18. Symbols
    • Does the worship area or sanctuary contain symbols, such as the cross, a religious tapestry, stained-glass windows, an ixthus, a baptistery, an altar, or none of these?

    COMMENTS: _____

19. Worship
    • Is the church's worship style traditional, classical (liturgical), or contemporary? Is there any liturgy?
    • What types of instruments, if any, are used in worship (organ, piano, guitars, drums, other)?
    • Is there a choir?
    • Does the choir consist mostly of men or women or both?
    • Is there a worship leader?
    • Do people worship by, for example, raising hands, weeping, swaying, dancing, or other?
    • Does the church sing from hymnals, words projected on a screen, or both?
    • Does worship attendance appear to be growing, plateaued, or declining?
    • Are people joining the church?

    COMMENTS: _____

20. Disciple-making ministries
    • Does the church have and communicate a clear, simple pathway for making disciples?
    • Does the church communicate well its primary ministries (worship/ preaching event, Sunday school, small groups)?

- Does the church communicate well that its secondary ministries (men and women's Bible studies, choir, and so forth) are important to its disciple-making process?
- Do you know what they are?
- Has the church identified and communicated well the characteristics of a mature disciple(they worship, study, and apply the Bible; fellowship with other Christians; do evangelism; and serve within or outside the church)?
- Does it have a nursery?
- Does it minister to toddlers?

COMMENTS: _____

_____

21. Outreach ministries
- Does the church have and make known its community outreach ministries?
- Do they advertise them well?
- Does the church reach out to poor and oppressed people in or outside its community?
- Does the church do evangelism projects in the neighborhood?
- Does the church minister outside its facilities as much as inside?

COMMENTS: _____

_____

22. Missions
- Does the church support in some way international missions?
- Does it support in some way local missions?

COMMENTS: _____

_____

23. Scripture
- Does the church teach and preach from the Bible?
- Do people carry their Bibles to church, classes, and small group meetings?
- Are the Scriptures projected on a screen during the worship service?

COMMENTS: _____

_____

24. Discipline
- Have you ever observed someone being disciplined?
- Have you ever heard of someone being disciplined?

COMMENTS: _____

_____

25. Visible behavior
   • Do people seem to manifest the fruit of the Spirit as found in Galatians 5:22–23 (love, joy, peace, patience, kindness, goodness, faithfulness, gentleness, and self-control)?
   • Do the majority of people appear to be spiritually mature?
   • Do people appear to be happy and excited?
   • Do the young people seem bored or excited about church?

   COMMENTS: _____

   _____

26. Vision
   • Does the church appear to have and communicate a vision?
   • Is the vision clear and understandable?
   • Is it compelling?
   • Is it written down anywhere?
   • Do you hear it regularly from the pastor or clergyperson when preaching?
   • Do you overhear people talking about it?
   • Do people appear to be in favor of the vision?

   COMMENTS: _____

   _____

27. Values
   • Has the church identified and does it communicate well its values?
   • Has it done the same for its core values?
   • Are they written down somewhere?
   • Does someone, such as the pastor, articulate them or preach on them at least annually?
   • Some churches even mount them on the walls of their sanctuary so people will see and remember them—are they on the wall of this church?
   • Based on what you observe, do you think you know the church's core values?

   COMMENTS: _____

   _____

28. Atmosphere
    - Do you sense that the church is warm and welcoming, cold and aloof, or somewhere in between?
    - Does the church appear to be fast- or slow-paced?
    - Do you feel excitement in the air?
    - Do you ever feel tension in the air?
    - Is there obvious conflict?

    COMMENTS: _____

29. Ceremonies
    - Does the church have baby dedications, infant baptisms, and ordination services?
    - Does it observe and celebrate certain holidays, such as Easter, Christmas, Lent, and others?

    COMMENTS: _____

30. Women
    - Does the church appear to have more women attending than men?
    - Are women involved in some way in worship?
    - Do they ever preach and teach?
    - Do they ever usher?
    - Do they serve communion or baptize people?
    - Do they seem to minister mostly to children?

    COMMENTS: _____

31. Myths and stories
    - Is there any particular person or persons that the church tells stories about? Who are its heroes?
    - Is one of its heroes the pastor or a former pastor, such as the founding pastor?
    - Does the church talk about villains, such as Satan, the Antichrist, atheists, and others?
    - Does the church make heroes of some of its missionaries or longtime members?

    COMMENTS: _____

32. Visitors
    - Does the church seem prepared for visitors?
    - Do they appear to care about visitors?
    - Do they have parking reserved for visitors?
    - Is there a welcome center that provides information about the church?
    - Is it manned by friendly people who can take visitors to where they need to go (classrooms, worship center, nursery, and so on)?
    - Does the church follow up visitors with a phone call and/or letter?

    COMMENTS: _____

    _____

33. Senior pastor
    - Is the senior pastor friendly and relational?
    - Is the pastor a good preacher?
    - Is the pastor a good leader?
    - Does the pastor's dress tell you about his style of leadership (formal, informal, and so on)?
    - Do you like him?
    - Do others appear to like him?
    - Do you sense that there may be others who lead or try to lead the church, such as a board person, a family, several families?
    - Is the church without a senior pastor?

    COMMENTS: _____

    _____

34. Staff
    - Does the church have any staff persons (paid ministry people other than the senior pastor) who lead ministries?
    - What ministries are they responsible for: youth, children, adults, women's/men's ministries, other?
    - Do the ministries of the church tell you what the church thinks is or isn't important?
    - Do people like the staff?

    COMMENTS: _____

    _____

35. Doctrinal beliefs
    - Does the church have doctrinal beliefs based on the Scriptures? Does it communicate these beliefs?

- Do the pastor and other teachers teach and preach regularly the church's doctrinal beliefs from the Bible?

COMMENTS: _____

_____

36. Leadership development
    - Have you heard if the church has a churchwide leader-development process for developing leaders?
    - Have you heard if the church develops its small group leaders?

COMMENTS: _____

_____

37. Finances
    - Does the church appear to be struggling financially?
    - Does the church appear to be doing well financially?
    - Does the church say little about its finances?
    - Does the church inform people of its finances in the bulletin, on the website, and in other visible places, such as a bulletin board?

COMMENTS: _____

_____

38. Politics
    - Have you heard if the church promotes certain political parties?
    - Have you heard if the church endorses certain people for political offices?
    - Is the church strongly affiliated with a particular denomination, as reflected in its name?
    - Have you heard if the church speaks out on what some would call political issues (abortion, homosexuality, and so forth)?

Appendix B

Core Values Audit

Directions: Using the scale below, circle the number that best expresses the importance of the following values to your church (actual values). Work your way through the list quickly, going with your first impression.

1 = not important
2 = somewhat important
3 = important
4 = most important

	1	2	3	4
1. **Family:** The relationships between husbands and wives and their children.	1	2	3	4
2. **Biblical instruction**: A familiarity with and desire to know the truths of Scripture.	1	2	3	4
3. **World missions**: Spreading the gospel of Christ around the globe.	1	2	3	4
4. **Encouragement**: Giving hope to people who at times need some hope.	1	2	3	4
5. **Giving**: Providing a portion of one's finances to support the ministry.	1	2	3	4
6. **Fellowship**: Relating to and spending time with others, primarily within the church.	1	2	3	4
7. **Leadership**: A person's ability to influence others to pursue God's mission for the church.	1	2	3	4
8. **Cultural relevance**: Communicating truth in a way that people who aren't like us understand.	1	2	3	4
9. **Prayer**: Communicating with God.	1	2	3	4

10. **Excellence**: Maintaining the highest of ministry standards that bring glory to God.	1	2	3	4
11. **Evangelism**: Telling others the good news about Christ.	1	2	3	4
12. **Team ministry**: A group of people ministering together.	1	2	3	4
13. **Creativity**: Coming up with new ideas and ways of doing ministry.	1	2	3	4
14. **Worship**: Attributing worth to God.	1	2	3	4
15. **Cooperation**: The act of working together in the service of the Savior.	1	2	3	4
16. **Ministry/service**: Christians actively involved and serving in the ministries of the church (a mobilized congregation).	1	2	3	4
17. **Obedience**: A willingness to do what God or others ask of a person.	1	2	3	4
18. **Innovation**: Making changes that promote the ministry as it serves Christ.	1	2	3	4
19. **Initiative**: The willingness to take the first step or make the first move in a ministry situation.	1	2	3	4
20. **Community**: The desire to reach out to the people who live within driving distance of the church (your Jerusalem).	1	2	3	4
21. **Other values**:	1	2	3	4

Note all the values that you rated with a 4. Rank these according to priority. The first four to six values are your core values as an organization. The rest, including some of the values you rated as a 3, will make up your organizational culture.

Appendix C

Core Values Statements

Jerusalem Church

Jerusalem, Israel

- We value Bible doctrine (Acts 2:42–43).
- We value fellowship (Acts 2:42, 44–46).
- We value praise and worship (Acts 2:42, 47).
- We value evangelism (Acts 2:40–41, 47).

Northwood Community Church

Dallas, Texas

The following presents the core values of Northwood Community Church. We desire that they define and drive this ministry in the context of a warm and caring environment.

CHRIST'S HEADSHIP

We acknowledge Christ as the Head of our church and submit ourselves and all our activities to His will and good pleasure (Eph. 1:22–23).

BIBLICAL TEACHING

We strive to teach God's Word with integrity and authority so that seekers find Christ and believers mature in Him (2 Tim. 3:16).

Authentic Worship

We desire to acknowledge God's supreme value and worth in our personal lives and in the corporate, contemporary worship of our church (Rom. 12:1–2).

Sense of Community

We ask all our people to commit to and fully participate in biblically functioning small groups where they may reach the lost, exercise their gifts, be shepherded, and thus grow in Christlikeness (Acts 2:44–46).

Family

We support the spiritual nurture of the family as one of God's dynamic means to perpetuate the Christian faith (2 Tim. 1:5).

Grace-Orientation

We encourage our people to serve Christ from hearts of love and gratitude rather than guilt and condemnation (Rom. 6:14).

Creativity and Innovation

We will constantly evaluate our forms and methods, seeking cultural relevance and maximum ministry effectiveness for Christ (1 Chron. 12:32).

Mobilized Congregation

We seek to equip all our uniquely designed and gifted people to effectively accomplish the work of our ministry (Eph. 4:11–13).*

Lost People

We value unchurched, lost people and will use every available Christ-honoring means to pursue, win, and disciple them (Luke 19:10).*

---

* These are aspirational values. While they are not yet our values, we are working hard at making them our core values.

Appendix D

Beliefs Audit

irections: This is an exercise to help you discover some but not all of your core church beliefs or assumptions. Which beliefs listed below are your church's beliefs? Place a check by the statement that most closely summarizes them in each area. There is a space for you to add information and make any comments you deem appropriate.

1. What is the nature of reality? What is real?
   - ☐ The church believes in a natural or material world and a spiritual world (angels, demons, the devil, and so on).
   - ☐ The church believes only in a natural world, not a spiritual world.
   - ☐ Other:

   COMMENT: _____

   _____

2. What is the nature of truth?
   - ☐ The church believes that truth is what works (pragmatism)—what consistently solves their problems.
   - ☐ The church believes that all truth is God's truth, and God has revealed his truth to man in the Bible (special revelation) and in nature (natural revelation).
   - ☐ The church holds to both beliefs above, though they appear inconsistent.
   - ☐ Other:

   COMMENT: _____

3. What is the nature of the church (the definition of the church)?
   - ☐ The church is the body of professing believers in Christ, who is the hope of the world.
   - ☐ The church is primarily a family made up of families. In some cases, people are actually blood relatives or family by marriage.
   - ☐ The church is an organization that provides certain services for people.
   - ☐ Other:

   COMMENT: _____

4. What is the purpose of the church? Why is the church on earth?
   - ☐ The church believes its purpose is to glorify God, which involves upholding his excellent reputation in the church's community, where the church conducts much of its ministry.
   - ☐ The church believes that it's here primarily to take care of its people, especially its elderly members.
   - ☐ The church believes that it exists to support certain social causes, such as women's rights, gay rights, world peace, minority rights, providing for the poor, feeding the hungry.
   - ☐ Other:

   COMMENT: _____

5. What is the mission of the church? What is it supposed to be doing?
   - ☐ The church believes its mission is primarily to make disciples, which involves both evangelism and edification.
   - ☐ The church believes its mission is primarily to take care of people.
   - ☐ The church believes it's here to make a better world for as many people as possible.
   - ☐ Other:

   COMMENT: _____

6. What is the church's view of a vision?
   - ☐ The church believes that today's emphasis on vision is overdone.
   - ☐ The church believes that casting a clear, compelling vision is vital to its future.
   - ☐ The church believes that vision isn't very important to its future.
   - ☐ Other:

COMMENT: _____

_____

7. What are the church's theological beliefs (the church's doctrine, traditions, and so on)?
   - ☐ The church holds to the orthodox interpretation of the faith. This includes the inspiration of the Bible, the Trinity, the virgin birth, deity of Christ, substitutionary atonement, the bodily resurrection and physical return of Christ.
   - ☐ The church is fairly open on what it believes, combining biblical teaching with church traditions.
   - ☐ The church holds to long-standing traditions, not biblical teaching.
   - ☐ The church has very few beliefs. People of all faiths and beliefs are welcome.
   - ☐ Other:

   COMMENT: _____

   _____

8. What is the church's view of salvation?
   - ☐ The church believes that, because all people are sinners, they need to be saved through faith in Christ alone as their Savior.
   - ☐ The church believes that all people are sinners and that faith in Christ helps but that one's individual good works are most important and play a role in one's salvation.
   - ☐ The church believes that people are basically good and will do good and don't need a Savior.
   - ☐ Other:

   COMMENT: _____

   _____

9. What is the church's view toward sign gifts, such as speaking in tongues, prophecy, and healing?
   - ☐ The church believes that these gifts were primarily for the first-century church and have since ceased.
   - ☐ The church believes that these gifts are for today and should be regularly practiced, especially during the church's worship times.
   - ☐ The church believes that these gifts may be available for today but doesn't practice them during services.
   - ☐ Other:

   COMMENT: _____

   _____

10. What is the role of the pastor of the church?
    - ☐ The church believes that the pastor and any ministry staff are to equip the people who, in turn, do the ministry of the church.
    - ☐ The church believes that the pastor functions as a chaplain who is at the church to do the ministry (marry, bury, counsel, visit, preach, and so on). The people do not do these ministries.
    - ☐ Other:

    COMMENT: _____

    _____

11. What is the role of the congregation?
    - ☐ The church believes that the congregation is to lead and do the ministry.
    - ☐ The church believes that the congregation is responsible to be in church every Sunday and to support the church with its tithes and offerings.
    - ☐ The church believes that its people should not be involved in the ministry as that is the domain of the pastor and any staff.
    - ☐ Other:

    COMMENT: _____

    _____

12. What role should women play in the church?
    - ☐ The church believes that a woman can do anything that a man can do, which includes preaching, teaching, and leading.
    - ☐ The church believes that a woman's role in the church is limited in that she is not to preach or teach, especially when men are present.
    - ☐ Other:

    COMMENT: _____

    _____

13. How does the church view worship?
    - ☐ The church believes that Christ-honoring worship should take place in a liturgical context.
    - ☐ The church believes that Christ-honoring worship should take place in a traditional context, with such instruments as an organ and possibly a piano.
    - ☐ The church believes that Christ-honoring worship can take place in a number of different contexts but emphasizes a more contemporary approach.

☐ Other:

COMMENT: _____

_____

14. How does the church view Christian community or fellowship?
    ☐ The church believes that Christians should spend some time together, possibly in small groups, ministering to one another and encouraging one another in the faith.
    ☐ The church believes that the Christian's fellowship needs can best be met by providing coffee and donuts before the worship time.
    ☐ The church believes that the Christian's need for fellowship will take care of itself and doesn't need to be addressed by the church.
    ☐ Other:

COMMENT: _____

_____

15. How does the church view biblical instruction?
    ☐ The church believes that, if people are to grow in their faith, they must receive regular instruction from the Scriptures when the church meets.
    ☐ The church believes that most Christians will meet their needs for biblical instruction on their own time and not during church.
    ☐ The church believes that Bible study isn't important.
    ☐ Other:

COMMENT: _____

_____

16. How does the church view evangelism?
    ☐ The church believes that evangelism is vital to the Great Commission; thus it provides instruction in evangelism for its people on a regular basis.
    ☐ The church believes that evangelism will happen on its own.
    ☐ The church believes that evangelism is akin to proselytizing and should be avoided.
    ☐ Other:

COMMENT: _____

_____

17. How does the church view small group ministries?
    ☐ The church knows little about small group ministries.

☐ The church values small group ministries and encourages all of its people to be part of a small group.

☐ The church has some small group ministries but doesn't encourage them.

☐ Other:

COMMENT: _____

18. How does the church view time?

☐ The church believes that its past was better than the present and primarily lives in the past.

☐ The church believes that the present is more important than its past and attempts to live in the present.

☐ The church has a clear, compelling vision for the future.

☐ Other:

COMMENT: _____

19. How does the church view space?

☐ The congregation believes that they have the right to a certain amount of personal space, as evidenced by their unwillingness to sit close to people they don't know in the worship service.

☐ While the church doesn't believe in reserved seating, people prefer to sit in the same seats every Sunday.

☐ Other:

COMMENT: _____

20. How does the church view change and innovation?

☐ The church is most comfortable with the status quo and turns a deaf ear to change and innovation.

☐ The church is most comfortable with the status quo but realizes that change and innovation are important to its survival.

☐ The church is attempting to change and innovate so as to be more relevant to the world outside the church.

☐ Other:

COMMENT: _____

21. How does the church view technology?

☐ The church is not comfortable with technology and uses it sparingly.

☐ The church is most comfortable with technology and believes that it can make life and ministry easier.

☐ The church has gone overboard with technology.

☐ Other:

COMMENT: _____

_____

22. How does the church view ministry to its community?

☐ The church believes that its entire ministry is in and only to its community.

☐ The church believes that it is responsible to minister in and to its community.

☐ The church has very little interest in ministering in and to its community.

☐ Other:

COMMENT: _____

_____

The purpose of this audit is to help you discover your church's primary, fundamental beliefs about important matters to the church. It's not meant to be exhaustive. If you are aware of any beliefs that you feel are important to the culture of the church that aren't listed here, add them in the space below.

Appendix E

Faith Statement

Northwood Community Church

Dallas, Texas

The members of Northwood Community Church have adopted the following twelve-point statement of the Evangelical Free Church of America as its faith statement.

1. We believe the Scriptures, both Old and New Testaments, to be the inspired Word of God, without error in the original writings, the complete revelation of His will for the salvation of men, and the divine and final authority for all Christian faith and life. 2 Timothy 3:16; 2 Peter 1:21.
2. We believe in one God, Creator of all things, infinitely perfect and eternally existing in three persons—Father, Son, and Holy Spirit. Deuteronomy 6:4; Matthew 28:19; Acts 5:3–4; John 5:18; 10:30.
3. We believe that Jesus Christ is true God and true man, having been conceived of the Holy Spirit and born of the virgin Mary. He died on the cross as a sacrifice for our sins according to the Scriptures. Further, He arose bodily from the dead, ascended into heaven, where at the right hand of the Majesty on High, He now is our High Priest and Advocate. John 1:3, 18; 1 Peter 2:21; Hebrews 10:1–10; John 5:18; Colossians 1:17.
4. We believe that the ministry of the Holy Spirit is to glorify the Lord Jesus Christ, and during this age to convict men, regenerate the believing sinner, indwell, guide, instruct, and empower the believer for godly living

and service. John 16:8–11; Titus 2:5; 1 Corinthians 6:19; 1 Corinthians 12:13; Ephesians 4:30; 5:18.

5. We believe that man was created in the image of God but fell into sin and is therefore lost and only through regeneration by the Holy Spirit can salvation and spiritual life be obtained. Genesis 1:26; 5:1, 3; Romans 3:23; 6:23.

6. We believe that the shed blood of Jesus Christ and His resurrection provide the only ground for justification and salvation for all who believe, and only such as receive Jesus Christ are born of the Holy Spirit, and thus become children of God. Acts 16:31; Ephesians 2:8–9; 2 Corinthians 5:21.

7. We believe that water baptism and the Lord's Supper are ordinances to be observed by the church during the present age. They are, however, not to be regarded as means of salvation. Acts 2:38; 1 Corinthians 11:24–26; Romans 6:1–4.

8. We believe that the true Church is composed of all such persons who through saving faith in Jesus Christ have been regenerated by the Holy Spirit and are united together in the body of Christ of which He is the Head. 1 Corinthians 1:2; 1 Thessalonians 1:1; Matthew 16:18.

9. We believe that only those who are members of the true Church shall be eligible for membership in the local church.

10. We believe that Jesus Christ is the Lord and Head of the Church, and that every local church has the right under Christ to decide and govern its own affairs. Matthew 16:18.

11. We believe in the personal, premillennial and imminent coming of our Lord Jesus Christ, and that this "Blessed Hope" has a vital bearing on the personal life and service of the believer. John 14:1–3; 1 Corinthians 15:51–57; 1 Thessalonians 4:13–18.

12. We believe in the bodily resurrection of the dead, of the believer to everlasting blessedness and joy with the Lord, of the unbeliever to judgment and everlasting conscious punishment. Matthew 25:31–46; Revelation 20:11–15; 1 Thessalonians 4:16.

Appendix F

The Culture Matrix

Beliefs, Values, Behavior

	Belief	Value	Behavior/Expression
Definition	A conviction of the existence or truth of something not subject to rational proof (scientific method). It is an assumption (we assume it is true).	A belief that guides and drives an individual or organization to act on a belief or assumption.	The results of acting on a value.
Action	A predisposition to action (people do evangelism, for example).	A belief that people act on. It guides/directs behavior—the reason we do what we do.	The resulting behavior—what we do.
Number	Organizations have many beliefs.	Organizations have fewer values.	Organizations have numerous actions, behaviors, or expressions.
Purpose	To guide or orient people in life—to make sense out of life.	To guide or direct behavior that affects life.	How a value affects life.
Change	Slow to change, making change in an organization difficult.	Slow to change but not as slow as beliefs.	Subject to change.
Synonyms	*conviction, assumption, church view; what we believe or assume*	*ideal, standard, precept; why we do what we do*	*action, presentation; what we do*

Beliefs Format: "We believe/assume _____."

Values Format: "We value _____."

Expressions Format: "We see/hear/feel _____."

Appendix G

Spiritual Maturity Audit

Directions: Read carefully each statement and circle the number (1, 2, 3, or 4) that best describes your church culture. Be sure to respond on the basis of what is actually true, not what you wish were true of your church.

1. The congregation knows the Bible well and applies its teachings to their daily lives.

   1. True   2. More true than false   3. More false than true   4. False

2. The church believes that the primary role of the pastor is to serve as a visionary leader, not a chaplain or the primary caregiver.

   1. True   2. More true than false   3. More false than true   4. False

3. The church believes that the people, not the pastor, are responsible to do the ministry.

   1. True   2. More true than false   3. More false than true   4. False

4. As many as 50 to 60 percent of the congregation are serving in some ministry capacity.

   1. True   2. More true than false   3. More false than true   4. False

5. The church prefers change and innovation over simply maintaining the status quo.

    1. True   2. More true than false   3. More false than true   4. False

6. The church's main mission is to make disciples, not simply to take care of its people—especially the elderly.

    1. True   2. More true than false   3. More false than true   4. False

7. The congregation is heavily involved in evangelism.

    1. True   2. More true than false   3. More false than true   4. False

8. Much of the church's ministry takes place out in its immediate community and not just within its facility.

    1. True   2. More true than false   3. More false than true   4. False

9. The church appears to be growing, not plateaued or declining in its worship attendance.

    1. True   2. More true than false   3. More false than true   4. False

10. The church in general is characterized by excellent spiritual leadership.

    1. True   2. More true than false   3. More false than true   4. False

11. The church has in place a process for developing lay and staff leaders at every level of ministry in the church.

    1. True   2. More true than false   3. More false than true   4. False

12. The church attracts people who are different from the majority of attenders.

    1. True   2. More true than false   3. More false than true   4. False

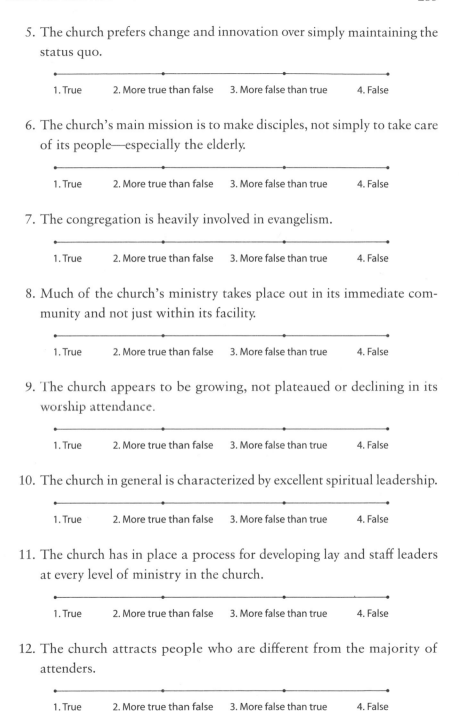

13. Most of the staff and lay leaders who are involved in the church's leader-development process have an individual, personal leader-development plan.

    1. True   2. More true than false   3. More false than true   4. False

14. The church takes very good care of its facilities.

    1. True   2. More true than false   3. More false than true   4. False

15. The church has a clear, compelling vision that attracts visitors as well as excites its members.

    1. True   2. More true than false   3. More false than true   4. False

16. Most of the members and regular attenders know and can recite from memory the church's mission and are involved in its fulfillment.

    1. True   2. More true than false   3. More false than true   4. False

17. The church provides excellent training for the many people who volunteer to serve in its ministries.

    1. True   2. More true than false   3. More false than true   4. False

18. People in the church make a point of greeting in some way those who are visiting the church.

    1. True   2. More true than false   3. More false than true   4. False

19. The pastor is a strong visionary leader who is a good preacher.

    1. True   2. More true than false   3. More false than true   4. False

20. The church's members see themselves not so much as members but as missionaries.

    1. True   2. More true than false   3. More false than true   4. False

21. Many people in the community are aware of the church and its presence in the community—if it were to disappear, it would be missed.

1. True   2. More true than false   3. More false than true   4. False

22. The church has a clear, simple pathway for making disciples that most understand and know where they are along that pathway.

1. True   2. More true than false   3. More false than true   4. False

23. The church has a good reputation in the community.

1. True   2. More true than false   3. More false than true   4. False

24. The church is open to change and new ideas for ministering to people.

1. True   2. More true than false   3. More false than true   4. False

25. The church invites constructive feedback and makes necessary changes.

1. True   2. More true than false   3. More false than true   4. False

26. There is a sense of excitement among people about the future of the church.

1. True   2. More true than false   3. More false than true   4. False

27. The congregation supports the ministry well with their tithes and offerings.

1. True   2. More true than false   3. More false than true   4. False

28. The church's worship is vibrant and inspiring.

1. True   2. More true than false   3. More false than true   4. False

29. People seem to be living a vibrant spirituality.

1. True   2. More true than false   3. More false than true   4. False

30. The church has small group ministries that address people's need for fellowship and spiritual accountability.

1. True   2. More true than false   3. More false than true   4. False

Scoring

Add the numbers (1, 2, 3, or 4) you circled for all thirty statements. The total will range somewhere between 30 and 120. Write the total in the space below.

The church's score is _____

If your score is:

30–45: Yours is a spiritually healthy, mature culture that is having a powerful impact for Christ. (This is especially true the closer your score is to 30.)

46–75: Yours is a somewhat spiritually healthy, moderately mature church that is having some impact for Christ. Note the statements where you scored a 3 or 4 and work on those. You would be wise to bring in someone from the outside to help you improve in these areas.

76–105: Yours is a somewhat spiritually unhealthy, moderately immature church that isn't reaching its potential for Christ. You need to bring in help from the outside to evaluate and totally revamp your ministry.

106–120: Yours is a spiritually unhealthy, immature church that likely is doing more harm than good. You should bring in someone from the outside to help you determine reasons you should not close this church.

Appendix H

Character Assessment for Leadership

Over the years, leaders have discovered that godly character is critical to effective ministry for Christ. However, no one is perfect, and all of us have our weaknesses and flaws as well as strengths. This character assessment is to help you determine your character strengths and weaknesses so that you can know where you are strong and where you need to develop and grow. The characteristics are found in 1 Timothy 3:1–7 and Titus 1:6–9.

Directions: Circle the number that best represents how you would rate yourself in each area.

1. I am "above reproach." I have a good reputation among people in general. I have done nothing that someone could use as an accusation against me.

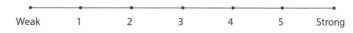

Weak   1   2   3   4   5   Strong

2. I am the "husband of one wife." If married, not only do I have one wife but I am not physically or mentally promiscuous, for I am focused only on her.

Weak   1   2   3   4   5   Strong

3. I am "temperate." I am a well-balanced person. I do not overdo my use of alcohol, my eating, my watching TV, or any other pastimes. I am not excessive or given to extremes in my beliefs.

Weak   1   2   3   4   5   Strong

4. I am "sensible." I show good judgment in life and have a proper perspective regarding myself and my abilities (humble).

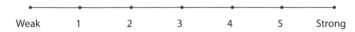

Weak   1   2   3   4   5   Strong

5. I am "respectable." I conduct my life in an honorable way, and people have and show respect for me.

Weak   1   2   3   4   5   Strong

6. I am "hospitable." I use my residence as a place to serve and minister to Christians and non-Christians alike.

Weak   1   2   3   4   5   Strong

7. I am "able to teach." When I teach the Bible, I show an aptitude for handling the Scriptures with reasonable skill.

Weak   1   2   3   4   5   Strong

8. I am "not given to drunkenness." If I drink alcoholic beverages or indulge in other acceptable but potentially addictive practices, I do so in moderation.

Weak   1   2   3   4   5   Strong

9. I am "not violent." I am under control. I do not lose control to the point that I physically or verbally strike out or cause damage to other people or their property.

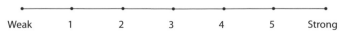

Weak   1   2   3   4   5   Strong

10. I am "gentle." I am a kind, meek (not weak), forbearing person who does not insist on his rights nor resort to violence.

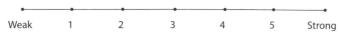

Weak   1   2   3   4   5   Strong

11. I am "not quarrelsome." I am an uncontentious peacemaker who avoids hostile situations with people.

Weak   1   2   3   4   5   Strong

12. I am "not a lover of money." I am not in ministry for financial gain. I seek first God's righteousness, knowing that God will supply my needs.

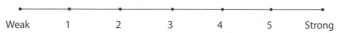

Weak   1   2   3   4   5   Strong

13. I "manage my family well." If I am married and have a family, my children are believers who obey me with respect. People do not think of or accuse them of being wild or disobedient.

Weak   1   2   3   4   5   Strong

14. I am "not a recent convert."

Weak   1   2   3   4   5   Strong

15. I have "a good reputation with outsiders." Though lost people may not agree with my religious convictions, they still respect me as a person.

Weak   1   2   3   4   5   Strong

16. I am "not overbearing." I am not self-willed, stubborn, or arrogant.

Weak   1   2   3   4   5   Strong

17. I am "not quick-tempered." I am not inclined toward anger (an angry person) and I do not lose my temper quickly and easily.

Weak   1   2   3   4   5   Strong

18. I am "not pursuing dishonest gain." I am not fond of nor involved in any wrongful practices that result in fraudulent gain.

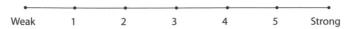

Weak   1   2   3   4   5   Strong

19. I "love what is good." I love the things that honor God.

Weak   1   2   3   4   5   Strong

20. I am "upright." I live in accordance with the laws of God and man.

Weak   1   2   3   4   5   Strong

21. I am "holy." I am a devout person, whose life is generally pleasing to God.

Weak   1   2   3   4   5   Strong

22. I "hold firmly to the faith." I understand, hold to, and attempt to conserve God's truth. I also encourage others in faith, while refuting those who oppose the truth.

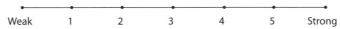

Weak   1   2   3   4   5   Strong

When you have completed this character assessment, note those characteristics that you gave the lowest rating (2 or below). The lowest of these should become the character goals or challenges on which you focus.

Appendix I

Spiritual Gifts Inventory for Leaders

irections: Work through each of the following fifty-five statements on spiritual gifts. After each, check the appropriate box that best describes to what extent the statement accurately describes you. Do not answer on the basis of what you wish were true or what another says might be true, but on the basis of what to your knowledge is true of you.

	Never	Rarely	Sometimes	Often	Always
	1	2	3	4	5
1. I enjoy working with others in determining ministry goals and objectives.	☐	☐	☐	☐	☐
2. I prefer to be involved in new ministries.	☐	☐	☐	☐	☐
3. I delight in telling lost people about what Christ has done for them.	☐	☐	☐	☐	☐
4. It bothers me that some people are hurting and discouraged.	☐	☐	☐	☐	☐
5. I have a strong ability to see what needs to be done and believe that God will do it.	☐	☐	☐	☐	☐
6. I love to give a significant portion of my resources to God's work.	☐	☐	☐	☐	☐
7. I have a strong capacity to recognize practical needs and to do something about them.	☐	☐	☐	☐	☐
8. I have a clear vision for the direction of a ministry.	☐	☐	☐	☐	☐

	Never	Rarely	Sometimes	Often	Always
	1	2	3	4	5
9. I always feel compassion for those in difficult situations.	☐	☐	☐	☐	☐
10. I have a strong desire to nurture God's people.	☐	☐	☐	☐	☐
11. I spend a significant portion of my time each week studying the Bible.	☐	☐	☐	☐	☐
12. I am motivated to design plans to accomplish ministry goals.	☐	☐	☐	☐	☐
13. I prefer to create my own ministry problems than to inherit others' problems.	☐	☐	☐	☐	☐
14. I have a strong attraction to lost people.	☐	☐	☐	☐	☐
15. I am very concerned that more people are not serving the Lord.	☐	☐	☐	☐	☐
16. I have a strong capacity to trust God for the difficult things in life.	☐	☐	☐	☐	☐
17. I am eager to financially support ministries that are accomplishing significant things for God.	☐	☐	☐	☐	☐
18. I enjoy helping people meet their practical needs.	☐	☐	☐	☐	☐
19. I find that I have a strong capacity to attract followers to my ministry.	☐	☐	☐	☐	☐
20. I am motivated to sympathize with those in the midst of a crisis.	☐	☐	☐	☐	☐
21. I am at my best when leading and shepherding a small group of believers.	☐	☐	☐	☐	☐
22. I have strong insight into the Bible and how it applies to people's lives.	☐	☐	☐	☐	☐
23. I feel significant when developing budgets.	☐	☐	☐	☐	☐
24. I am motivated to minister in places where no one else has ministered.	☐	☐	☐	☐	☐
25. I find that I get along well with unsaved people.	☐	☐	☐	☐	☐
26. I have a strong desire to encourage Christians to mature in Christ.	☐	☐	☐	☐	☐
27. I delight in the truth that God accomplishes things that seem impossible to most people.	☐	☐	☐	☐	☐
28. God has greatly blessed me with life's provisions in order to help others.	☐	☐	☐	☐	☐

	Never	Rarely	Sometimes	Often	Always
	1	2	3	4	5
29. I enjoy making personal sacrifices to help others.	☐	☐	☐	☐	☐
30. I prefer to lead people more than to follow them.	☐	☐	☐	☐	☐
31. I delight in extending a hand to those in difficulty.	☐	☐	☐	☐	☐
32. I enjoy showing attention to those who are in need of care and concern.	☐	☐	☐	☐	☐
33. I am motivated to present God's truth to people so they can better understand the Bible.	☐	☐	☐	☐	☐
34. I am at my best when creating an organizational structure for a plan.	☐	☐	☐	☐	☐
35. I am definitely a self-starter with a pioneer spirit.	☐	☐	☐	☐	☐
36. I derive extreme satisfaction when lost people accept Christ.	☐	☐	☐	☐	☐
37. I have been effective at inspiring believers to a stronger faith.	☐	☐	☐	☐	☐
38. I am convinced that God is going to accomplish something special through my ministry.	☐	☐	☐	☐	☐
39. I am convinced that all I have belongs to God.	☐	☐	☐	☐	☐
40. I work best when I serve others behind the scenes.	☐	☐	☐	☐	☐
41. If I am not careful, I have a tendency to dominate people and situations.	☐	☐	☐	☐	☐
42. I am a born burden-bearer.	☐	☐	☐	☐	☐
43. I have a deep desire to protect Christians from people and beliefs that may harm them.	☐	☐	☐	☐	☐
44. I am deeply committed to biblical truth and people's need to know and understand it.	☐	☐	☐	☐	☐
45. I delight in staffing a particular ministry structure.	☐	☐	☐	☐	☐
46. I am challenged by a big vision to accomplish what some believe is impossible.	☐	☐	☐	☐	☐
47. I feel a deep compassion for people who are without Christ.	☐	☐	☐	☐	☐

	Never	Rarely	Sometimes	Often	Always
	1	2	3	4	5
48. I have the ability to say the right things to people who are experiencing discouragement.	☐	☐	☐	☐	☐
49. I am rarely surprised when God turns seeming obstacles into opportunities for ministry.	☐	☐	☐	☐	☐
50. I feel good when I have the opportunity to give from my abundance to people with genuine needs.	☐	☐	☐	☐	☐
51. I have a strong capacity to serve people.	☐	☐	☐	☐	☐
52. I am motivated to be proactive, not passive, in my ministry for Christ.	☐	☐	☐	☐	☐
53. I have the ability to feel the pain of others who are suffering.	☐	☐	☐	☐	☐
54. I get excited about helping new Christians grow to maturity in Christ.	☐	☐	☐	☐	☐
55. Whenever I teach a Bible class, the size of the group increases in number.	☐	☐	☐	☐	☐

Instructions for determining your spiritual gifts:

1. Write the number for each of your answers on the line corresponding to the question number.
2. Add the numbers horizontally and place the total for each row in the space before the name of each gift.

1.__	12.__	23.__	34.__	45.__	___Administration
2.__	13.__	24.__	35.__	46.__	___Apostleship
3.__	14.__	25.__	36.__	47.__	___Encouragement
4.__	15.__	26.__	37.__	48.__	___Evangelism
5.__	16.__	27.__	38.__	49.__	___Faith
6.__	17.__	28.__	39.__	50.__	___Giving
7.__	18.__	29.__	40.__	51.__	___Helps
8.__	19.__	30.__	41.__	52.__	___Leadership
9.__	20.__	31.__	42.__	53.__	___Mercy
10.__	21.__	32.__	43.__	54.__	___Pastor
11.__	22.__	33.__	44.__	55.__	___Teacher

3. Write the names of your five highest-scoring gifts in the spaces below under "Spiritual Gifts Inventory."

Spiritual Gifts Inventory

    1. _____

    2. _____

    3. _____

    4. _____

    5. _____

Instructions for determining your gift-mix and gift-cluster

    1. To determine your gift-mix, write the names of the five gifts that ranked the highest, in descending order in the spaces below "Gift-Mix."
    2. To determine if you have a gift-cluster, decide if the first gift or another gift in your mix is dominant and supported by the other gifts. If this is the case, place it in the center space under "Gift-Cluster" and place the other gifts in the spaces above and below it.

Gift-Mix

    1. _____

    2. _____

    3. _____

    4. _____

Gift-Cluster

_____

_____

Dominant gift: _____

_____

_____

Appendix J

Temperament Indicator 1

Directions: Read the four terms listed across each row. Then rank the four characteristics for how well each one describes you in a ministry or work-related situation. Number 4 is most like you, and number 1 is least like you. Rank each word with 1, 2, 3, or 4. When you are finished, total the numbers in each column and write that number in the space provided below that column.

1.	___Direct	___Popular	___Loyal	___Analytical
2.	___Decisive	___Outgoing	___Dependable	___Logical
3.	___Controlling	___Expressive	___Steady	___Thorough
4.	___Competent	___Influential	___Responsible	___Skeptical
5.	___Blunt	___Enthusiastic	___Sensible	___Compliant
6.	___Competitive	___Persuasive	___Cooperative	___Serious
7.	___Callous	___Impulsive	___Submissive	___Accurate
8.	___Volatile	___Manipulative	___Conforming	___Picky
9.	___Persistent	___Personable	___Harmonious	___Creative
10.	___Productive	___Animated	___Restrained	___Fearful
11.	___Self-reliant	___Articulate	___Predictable	___Diplomatic
	___Total	___Total	___Total	___Total
	(Doer)	*(Influencer)*	*(Steady)*	*(Thinker)*

Appendix K

The Personal Profile

The Persuader Pattern

In several places I have noted that the Persuader Pattern on the *Personal Profile* is characteristic of revitalization pastors. But what is the Persuader Pattern? I have included this appendix to supply the reader with more information on this particular pattern.

The Persuader Pattern results from bringing the high I temperament together with a secondary D. The high I predominates but the D also influences the temperament. What does this look like in an individual? The *Personal Profile* (which may be obtained online) supplies the following description of the Persuader Pattern.

Persuaders work with people, striving to be friendly while pushing forward their own objectives. Outgoing and interested in people, Persuaders have the ability to gain the respect and confidence of various kinds of people. Persuaders can impress their thoughts on others, drawing people to them and retaining them as clients and friends. This ability is particularly helpful when Persuaders sell themselves or their ideas to win positions of authority. The most favorable environment for Persuaders includes working with people, receiving challenging assignments, and experiencing a variety of work activities that require mobility. They seek work assignments that will give them the opportunity to look good. As a result of their naturally positive outlook, Persuaders may be too optimistic about a project's result and others' potential. Persuaders also tend to overestimate their ability to change the behavior of others. Although Persuaders desire freedom from routine and regimentation, they need to receive analytical data on a systematic basis. Once alerted to the importance of the "little things," Persuaders can use the information to balance their enthusiasm with a realistic assessment of the situation.[1]

In addition, the *Personal Profile* breaks the Persuader Pattern down into nine specific areas:

emotions	trusts others; is enthusiastic
goals	authority and prestige; status symbols
judges others by	ability to express themselves; flexibility
influences others by	a friendly, open manner; verbal skills
value to the organization	sells and closes; delegates responsibility; is poised and confident
overuses	enthusiasm; selling ability; optimism
under pressure	becomes indecisive and is easily persuaded; becomes organized in order to look good
fears	a fixed environment; complex relationships
would increase effectiveness with more	challenging assignments; attention to task-oriented service and key details; objective data analysis[2]

Appendix L

Temperament Indicator 2

Directions: As you take this indicator, please keep in mind that there are no correct or incorrect answers. Read each statement and circle the item (a or b) that best represents your preference in a ministry or work-related environment. Do not spend a lot of time thinking about your answers. Go with your first impulse.

1. When around other people, I am
   a) expressive
   b) quiet
2. I tend to
   a) dislike new problems
   b) like new problems
3. I make decisions based on my
   a) logic
   b) values
4. I prefer to work in a
   a) structured environment
   b) nonstructured environment
5. I feel more energetic after being
   a) around people
   b) away from people

6. I work best with
   a) facts
   b) ideas
7. People say I am
   a) impersonal
   b) a people-pleaser
8. My friends at work say I am very
   a) organized
   b) flexible
9. I get more work accomplished when I am
   a) with people
   b) by myself
10. I like to think about
    a) what is
    b) what could be

11. I admire
    a) strength
    b) compassion
12. I make decisions
    a) quickly
    b) slowly
13. I prefer
    a) variety and action
    b) focus and quiet
14. I like
    a) established ways to do things
    b) new ways to do things
15. I tend to be rather
    a) unemotional
    b) emotional
16. Most often I dislike
    a) carelessness with details
    b) complicated procedures
17. In my relationships I find that over time it is easy to
    a) keep up with people
    b) lose track of people
18. I enjoy skills that
    a) I have already learned and used
    b) are newly learned but unused
19. Sometimes I make decisions that
    a) hurt other people's feelings
    b) are too influenced by other people
20. When my circumstances change, I prefer to
    a) follow a good plan
    b) adapt to each new situation

21. In conversations I communicate
    a) freely and openly
    b) quietly and cautiously
22. In my work I tend to
    a) take time to be precise
    b) dislike taking time to be precise
23. I relate well to
    a) people like me
    b) most people
24. When working on a project, I do not
    a) like interruptions
    b) mind interruptions
25. Sometimes I find that I
    a) act first and ask questions later
    b) ask questions first and act later
26. I would describe my work style as
    a) steady with realistic expectations
    b) periodic with bursts of enthusiasm
27. At work I need
    a) fair treatment
    b) occasional praise
28. In a new job I prefer to know
    a) only what it takes to get it done
    b) all about it
29. In any job I am most interested in
    a) getting it done and the results
    b) the idea behind the job

30. I have found that I am
   a) patient with routine details
   b) impatient with routine details
31. When working with other people, I find it
   a) easy to correct them
   b) difficult to correct them
32. Once I have made a decision, I consider the case
   a) closed
   b) still open

33. I prefer
   a) lots of acquaintances
   b) a few good friends
34. I am more likely to trust my
   a) experiences
   b) inspirations
35. I consistently decide matters based on
   a) the facts in my head
   b) the feelings in my heart
36. I prefer to work
   a) in an established business
   b) as an entrepreneur

Instructions for Scoring:

1. Place a check in the a or b box below to indicate how you answered each question.
2. Add the checks down each column and record the total for each column at the bottom.
3. The highest score for each pair indicates your temperament preference.
4. For each pair, subtract the lower from the higher score to discover the difference in your preferences. A higher number indicates a clear choice or preference but does not indicate the measure of development. For example, a higher score for extraversion means that you prefer it over introversion. It does not mean that you are a strong extravert.

	a	b		a	b		a	b		a	b
1	☐	☐	2	☐	☐	3	☐	☐	4	☐	☐
5	☐	☐	6	☐	☐	7	☐	☐	8	☐	☐
9	☐	☐	10	☐	☐	11	☐	☐	12	☐	☐
13	☐	☐	14	☐	☐	15	☐	☐	16	☐	☐
17	☐	☐	18	☐	☐	19	☐	☐	20	☐	☐
21	☐	☐	22	☐	☐	23	☐	☐	24	☐	☐
25	☐	☐	26	☐	☐	27	☐	☐	28	☐	☐
29	☐	☐	30	☐	☐	31	☐	☐	32	☐	☐
33	☐	☐	34	☐	☐	35	☐	☐	36	☐	☐
Total	—	—	Total	—	—	Total	—	—	Total	—	—
	E	I		S	N		T	F		J	P
	Extravert	Introvert		Sensing	Intuition		Thinking	Feeling		Judgment	Perception

Appendix M

Temperament Indicator 2

Further Explanation

The *Myers-Briggs Temperament Indicator* (*MBTI*) works with four sets of preferences: E-I, S-N, T-F, and J-P. The first preference set (E-I) relates to where leaders focus their attention and derive their energy. The E represents extraverts who like to work with the outer world of people and things. They are energized by contact with people. The I represents introverts who prefer the inner world of ideas. They draw energy from solitude and find themselves drained if around a lot of people for a lengthy period of time. In *Personality Type and Religious Leadership*, Roy Oswald and Otto Kroeger conclude from a study of the functions normally expected in ministry "that the parish ministry is primarily an Extroverted profession."[1] In my work with the *MBTI* and pastoral leaders, I have observed that God uses both Es and Is to lead churches that need strong direction and numerical growth. Often pastors of large churches are Is. I would grant a slight edge to extraverts.

The second set (S-N) looks at how people find out about things and how they prefer to take in and process information. The S represents people who take in information through the five senses. They prefer to focus on observable facts and details—what they can see, hear, touch, taste, and smell. They tend to dwell on present reality (the here-and-now), and for them "seeing is believing." The N represents people who take in information holistically, preferring the world of ideas, possibilities, and relationships. They are the world's visionaries who thrive on change and new ideas. For them "believing is seeing." The last two sentences indicate that culture changers are clearly Ns. Change agents must be strong visionary leaders who prefer change and innovation, which encourages growth in plateaued and declining cultures.

The third set (T-F) relates to what people do with the information they take in or how they make decisions. The T represents leaders who make their decisions on the basis of logic and objective analysis. They prefer to win people over by their logic. They take a more impersonal approach to decision making and can come across at times as insensitive. The F represents leaders who make their decisions on the basis of personal values and motives. They prefer to win people to their ideas through persuasion. They take a personal approach to decision making and communicate warmth and harmony. Human values are very important; consequently, they are more people oriented.

Various studies on change indicate that those who have a strong people orientation and are sensitive to people and their feelings and ideas are culture change agents. This is true of F-type leaders. The problem is they eventually stop exercising consistent strong leadership, which only serves to plateau a church's growth. This is not true of NT clergy.[2] Ts and NTs in particular serve well as change agents because they are strong visionary leaders who press for change.[3]

The fourth set (J-P) reflects how people orient to the outer world in terms of structure and the time it takes to make decisions. J-type leaders prefer a more structured approach to life because they like to control and regulate life. They are very organized and deal with the world in a planned and orderly manner. Preferring to have matters settled, they tend to be quick decision makers. The P-type leader takes a less structured approach to life because he seeks to understand and adapt to life. These leaders tend to be very adaptable, flexible, and spontaneous. They have little need for closure and prefer to make decisions after all the facts are in.

The Js have an advantage in their ability to make hard decisions, take a strong stand, and commit themselves to a clear course of action.[4] However, when combined with the sensing-type (SJs), they can become very rigid and inflexible, preferring the status quo.[5] Consequently, SJs do not serve well as change agents. The Ps have an advantage in their openness to change, which brings both new options and a freshness to their leadership. However, their openness and flexibility may result in indecisiveness and the failure to take a stand and commit to a plan for the future.[6] Consequently, either Js or Ps can involve themselves in change but must work on the characteristics that inhibit their leadership toward change.

Appendix N

Implementation Team Worksheet

Directions: The following is a list of twelve ministry objectives along with their implementation teams that review the strategic planning process. (Note that the last two objectives are optional.)

1. Assign each objective (community outreach, for example) to a leader/ champion who will recruit a team from the strategic leadership team and the congregation for their implementation.
2. Note that each objective lists a number of measurable goals that when accomplished will form your strategy for each ministry objective. They will also serve to keep you on track and focused on your ministry tasks.
3. Each team needs to prioritize their goals and look for potential "short-term wins."
4. Determine who on the team will work through and develop each goal.
5. Observe the deadline (date) for the completion of the goals.
6. You may add or subtract goals (be sure to clear this with the Lead Implementation Team).
7. Use the space in front of each goal to check off completed goals and/or to prioritize the goals.

Objective 1. What: *Recruit a Lead Implementation Team and begin the process.* (Who: Lead Implementation Team. When: completion date _____.)

    Team leader:

    Team members:

____ Recruit a leader/champion (could be a lay leader, a staff person, or the senior pastor) over the entire process.

____ The leader will recruit an assistant leader and one or two other team members from the SLT and congregation to assist him/her.

____ Assist the pastor or person responsible for recruiting the other team leaders who, in turn, will recruit their team persons.

____ Exercise general oversight over the implementation process.

____ Create an overall process time line (Gantt Chart) and use it to coordinate the various launch dates, etc.

____ Regularly monitor and update the time line.

____ Regularly communicate with each team and its leader (track progress, address problems, etc.).

____ Regularly assess the overall progress (the "big picture") of the implementation process and keep the pastor informed.

____ Troubleshoot when necessary.

____ Schedule and conduct the MIR (Monthly Implementation Reviews) meetings.

____ Set up and monitor a strategic planning website.

____ Assemble and edit the final draft of the strategic plan (if necessary).

____ Regularly evaluate and seek to improve the overall implementation process.

Objective 2. What: *Pray for the implementation process.* (Who: Intercessory Prayer Implementation Team. When: completion date _____.)

    Team leader:

    Team members:

____ Determine if such a prayer team already exists.

____ Pray specifically for the SLT while it is meeting, usually Friday evenings and Saturday mornings.

____ Pray for the senior pastor, staff, and SLT as they're involved in the process.

____ Pray for the various implementation teams and their leaders.

____ Pray for the congregation to accept and be involved in the process.

Objective 3. What: *Design and implement a congregational communication plan.* (Who: Congregational Communication Implementation Team. When: completion date _____.)

    Team leader:

    Team members:

____ Draft your core values statement (credo).

____ Decide how you will best communicate in particular your values and mission to the congregation (see "best practices" for communication below).

____ Regularly remind the pastor to communicate the mission and vision to the congregation.

____ Investigate and evaluate how the church currently communicates.

____ Apply the following communication tool to your board meetings, staff meetings, team ministries, etc. (Communication tool: what needs to be communicated, by whom, to whom, where, when, how, how often, and why).

____ Recruit a lay- or staff person who clears and coordinates what gets communicated publically (often this is the senior pastor or chairman of the board).

____ Determine some "best practices" for communication (website, bulletin board, bulletins, newsletters, emails, sermons, a magazine, announcements, annual congregational survey, new members class, etc.).

____ Survey other churches in your area that are known for good communication and find out what they are doing that would help you.

____ Decide how best to communicate with those outside the church and design a marketing strategy to get your message to them.

____ Draft the overall church vision statement.

____ Decide along with the senior pastor how you will best communicate your vision in particular to the congregation.

____ Regularly evaluate and improve your communication process.

Objective 4. What: *Develop and implement a strategy to reach your community.* (Who: Community Outreach Implementation Team. When: completion date _____.)

Team leader:
Team members:

___ Attend the instructional meeting led by the staff or a consultant from The Malphurs Group (TMG).

___ Identify your Jerusalem (Acts 1:8)—set "soft" community boundaries.

___ Discover who lives in your community, using demographics and psychographics (community report).

___ Keep abreast of your community's demographics and psychographics.

___ Identify the issues your community struggles with and how your church will address them.

___ Identify some key initial and long-term ministries that would help you reach your community.

___ Discover your congregation's self-identity—how you view yourselves (missionaries, disciples, servants, witnesses, evangelists, members, etc.).

___ Provide evangelistic training for the congregation (a premier evangelistic training course, gospel presentation, style of evangelism, etc.).

___ Identify other implementation teams you need to communicate with and meet or somehow connect with periodically.

___ Develop a one-paragraph vision statement for community outreach.

___ When you have addressed most if not all these goals, you'll have your strategy to accomplish community outreach. Draft a statement that will capture and communicate this strategy for community outreach, and present it to the LIT (Lead Implementation Team) or appropriate person(s) (pastor, executive pastor, SLT, board, etc.) for evaluation, input, and final approval.

___ Observe the deadline (date) for when you plan to launch this ministry churchwide.

___ Regularly evaluate and update long term your community outreach strategy.

Objective 5. *Develop and implement your strategy to make disciples.* (Who: Disciple-Making Implementation Team. When: completion date _____.)

> Team leader:
> Team members:
> ____ Attend the instructional meeting led by the staff or a TMG consultant.
> ____ Identify the characteristics of a mature disciple.
> ____ Identify your primary ministries—"disciple-making pathway": preaching/worship service, Bible study, small groups, etc.
> ____ Determine which characteristics are accomplished currently by each primary ministry.
> ____ Evaluate and tweak or develop the primary ministries—your disciple-making pathway. If you have time, do the same with the secondary ministries.
> ____ Create or embrace a figure or image to communicate your disciple-making strategy.
> ____ Decide how you'll measure or evaluate progress.
> ____ Identify other implementation teams you need to communicate with and meet or somehow connect with periodically.
> ____ Develop a one-paragraph vision statement for making disciples.
> ____ When you have addressed most if not all these goals, you'll have your strategy to accomplish disciple making. Draft a statement that will capture the church's strategy for making disciples and present it to the LIT or appropriate person(s) (pastor, executive pastor, SLT, board, etc.) for evaluation, input, and final approval.
> ____ Regularly evaluate and update long term your disciple-making strategy.

Objective 6. *Develop and implement a strategy to mobilize your congregation.* (Who: Mobilization Implementation Team. When: completion date _____.)

> Team leader:
> Team members:
> ____ Attend the instructional meeting led by the staff or TMG consultant.
> ____ Articulate and communicate to all the importance of mobilizing your congregation (work with the Communication IT).
> ____ Identify the mobilization problem.

____ Determine or guess what percent of your congregation is mobilized.

____ Embrace and communicate the biblical solution for mobilization.

____ Understand and be able to explain the divine design concept.

____ Develop and put in place a three-phase mobilization process: discovery, consulting, and placement or something similar.

____ Train ministry leaders (children, youth, adults, etc.) in the process.

____ Decide on the appropriate mobilization tools (gifts inventory, passion audit, temperament tool, etc.). Assess costs.

____ Develop a one-paragraph statement that captures and communicates your vision for church mobilization.

____ Identify other implementation teams you need to communicate with and meet or somehow connect with periodically.

____ When you have addressed most if not all these goals, you'll have your strategy to mobilize your congregation. Draft a paper that will capture the church's strategy for mobilizing its people, and present it to the appropriate person(s) (pastor, executive pastor, SLT, board, etc.) for evaluation, input, and final approval.

____ Observe the deadline (date) for when you plan to launch this ministry churchwide.

____ Regularly evaluate and update long term your congregational mobilization strategy.

Objective 7. What: *Develop and implement your strategy to build a ministry staff team.* (Who: Staffing Implementation Team. When: completion date _____.)

Team leader:

Team members:

____ Attend the instructional meeting led by the staff or TMG consultant.

____ Determine how many staff you should have.

____ Address whether you have a balanced staff (functional and age-specific).

____ See that all ministry staff have a job/ministry description.

____ Determine if staff will equip laypersons for ministry.

____ Determine if staff will primarily train leaders for ministry.

____ Develop a staff organizational chart.

____ Create a staffing blueprint for the future.

____ Address staff deployment. (Are staff in the right positions?)

____ Design and conduct a staff evaluation process.

____ Evaluate staff chemistry.

____ Develop a one-paragraph vision statement for building staff.

____ Identify other implementation teams you need to communicate with and meet or somehow connect with periodically.

____ When you have addressed most if not all these goals, you'll have your strategy to build your staff. Draft a statement that will capture the church's strategy for building its ministry staff, and present it to the LIT or appropriate person(s) (pastor, executive pastor, SLT, board, etc.) for evaluation, input, and final approval.

____ Observe the deadline (date) for when you plan to launch this ministry churchwide.

____ Regularly evaluate and update long term your strategy to build ministry staff.

Objective 8. What: *Develop and implement a strategy to determine your best ministry setting.* (Who: Location and Facilities Implementation Team. When: completion date _____.)

Team leader:

Team members:

____ Attend the instructional meeting led by the staff or TMG consultant.

____ Determine how best to address your location issues.

____ Draft a church campus master plan.

____ Evaluate the church's "visitor friendliness" and propose corrections.

____ Evaluate the church's cleanliness and propose corrections.

____ Evaluate whether facilities are functional and propose corrections.

____ Identify any facility "blind spots" and propose corrections.

____ Evaluate current parking and propose corrections.

____ Evaluate seating capacity (rule of thumb is that it should not be more than 80 to 90 percent full) and propose corrections.

____ Evaluate acreage (1 acre per 100 people) and propose corrections.

____ Address whether or not the church should consider a relocation.

____ Identify other implementation teams you need to communicate with and meet or somehow connect with periodically.

____ Develop a one-paragraph vision statement for location and facilities.

____ When you have addressed most if not all these goals, you'll have your strategy to best determine your ministry setting. Draft a statement that will capture the church's strategy for determining its best ministry setting and present it to the LIT or appropriate person(s) (pastor, executive pastor, SLT, board, etc.) for evaluation, input, and final approval.

____ Regularly evaluate and update long term your strategy for determining your best ministry setting.

Objective 9. What: *Develop and implement a strategy to evaluate and raise significant finances for ministry.* (Who: Finances/Stewardship Implementation Team. When: completion date _____.)

Team leader:

Team members:

____ Attend the instructional meeting led by the staff or TMG consultant.

____ Determine who will lead the fund-raising efforts.

____ Reconstruct the budget around the four major allocation areas (missions and evangelism, personnel, ministries, and facilities).

____ Determine the proper allocation of funds to each area.

____ Monitor and assess your current giving.

____ Decide how you'll raise funding for ministry.

____ Consider alternative sources for funding (capital campaigns, trusts, etc.).

____ Develop a one-paragraph vision statement for your stewardship ministry.

____ Identify other implementation teams and/or committees you need to communicate with and meet or somehow connect with periodically.

____ Observe the deadline (date) for when you plan to launch this ministry churchwide.

____ When you have addressed most if not all these goals, you'll have your strategy to evaluate and raise finances for your church. Draft a statement that will capture the church's strategy for fund-raising and present it to the LIT or appropriate person(s) (pastor, executive pastor, SLT, board, etc.) for evaluation, input, and final approval.

____ Regularly evaluate and update long term your funding strategy.

Objective 10. What: *Build a creative, innovative church that can adapt quickly to change in the culture.* (Who: Creativity and Innovation Implementation Team. When: completion date _____.)

Team leader:

Team members:

____ Determine if the church keeps up with and relates well to the culture (through congregational scorecard and surveys of congregation).

____ Interview people within and outside the congregation and ask what you are doing that's become outdated and irrelevant. (What's not changed in the last five years?)

____ Develop and apply a biblical theology of change (should include the church's *functions* such as worship, evangelism, and others; the *form* these functions will take, i.e., traditional or contemporary worship; and the leader's *freedom* to change those forms but not the function).

____ Constantly challenge your views and assumptions about what you think is true about your community, your congregation, your ministries, your leaders, and the way you do things inside your organization. Take nothing for granted.

____ Develop a process for generating hundreds of new, strategic ministry ideas each year (brainstorming sessions, etc.).

____ Gain congregational permission to experiment with and try new things. (This means they and you will have to become comfortable with failure. It's far better to have tried and failed than not to have tried at all.)

____ Consider and evaluate creative and innovative ideas from the congregation and others.

____ Identify innovative and creative churches in America and discover what they are doing and how they may help you in your ministry.

____ Allocate funds in the budget to fund new ideas (recommend 1 to 5 percent of the ministries budget).

____ Read books and articles on creativity and innovation (for example, *Fast Company*) and on innovative, creative churches.

____ Invite new staff and new members and even outsiders to tell you what they think you need to change to be more effective as a church.

Optional Objective 11. What: *Craft a process to develop leaders in the church.* (Who: Leadership Development Implementation Team. When: completion date _____.)

    Team leader:

    Team members:

___ Attend the instructional meeting led by the staff or TMG consultant.

___ Articulate why leadership development is so important.

___ Articulate why churches are not developing leaders.

___ Determine if you believe that leaders are born or made.

___ Define leader development.

___ Articulate Jesus's leader development phases, principles, and steps.

___ Determine if your empowered leaders (board, staff, pastor, patriarch, etc.) will support the leader-development process.

___ Decide who will initiate, support, and lead the development process.

___ Determine who will actually develop leaders.

___ Arrive at a consensus definition of leadership.

___ Identify the various leadership levels in your church.

___ Discover new, emerging leaders for development.

___ Deploy new leaders into their positions of leadership.

___ Develop new and present leaders for their ministries in the church.

___ Regularly evaluate your leader-development process.

___ Consistently reward those who are developing leaders.

___ Identify other implementation teams you need to communicate with and meet or somehow connect with periodically.

___ Develop a one-paragraph vision statement for leader development.

___ When you have addressed most if not all these goals, you'll have your process for developing leaders in your church. Draft a statement that will describe the leader-development process and present it to the LIT or appropriate person(s) (pastor, executive pastor, SLT, board, etc.) for evaluation, input, and final approval.

___ Observe the deadline (date) for when you plan to launch this ministry churchwide.

___ Regularly evaluate and update long term your leader-development strategy.

Optional Objective 12. What: *Develop a strategy that equips the board for leadership excellence.* (Who: Board Strategy Implementation Team. When: completion date _____.)

Team leader:

Team members:

____ Attend the instructional meeting led by the staff or TMG consultant.

____ Define your governing board.

____ Evaluate current board performance.

____ Limit the board's size.

____ Determine the spiritual qualifications for the board.

____ Determine the relationship between the board, pastor, and ministry staff.

____ Evaluate and establish clear board functions (what it does).

____ Review and set the composition of the board.

____ Identify the characteristics of a healthy board.

____ Establish guidelines with the pastor and board for power checks and balances.

____ Implement a church policies approach.

____ Set up an orientation and training process for new board members.

____ Identify other implementation teams you need to communicate with and meet or somehow connect with periodically.

____ Develop a one-paragraph vision statement for the board.

____ When you have addressed most if not all these goals, you'll have your strategy to equip your board for leadership excellence. Draft a statement that will describe the church's strategy for board excellence and present it to the LIT or appropriate person(s) (pastor, executive pastor, SLT, board, etc.) for evaluation, input, and final approval.

____ Regularly evaluate and update long term your board-development strategy.

Notes

Chapter 1 Why Leaders Should Read This Book

1. Dick Clark, "Corporate Culture Is the Game," *Executive Leadership* (November 2008): 3.

Chapter 2 What Are We Talking About?

1. Edgar H. Schein, *Organizational Culture and Leadership,* 2nd ed. (San Francisco: Jossey-Bass, 1997).

Chapter 4 Why We Do What We Do

1. Lyle E. Schaller, *Getting Things Done* (Nashville: Abingdon, 1986), 152.
2. Ibid., 153.
3. James C. Collins and Jerry I. Porras, *Built to Last* (New York: Harper Business, 1994), 74, 219.
4. Ken Blanchard and Phil Hodges, *The Servant Leader* (Nashville: Thomas Nelson, 2003), 50.

Chapter 5 What We Believe

1. James W. Sire, *The Universe Next Door* (Downers Grove, IL: InterVarsity, 1988), 17.

Chapter 9 The Church Planter as Culture Architect

1. "Back from the Brink: A *Leadership* Special Report," *Leadership Journal* 26, no. 4 (fall 2005): 24.
2. David T. Olson, *The American Church in Crisis* (Grand Rapids: Zondervan, 2008), 28–29.
3. Ibid., 179.
4. Aubrey Malphurs, *Planting Growing Churches for the 21st Century* (Grand Rapids: Baker, 1992).

Chapter 11 The Church Pastor as Culture Sculptor: Part 2 Personnel

1. Gordon E. Penfold, "Defining Characteristics of Turnaround Pastors among Evangelical Churches in the Rocky Mountain States" (DMin diss., Biola University, 2011), 136–38.
2. Ibid.
3. Ibid.
4. Ibid.
5. Lyle E. Schaller, *Create Your Own Future!* (Nashville: Abingdon, 1991), 24–25.
6. C. Peter Wagner, *Leading Your Church to Growth* (Ventura, CA: Regal, 1984), 97.

7. The *Personal Profile* and the *Biblical Personal Profile* are essentially the same tools. The latter connects the temperaments with those of biblical characters.

8. Robert W. Thomas, "Personality Characteristics of Effective Revitalization Pastors in Small, Passive Baptist General Conference Churches" (DMin diss., Talbot School of Theology, 1989), 102.

9. Ken R. Voges, *Workbook: Level 1 Part A,* The Biblical Behavior Series (Minneapolis: Performax Systems International, 1986), 6.

10. Gordon Penfold, "Turnaround Pastors: Characteristics of Those Who Lead Churches from Life-Support to New Life" (paper presented to the Great Commission Research Network, Biola University, November 11, 2011), 4–5.

11. Ibid.

12. Roy M. Oswald and Otto Kroeger, *Personality Type and Religious Leadership* (Washington, DC: Alban Institute, 1988), 65.

13. Joel A. Barker, *Discovering the Future* (St. Paul: ILI Press, 1989), 25.

14. Ibid., 26–27.

15. Ibid., 37.

16. Penfold, "Defining Characteristics of Turnaround Pastors," 161–62.

17. Barker, *Discovering the Future*, 35.

18. Penfold, "Defining Characteristics of Turnaround Pastors," 161–62.

19. Barker, *Discovering the Future*, 27.

20. Penfold, "Defining Characteristics of Turnaround Pastors," 161–62.

21. Schaller, *Create Your Own Future!*, 24–25.

22. Penfold, "Defining Characteristics of Turnaround Pastors," 150–51.

23. Ibid. 162.

24. Ibid.

25. Ibid.

26. Ibid.

27. Ibid.

28. Ibid.

29. Ibid.

30. Ibid.

31. Penfold, "Turnaround Pastors," 19.

Chapter 12 The Church Pastor as Culture Sculptor: Part 3 The Process

1. Some will object to my using what they would refer to as a secular model for the change process. While I don't know if Lewin was a Christian, I do believe that all truth is God's truth regardless. And I'm convinced that God has allowed Lewin to tap into his truth (natural revelation) when it comes to the change process and how it takes place.

2. Jeff Chu, "Teachings from the Summit: Highlights from the 2010 Conference," *Fast Company* (December 2010–January 2011): 131.

Appendix K The Personal Profile: The Persuader Pattern

1. *DiSC Classic Version 9.0* (Minneapolis: Inscape Publishing, 2001), 17.

2. Ibid.

Appendix M Temperament Indicator 2: Further Explanation

1. Roy M. Oswald and Otto Kroeger, *Personality Type and Religious Leadership* (Washington, DC: Alban Institute, 1988), 30.

2. Ibid., 69.

3. Ibid., 68.

4. Ibid., 41.

5. Ibid., 81.

6. Ibid., 41.

Index

Advanced Strategic Planning (Malphurs), 151, 190, 192

Bacon Heights Baptist Church, 54
Barker, Joel, 166–69
Barna, George, 180
Bates, Marilyn, 165
behavior
  church culture, 26–32
  examples of, 27–31
Behaviors Audit, 209–19
beliefs, discovering church, 89–90
Beliefs Audit, 224–30
Blanchard, Ken, 52
Buckingham, Marcus, 113
Built to Last (Collins and Porras), 52

Character Assessment for Leadership, 239–42
church
  budget, 50
  change
    application worksheet, 152–53
    complexity of, 138–39
    four categories of response to, 140–43
    kinds of, 149–50
    leadership levels influencing, 143–46
    levels of, 150–51
    preparation for, 130–32
    resistance to, 134–36
    self-centeredness, 139–40
    stress of, 137–38
    tools that facilitate, 146–49, 151
  core values, 119, 191–92

culture, 20–22, 25
  application to, making, 90–95
  decline of American, 111, 177, 199–200
  growth factors, 125–26
  interpreting, 86–90, 119–21
  observing, 84–86, 117–19
  reading, 94–95, 176–78
  shaping an established, 176, 178, 188, 193
  life cycle of, 183
  mergers, 201–5
  plateauing churches, options for, 200–205
  practicing it in culture, 74–78
  responses to culture
    accommodation, 69–71
    contextualization, 71–73
    isolation, 68–69
  strategy for mission, 192–93
Church of the Resurrection, 204
church planting, 16, 186
  application to culture, 120–21
  core beliefs/values, 119–20
  interpreting culture, 119–20
  five stages of, 122–28
  gifts of, 115
  observing culture, 117–19
  preparation for, 130
  profile, 113–16
church revitalization, 129–30, 141, 164, 200
  interventions motivating, 182–88
church view, 64–66
Clark, Dick, 17
Collins, James, 52

congregational beliefs
  communicating, 66–67
  defining, 60–66
  importance of, 56–60
  values, versus, 62–63
congregational (church) culture, 20–22, 25
  reading, 83–95
  reading and shaping, 112–13, 132–34, 176–
    77, 188–89, 193
  re-form new, 193–97
  thawing current, 178–88
  transition to new level, 188–93
Core Values Audit, 49–50, 220–21
Core Values Statements, 222–23
culture, 7–8, 13, 17, 19–20, 22–24, 68–78
  environmental scans of, 194–96
  five sectors of, 194
Culture Apple 21–22, 25–27, 34, 50, 56, 83,
    87, 112, 132–33, 176, 188
Culture Matrix, 26, 32, 54, 56, 67, 83, 233

Discover Your Strengths (Buckingham), 113
Discovering the Future (Barker), 168

Executive Leadership, 17

Fellowship Bible Church, 120
Fort McKinley United Methodist Church,
  204

Ginghamsburg United Methodist Church,
  204
gospel and culture relationship, 73–74
Graham, Billy, 69
Grand Avenue Temple, 204

Hendricks, Howard, 84–85
Hodges, Phil, 52
Hutton, E. F., 47
Hybels, Bill, 115, 160, 179

Implementation Team Worksheet, 256–66
Irving Bible Church, 185

Jerusalem Church, the, 50, 53, 93, 119, 223
  core values of, 43, 191–92
Joplin, Jerry, 54

Keirsey, David, 165
Keirsey Temperament Sorter II, 161, 164
Kinnaman, David, 111

leader(ship), 37, 57, 91–94, 97, 114–16, 121,
    125, 136, 143–46
leadership team, 187–88, 190, 196–97
Leading Leaders (Malphurs), 181
Lewin, Kurt, 175, 193

Malphurs Group, The (TMG), 92, 118, 132,
    166, 179–80, 187, 190, 192–93, 200
McQuitty, Andy, 185
multicultural America, 14–15
Myers–Briggs Temperament Indicator, 115–
    16, 161, 164–65

Natural Church Development (Schwarz),
    195–96
Nehemiah, leadership characteristics exem-
    plified in, 165–70
Northwood Community Church, 52–53, 66,
    223, 231–32

Olson, David, 111
organizational culture, 22

passion in ministry, 160–61
pastor as church sculptor, qualifications for,
    155–57
pastor, reading the
  application to leader's culture, 103–6
  interpreting leader's culture, 101–3
  observing leader's culture, 100
  source of leader's culture, 98–99
pastors, turnaround, 157, 169–73
  leadership characteristics of, 165–71
Paul, the apostle, 156, 160
Penfold, Gordon, 157, 159, 163–66, 168–71,
    184
(Biblical) Personal Profile, 161–63, 249–50
Persuader Profile, 162
plateaued church statistics, 111, 177, 179, 200
Porras, Jerry, 52

Resurrection Downtown, 204

Schaller, Lyle, 34–35, 157, 159, 169, 179
Schein, Edgar, 20
Schwarz, Christian, 195–96
Sire, James, 64
Sixteen Make-or-Break Questions, 180–82
spiritual gifts, 157–60
Spiritual Gifts Inventory for Leaders, 243–47
Spiritual Maturity Audit, 234–38

Stanley, Andy, 115, 160
Strategic Disciple Making (Malphurs), 192

Temperament Indicator 1, 248
Temperament Indicator 2, 251–55
temperament in ministry, role of, 161–65
Thomas, Robert, 162–64, 167

values
  of American Evangelical Churches, 44–45
  communicating core, 53–54
  defining, 39–41, 62–63
  developing core, 51–54

discovering church, 87–89
discovering core, 45–50, 191–92
importance of, 34–39
kinds of, 41–44
Voges, Ken, 163

Wagner, Peter, 161
Warren, Rick, 115, 118, 160, 185
Willow Creek Association, 185
Willow Creek Community Church, 125
worldview, 63–64

Young Jr., Ed, 120

THEMALPHURSGROUP
—————— *ENVISION TOMORROW TODAY*

Are there areas of your ministry that you could use help with? Professionals in our group are available for onsite and online consulting and coaching. We offer

- Strategic Planning
- Leadership Training
- Leadership Coaching
- Ministry Analysis / Change Audits
- Mystery Shopper Assessments
- Church Planting Coaching

FOR MORE INFORMATION

Email: info@malphursgroup.com
Twitter: twitter.com/malphursgroup
Facebook: facebook.com/malphursgroup

Phone: 469.585.2701
Web: malphursgroup.com
Blog: malphursgroupblog.com

CHECK OUT OUR FREE MONTHLY LEADERSHIP RESOURCE